2nd Edition

WILD
running

wild-running *(n.):*

1. running in the wild or in the elements; escaping the modern world and reconnecting to nature.

2. running freely, with exhilaration; without limits or restrictions.

3. running to the peak of our evolutionary ability; running extraordinary distances and achieving the extraordinary.

Jen Benson and Sim Benson

for E & H

WILD
running

Contents

Runs by Region

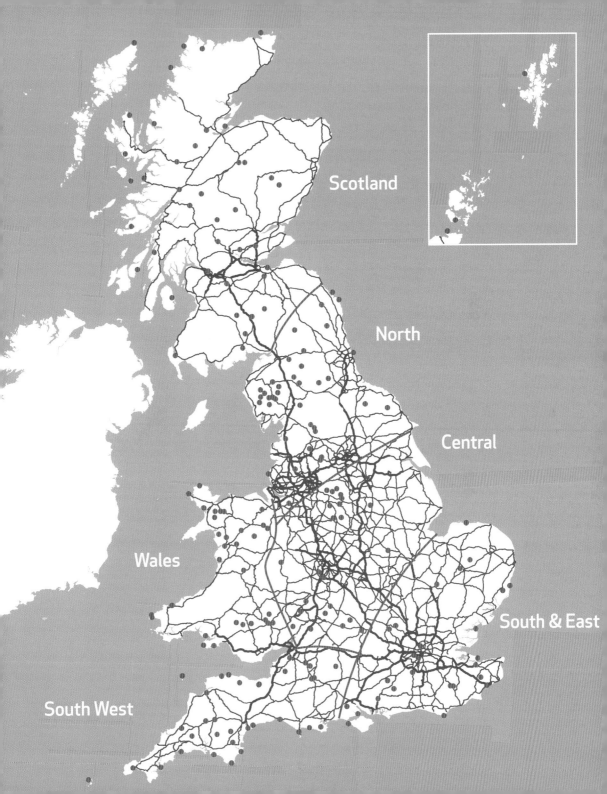

Scotland

North

Central

Wales

South & East

South West

Introduction

"For every runner who tours the world running marathons, there are thousands who run to hear the leaves and listen to the rain, and look to the day when it is suddenly as easy as a bird in flight."

George Sheehan

A brief history of running

While we all have days when it may not feel like it, human beings are perfectly evolved for distance running. With our upright posture, long legs, efficient bodies and hands that can carry water and food as we run, we are brilliantly adapted for covering many miles at a time over a variety of terrain and in a range of conditions. So well adapted, in fact, that many experts believe that when it comes to steady paced, long-distance running, we are among the best in the animal kingdom. It is likely that the combination of our big brains – giving us the strategic edge over our prey – and our ability to keep running all day long, efficiently dealing with heat through sweating, and fuelling on the go, meant that early humans were able to survive where many species would have died out.

History is filled with great running stories, from the Greek messenger Pheidippides, said to have run from Marathon to Athens to deliver news of a military victory against the Persians at the Battle of Marathon, to the more recent legends of the sport. Some of these include Lizzy Hawker, 5 times winner of the UTMB; Steve Birkinshaw, Wainwrights record holder; Joss Naylor and Billy Bland, Lake District fell running legends; and Kilian Jornet who, as we write this introduction, has just broken the 36-year-old record for the Bob Graham Round, running 64 miles over 42 Lakeland peaks in 12 hours 52 minutes.

Today, running as a recreational pastime is more popular than it has ever been. From the big city road marathons where you can run surrounded by an almost overwhelming depth and breadth of humanity, to the multi-day mountain ultramarathons, completed only by the fittest few, there's an event to suit everyone. Many more runners simply leave the house each day in order to run, and the reasons we run differ from person to person and from day to day. Every run is unique, whether that's because of its individual

characteristics or because of what we bring to it, making the experience of running a different one every time.

Whatever our reasons for running, more and more of us are doing it. During 2016, UK runners logged a staggering 16.9 million runs over 132 million kilometres, including 60,264 marathon races, on Strava. Sport England's Active Lives Survey, published in 2018, found that 7 million adults take part in running or athletics on a regular basis. The global success of Parkrun – free, timed 5km runs held each weekend – is testament to the sport's wide appeal, with an astonishing 4.5 million Parkrunners registered worldwide as of 2018. Off-road running in particular is blossoming in Britain, with trail races of all distances drawing large numbers of participants, and the big trail, mountain and fell challenges generating more interest and excitement than ever before, both here and abroad.

Running wild

One of the many joys of running lies in its simplicity. Whatever level of runner you are, this is a time-efficient and cost-effective way to improve your physical and mental health and explore the great outdoors. Kitted out with little more specialist equipment than a good pair of shoes, the opportunities for adventure are endless. Whether you're just starting out or you're a seasoned ultrarunner, you enjoy running alone or with friends, you're into jungles of the urban or leafy variety, running has it all.

For us, a great running route – one that makes it into this book – has to have three ingredients: an amazing setting, great running terrain and just a little magic. We'll choose a place because it's a delight to be there, whether it's peaceful, leafy woodland, a mountain valley or a hidden wave-washed beach. Underfoot, the terrain must feel fantastic to run on: winding singletrack, springy grass, soft peat, firm sand, shingle, even smooth tarmac… The variety is endless but the feeling – that thrilling interaction between body and earth – is always there. And, finally, to the magic. This is the ingredient that is perhaps the hardest to define but we always know when it's there. In some cases it's the story behind the route – perhaps it holds an important place in running legend, or there's some interesting history or archaeology about it. Perhaps some rare geological phenomenon has shaped the landscape or the view was a favourite of someone of note. Sometimes it's a place that's special for its wildlife, and one of the many joys of running for us is the opportunity it's given us

to see rare wildlife, from red squirrels and ptarmigans to seals, puffins and dolphins. We're confident you'll agree that every route in this book has all three ingredients in abundance.

Our story

We met through a mutual love of wild places and tough, physical challenges. During the decade we have spent adventuring together so far, we have explored the length and breadth of the country in our quest to seek out the most amazing places to run. These days we're lucky enough to count the bringing of these great outdoor experiences to others as work. Since the publication of the first edition of *Wild Running* we've become routes editors for *Trail Running* magazine and regular contributors to a number of other magazines, websites and newspapers. We also have the pleasure of working closely with organisations such as Ordnance Survey, the National Trust, the Forestry Commission and the South West Coast Path Association, bringing running and other outdoor adventures to Britain's beautiful places. We're passionate about encouraging people to get outside and explore, and we're also passionate about doing so sustainably, with care and respect for the people, places and wildlife that make Britain such an incredible place to be.

Around Britain in the second edition

For us, running is the very best way to explore new places, challenge our physical limits and have incredible adventures, but when we started out we found very few guides aimed specifically at runners. Walking guides gave us route directions; mountain bike guides focused on the terrain and the great ascents and descents. We felt that the perfect running book lay somewhere between the two – using pure human power to access and discover incredible and beautiful places while making sure the terrain encountered made for exciting, varied and enjoyable running. This was our brief for the first edition of this book and writing it was an incredible experience that challenged, taught and excited us more than we could have imagined.

Nearly 5 years later our knowledge of Britain and the very best places to run here is even better – we've written several more books and taken several thousand more photos along the way, too. We loved the format and the feedback from our first book, so the essence in this update remains the same but with lots of brand new routes. As in the previous edition, many

Did you know...?

The *Urban Mind* study by King's College London (published 2018) found that the positive effects of a stint spent in nature could be felt for seven hours afterwards, and that people at greater risk of developing mental health problems benefit even more from spending time outdoors than others.

An analysis of previous studies published in the journal *Sports Medicine* in 2015 found that endurance running is effective in providing substantial, long-term health benefits.

A 20-year study by researchers at Stanford University found that older habitual runners have fewer disabilities, a longer span of active life and a better life expectancy than non-runners. And their knees were in better shape, too.

of our runs combine several different types of terrain, as we felt it was important to prioritise the experience of running the route rather than to be restrictive about what lay underfoot. As a result there are some that include gentle running on quiet country lanes, fun muddy wading through boggy ground and scrambling over boulders and scree slopes, alongside the more usual trails and paths. We strongly believe this adds to the variety and interest of the runs themselves. The routes included are deliberately diverse in their length, terrain and navigability, showcasing the rich diversity of running on offer and providing runs to suit and challenge as many people as possible.

Join us for a run around Britain, beginning in the South West, where we visit the idyllic Isles of Scilly and take to the spectacular coast path, winding its way around the edge of the peninsula. The wild expanses of Bodmin, Exmoor and Dartmoor follow, while the South and East section heads out across the rolling South Downs to the towering white cliffs at Beachy Head. East Anglia has great beach running and access to the classic long-distance trails of the Peddars Way and Icknield Way, the latter stretching across the country to the Chilterns, a delightful hilly escape from nearby London.

Central England is home to the Peak District, from the limestone trails of the White Peak to testing sections of the Pennine Way across the rugged and remote Dark Peak. Venturing into the North, the Lake District's majestic landscape contrasts high-level traverses with gentler lakeside excursions. The dales and moors of Yorkshire offer wilderness and fascinating geological features, with wonderful trails and exciting running. Wales boasts a great variety of landscapes, from the rolling, grassy hills of the south, along its rugged coast path to the towering mountains of Snowdonia in the north. Scotland's rugged peaks provide challenging ascents and dramatic vistas alongside gentler tours of the coastline and an escape to the remote and windswept Scottish islands.

Wherever you chose to go, our aim for this book is to inspire you to get out and try running in its most unadulterated form, experiencing our natural environment to the full: on foot, as one with the landscape and the elements, using only the power of your body. This is where some of the most pleasurable, fulfilling and exhilarating experiences happen, and where running becomes truly wild.

How to use this book

This book is organised geographically, starting in the south-west and progressing northwards to finish in the Scottish islands.

Each chapter provides an overview of the area, including any relevant or interesting running-related information, along with highlights of the routes. Detailed directions are provided for each run, including distance, start/finish postcode and step-by-step instructions.

Each run also has a unique web page where you'll find .gpx files to upload onto a smartphone, watch or GPS device; maps; printable route cards and elevation profiles. Simply enter the wildrunning.net address given in each route information box.

Finally, there's a 1:250,000 map for each route in the back of the book to allow you to locate it in relation to its surroundings. We strongly recommend taking the relevant 1:25,000 map with you, particularly when venturing into remote and/or unfamiliar areas; no book can provide a large enough map area to allow you to navigate safely should you become lost or stray off the area of map provided. OS Maps Online (subscriptions from osmaps.ordnancesurvey. co.uk) is a fantastic resource for runners, allowing you to view and print maps of most parts of the UK at up to 1:25,000.

Getting Started

One of the many great reasons to run lies in its simplicity and lack of need for complicated equipment. However there are items that will make running safer and more enjoyable if chosen with care. Each run is different, so carefully consider your requirements - and those of the run- before setting out.

Shoes A well-fitting pair of shoes appropriate to the terrain, and conditions of your run are essential. For hard-pack and road-based runs, a pair of road shoes will provide protection and cushioning for your feet. On trails and dry off-road surfaces trail shoes which combine a more rugged, grippy sole with some cushioning will give you traction and make running fast over uneven terrain easier. In wet, muddy conditions, a pair of fell shoes with deep lugs will grip the ground and stop you slipping and sliding as you run, greatly improving comfort, performance and safety. Many runs involve a combination of terrain so shoe choice is an important but not always straightforward decision. And remember, good fit is key, so be prepared to try several.

Clothing Running generates large amounts of heat, even in cold weather, so it's a good idea to layer your clothing to allow for easy ventilation. A lightweight windproof jacket is invaluable, as it can be worn over other clothing when required or stashed easily in a pocket. Bear in mind that in cooler weather you will lose heat rapidly if you need to slow down or stop for any reason. Other than this, dress for the conditions you will encounter and the length of your run, from tights, long-sleeved base layers, hats and gloves in winter to shorts and a vest in summer; most choices are common sense. Well-fitting, supportive underwear is essential for comfort whilst running and worth time and effort to get right.

Socks! A good pair of running socks is essential, providing warmth, cushioning and protection and wicking away sweat from the skin to reduce the chances of blisters. Make sure they fit really well and don't ruck up in your shoes, and consider taking a change of socks on really long runs. Waterproof socks are a great investment for wet-weather running.

Building fitness and technique

Routes have been included to provide for all levels of fitness and experience. Some of the longer and/or more mountainous routes require high levels of fitness and endurance to complete. Here are some tips for building fitness if you are just starting out:

Run regularly It is important to run regularly to allow your body to become conditioned to the forces exerted upon it during running and to maximise gains in fitness. Occasional hard runs interspersed with long gaps are more likely to leave you tired, sore and demotivated.

Build up gradually It's old advice but good. There's no proven maximum amount that you should increase by each week, and progress will be highly individual,

however take the time to increase the intensity and duration of your runs gradually to allow your body to adapt.

Find a training plan Having a set number and type of runs to complete each week is great for keeping your training fresh and varied. Make sure you listen to your body though, as no training plan will suit everybody all the time.

Enter a race Having a goal, such as race, on the horizon is great for motivation and helps get you out running even when the sofa seems like a much better option.

Technique Off-road running takes time and practice to perfect, and requires your body to work differently to road running. If you are new to running off-road, start with well-used trails and less

technically challenging terrain and work up to the more demanding routes. This will make them all the more enjoyable when you get there. As with most activities, the more you do the better you will get, but there are some specific areas to work on that will help you improve more rapidly:

Build strength Incorporate strength and conditioning work into your routine. Stronger muscles will make you more efficient in your running and protect against injury.

Practise balancing Good balance is key to running off-road successfully, yet it is something we rarely train ourselves to do. Incorporate balance work into your daily routine to increase body awareness and improve co-ordination.

Resources for Runners

The running community is a supportive and inclusive one and running clubs are a great way to get started, learn new routes and meet other runners. Magazines provide a regular dose of motivation and are a good way to keep up with events, advice and stories from the world of running – *Trail Running*, *Runner's World* and *Outdoor Fitness* are all a good place to start.

Ordnance Survey OS Mapping (osmaps.ordnancesurvey.co.uk) is a subscription service that allows you to view any part of Britain at up to 1:25,000 scale.

Fell Runners Association (fellrunner.org.uk) has race listings and useful information on running in the fells.

Long Distance Walkers Assoc. (ldwa.org.uk) has a huge database of routes and organised non-competitive events.

Trail Running Association (tra-uk.org) is full of information on trail running.

BMC (thebmc.co.uk) offers expert advice and information on mountain safety, scrambling, weather and lots more.

The National Trust and National Trust for Scotland (nationaltrust.org.uk/nts.org.uk) protects a multitude of places that are ideal for wild running.

The John Muir Trust (johnmuirtrust.org) is a Scottish charity dedicated to protecting wild places in the UK.

Bags A lightweight rucksack or waist pack can be really useful for carrying spare clothing, food, water and safety kit. It can take many attempts to find the perfect one for you, so be prepared to try several and always take the time to adjust them to fit you properly to avoid discomfort, bouncing around and chafing. There are many different types on the market and much is down to personal preference. Those with easy-to-reach zipper pockets for food are great for longer runs. Water-carrying options range from side, rear and strap arrangements to integrated bladder pouches, all of which have strengths and weaknesses in terms of comfort, accessibility and ease of refilling, with most runners having a personal preference.

Food and drink Again, the need for carrying refreshments will depend hugely on the run you are doing and the availability of stops along the way. In general it is important to take supplies if you are running for more than about 90 minutes. Many runners drink energy drinks, however these may become unpalatable on longer runs and are often expensive and sugary. Plain water is perfectly adequate in most cases and straightforward to replenish. Drink to thirst and, on longer runs especially, make sure you also replace salts which are lost through sweating, either through electrolyte tablets which can be added to water or simply by eating little and often. Hyponatraemia is a serious condition caused by over overdrinking, and a far greater danger to distance runners than dehydration. Snacks should be easy to carry, palatable and easy to stomach and can range from expensive energy bars to a handful of dried fruit, depending upon taste. In general, runners find their preference for sweet foods declines as the run duration increases, so try out different foods and see what works for you.

Emergency items When venturing out on longer runs or into remote or weather-affected areas, even more careful kit consideration is required. Packing the right safety equipment can prevent a run becoming an epic and may save your own or someone else's life. Carrying, and being able to use, kit is an important part of being prepared. The following list is not exhaustive and intended as a guide only: route description, map, compass, mobile phone, money, food, water, warm clothing, waterproof clothing, hat and gloves, first aid kit, whistle, survival bag, head torch, sunscreen. Clothing and equipment choices should always reflect the conditions and the route.

10 ways to be wild and safe

1 Take a compass and map and know how to use them, particularly when running in remote or unfamiliar places. Bring a mobile phone but don't rely on it.

2 Tell someone where you're going and when you'll be back.

3 Wear the right shoes. Enjoyable and safe off-road running requires shoes with good grip.

4 Dress right. When undertaking longer runs or venturing into remote or high areas, take extra clothing to allow you to keep warm should the weather deteriorate or should you need to stop or slow down.

5 Consider not wearing headphones, particularly if there are road crossings.

6 Ensure that you have enough food and water for the duration of your run.

7 Take a basic emergency kit on longer runs, and those in remote areas. Include a head torch, whistle, space blanket and emergency rations.

8 Research your run. Be prepared for the terrain, navigation and the weather involved. Find out where there are places to shelter, refuel and get information. We cannot guarantee that routes will still be in the condition described.

9 Run with a friend! A running adventure is a fantastic thing to share and is safer with company. Alternatively there are many running groups and guides with whom running in remote areas can be made safer and more enjoyable.

10 The routes in this book are described for fine, summer conditions only. In poor weather they may be vastly different, particularly those in high and mountainous areas, presenting a considerably tougher challenge or requiring specialist equipment and techniques and the skills and experience to use them.

Best for Beginners

Shorter, gentler runs on easier terrain with simple route finding. Perfect for those new or recently returned to running.

7 Dartington
22 Corfe Castle
52 Tamsin Trail
65 Port Meadow
72 Lickey Hills

86 Frogatt & Curbar Edge
108 Buttermere
119 Souter Lighthouse
132 Sugar Loaf
166 Chatelherault

Best for Fastpacking & Ultradistance

Pack everything you need for a fast-and-light multi-day running adventure and explore the country under your own steam.

2 Penzance to St Ives
32 Imber Perimeter
48 Royal Military Canal
90 Mary Towneley Loop
156 Dee Valley/North Berwyn Way

161 Romans & Reivers
165 Glasgow to Edinburgh
174 Lairig Ghru
184 Great Glen Way
198 Hebridean Way

Best for Urban Escapes

Discover hidden wild trails within easy reach of the city.

20 Exe Estuary Trail
34 Bath Skyline
42 Box Hill Circular
52 Tamsin Trail
71 Clent Hills

81 Kinder Trespass
88 Formby
125 Rhossili
166 Chatelherault
167 Arthur's Seat

Best for Summits & Views

Tough climbs to some of the highest places in each area are more often than not rewarded with glorious views – and a fun, fast descent, too.

Best for Coast & Beach

The finest coastal running from involving, technical, clifftop trails to firm, flat sand for running barefoot at the water's edge.

Best for Islands

Escape to one of Britain's beautiful islands for a really wild adventure.

Best for Woods & Forest

Winding woodland trails and peaceful, ancient forest: perfect routes for immersing yourself in the trees.

Best for Wild Swimming

The best places for a post-run dip or an adventurous wild swimrun.

Best for History & Culture

Wild runs with a story, from ancient monuments to places of great literary inspiration.

Best for Rocks & Scrambling

Add some extra excitement to your run with an airy ridge to scramble or rocky features for exploring.

5 Bodmin
11 Haytor & Hound Tor
75 Chrome Hill & Parkhouse Hill
82 Crowden Clough
103 Langdale Pikes
140 Cadair Idris

147 The Glyder Ridge
148 Around Tryfan
151 Nantlle Ridge
181 Silver Sands of Morar
194 Fossil Tree, Mull
192 Goat Fell, Arran

Best for Wildlife

Great trails through beautiful landscapes, nature reserves and SSSIs, perfect for spotting Britain's rich diversity of flora and fauna.

3 St Anthony Head
14 Roadford Lake
16 Lundy
58 Dunwich Beach
88 Formby
107 Aira Force & Gowbarrow Fell

129 St David's Head
146 Newborough Forest
156 The Dee Valley Way
170 Loch Leven
176 Chanonry Point
189 Sandwood Bay

Best for Wheels

Accessible adventures for running buggies, wheelchairs and bikes – please check for specific access information before you go.

20 Exe Estuary Trail
43 Bedgebury
52 Tamsin Trail
56 Thetford
74 Rutland Water

78 Around Carsington Water
141 Coed-y-Brenin
166 Chatelherault
173 Loch an Eilein

Best for Weekends

Perfect pairings for weekends away, one route for each day and a great adventure base.

Kynance Cove

South West

Discover white-sand beaches and peaceful rocky coves on the Isles of Scilly, dramatic coast path and windswept moorland in Devon and Cornwall, spectacular geology along the Jurassic Coast and the quintessential English countryside of Wiltshire and Somerset.

Highlights
South West

1 Explore the wild and beautiful Isles of Scilly with a run around the islands of Bryher and Tresco.

2-4 Discover some of the best of Cornwall's coast, traversing rugged granite headlands in the north and peaceful wooded creeks along the Fowey Estuary to the south.

7-13 Experience the great variety of running to be found in Devon, from the high wilds of Dartmoor to the South Hams' blue seas and rolling hills.

20-25 Take a run through time on the Jurassic Coast World Heritage Site or explore the castles and hill forts of East Devon and Dorset.

29-34 Find yourself in the green spaces surrounding the cities of Bristol and Bath or plan a great escape to the vast expanses of the Wiltshire plains.

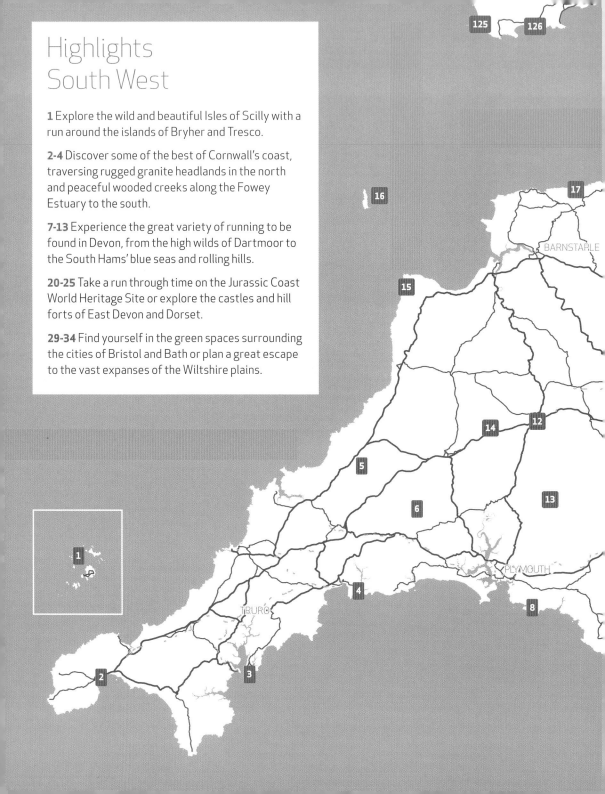

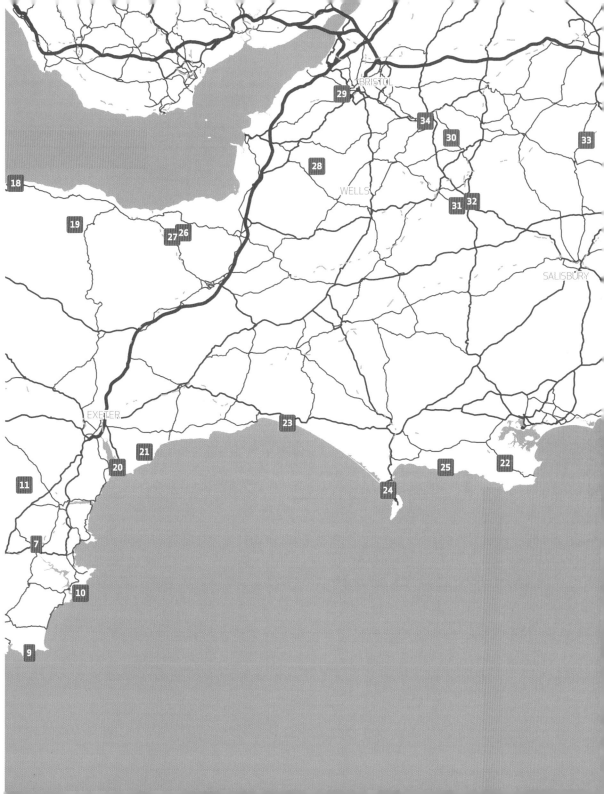

Tresco

Cornwall &
the Isles of Scilly

Twenty-eight miles off the coast of mainland Cornwall lie the Isles of Scilly. Of these 140 or so islands, 5 are inhabited, with each one having its own distinct character. Circumnavigations of the islands make for wonderful running adventures, hopping between them on one of the regular ferry services. The growing sport of swimrun is a perfect way to explore the archipelago, swimming the wide sheltered bays and running between them; the UK stage of the ÖTILLÖ swimrun world series is held here each summer.

Across to mainland Cornwall and there's a heady mix of dramatic coastline, colourful fishing harbours, white sandy beaches and windswept moorland to discover, along with some of the most spectacular sections of the 630-mile South West Coast Path. Expect well signed, interesting and varied running and plenty of opportunities for traditional Cornish refuelling with cream teas, pasties and the local seafood. Spring is a great time to visit, before the summer crowds descend and while the countryside is bright with daffodils and primroses.

As you make your way along the winding, undulating coast path take a moment to catch your breath and spot seals bobbing in the waves, buzzards circling overhead and, if you're lucky, rare Cornish choughs with their glossy black plumage and bright red beaks. The cliffs that form the base of many of the routes in this section are granite, and the resulting terrain is often rocky, steep and strewn with large boulders. Many of the features of the coast path, such as the stepped ascents and descents, stiles, stream crossings and walls, are hewn from this rock and require some negotiating, especially on tired legs. The remote high ground of Bodmin Moor in the east of the county is a fascinating contrast to the sunny beaches, popular with surfers, sunbathers and sandcastlers. Scattered with rocky tors and intriguing reminders of human activity, from disused quarried to stone circles, this is a perfect place to escape for some really wild trails.

1

2

3

Our south-west adventures begin on the Isles of Scilly with circumnavigation of two very different but equally wonderful islands: Bryher and Tresco (run 1). At just 1.5 miles long by half a mile wide, Bryher is the smallest of Scilly's inhabited islands; however, its landscape is still incredibly varied, from rugged headlands to beautiful beaches. Popplestone Bay, named for the sound the waves make as they break on the shingly shore, is a perfect spot to relax and watch the sunset after a long day's running. On neighbouring Tresco you'll find the exotic Abbey Gardens in the south and a wild and wave-washed coast in the north, topped with the ruins of Cromwell's Castle; catch a ferry between the islands for a full day of adventure.

Our Penzance to St Ives run (2) takes you along a stunning section of the South West Coast Path linked by train stations at either end. At over 40 miles this is an epic undertaking in one go; however, it lends itself brilliantly to a weekend or more as a fastpacking adventure. Highlights include rounding the headlands at Land's End and Cape Cornwall and the breathtaking technical trails around Bosigran and Zennor, passing the ruined remnants of Cornwall's lengthy mining history. Whether camping or B&B is your preference there are plenty of places to stay along the way, along with clear blue seas to bathe your weary legs and lots to explore in arty St Ives at the finish.

Bordered by the Fal Estuary to the west and the Atlantic Ocean to the east, the Roseland Peninsula has a character all of its own, quite different from much of Cornwall. Our run around St Anthony Head (3) takes in an enjoyable and brilliantly varied loop of the remote headland, right at the southernmost tip of the peninsula, a route that feels secret and wild. Starting at the former gun placements with views out across the Carrick Roads, a flooded ancient river valley which today forms one of the largest natural harbours in the world, it follows the South West Coast Path to Towan Beach. As well as the seals that lounge on the rocks here you may spot Earl, the Thirstea Company's vintage Citroen H van, serving everything from the finest loose-leaf teas to traditional Cornish pasties.

Routes 1-3

1 AROUND BRYHER & TRESCO

Distance 10.5 miles/17km
Ascent 346 metres
Start New Grimsby Quay, Tresco, TR24 0QE
Finish Bar Jetty, Bryher, TR23 0PR
Info wildrunning.net/201

Join the coast path north to Cromwell's Castle, turn R uphill and inland to King Charles Castle (0.75 miles/1.2km). Turn L along the coast path around the northern end of Tresco before trending south into Old Grimsby (2.1 miles/3.4km). Continue on the coast path south to Carn Near, then follow the west coast north to return to New Grimsby Quay. Ferry crossing to Bar Quay, Bryher (5.8 miles/9.4km). Take the road inland into The Town and L over the hill, taking a sharp L downhill and onto a footpath. Run around the southern end of Bryher to Droppy Nose Point (7.6 miles/12.3km). Trace the western coast around Great Porth, Gweal Hill and Popplestone beach and onto the wilder northern end of Bryher towards Shipman Head (9.7 miles/15.6km). Run along the coast path back along the eastern coast, above Hangman Island, behind the pub and through the boatyard back to Bar.

2 PENZANCE TO ST IVES

Distance 41 miles/66km
Ascent 3211 metres
Start Penzance Station, TR18 2NF
Finish St Ives Station, TR26 2EQ
Info wildrunning.net/202

This route follows the waymarked South West Coast Path from Penzance railway station to St Ives via these points: Mousehole (3.6 miles/5.8km), Lamorna Cove (5.9 miles/9.5km), the Minack Theatre (11.7 miles/18.9km), Land's End (16.7 miles/26.8km), Sennen Cove (18.3 miles/29.5km), Cape Cornwall (23.4 miles/37.7km) and Gurnard's Head (32 miles/51.6km). On reaching St Ives join the road through the town and around the harbour towards Porthminster Beach, and the station is just inland of this.

3 ST ANTHONY HEAD

Distance 6 miles/9.5km
Ascent 564 metres
Start St Anthony Head, TR2 5HA
Info wildrunning.net/203

Take the track to the gun emplacements on the headland and turn L onto the South West Coast Path. Follow this around Zone Point and along the coast to Towan Beach (2.4 miles/3.8km). Turn L inland then R onto the road, after a short distance turn L off the road and across a footbridge. Turn R after the bridge onto a footpath along Porth Creek and south along the Percuil River estuary to the road at St Anthony (4.2 miles/6.8km). Turn R past the church and along the creekside track, over a hill then down to the coast of St Mawes Harbour, turn L onto the coast path around Carricknath Point to the lighthouse at St Anthony Head. Join the signed and surfaced path uphill back to the car park.

4

5

6

Our next run (4) visits the picturesque peninsula below the town of Fowey (pronounced 'foy'), home to author Daphne du Maurier whose former residence, Ferryside, stands on the edge of the Fowey River. Starting at Readymoney Cove, overlooked by the 16th-century St Catherine's Castle, enjoyable running follows the South West Coast Path around Gribbin Head with its 26m red and white striped Daymark. The views along the coast from the National Trust-owned headland are outstanding – at certain times you can also climb the 109 steps to the top of the tower for an even better vantage point. From Polkerris the run joins the Saints Way, a 27-mile waymarked route across Cornwall from Padstow to Fowey, crossing the peninsula back to Readymoney Cove. Refuel at the quirky Lifebuoy Café in Fowey.

At 420 metres above sea level, Brown Willy is the amusingly named highest point of Bodmin Moor, and indeed the whole of the county of Cornwall. Its name in Cornish, Bronn Wennili, means 'hill of swallows'. Our Bodmin run (5) climbs straight up from the start to reach the summit of Rough Tor (Rough is pronounced row as in cow), from where there are grand views out across the rock-scattered moorland. From here it crosses, via a leg-sappingly steep valley, to Brown Willy before a fabulous, long descent plunges you into dense woodland at Roughtor Plantation. Following the line of trees through Low Moor Plantation brings you back to the start.

Bodmin Moor has a long history of human activity etched into its landscape, from Neolithic stone circles to the scars of modern-day quarries. Run 6, The Hurlers and the Cheesewring, takes in some of the most interesting spots including the Hurlers, a line of three late Neolithic or Early Bronze Age stone circles. According to local legend, they are the remains of men petrified for playing hurling on a Sunday. Starting at Minions, Cornwall's highest village, the run heads up onto open moorland, eventually gaining the rocky ridgeline of Kilmar Tor. A long downhill over Langstone Downs followed by a short, sharp climb up Stowes Hill brings you to the Cheesewring with its quarry and uneven pile of boulders – a naturally occurring feature that is said to have been built by an angry giant. The final stretch passes the Hurlers before returning to Minions.

Routes 4-6

4 FOWEY

Distance 7 miles/11km
Ascent 973 metres
Start Readymoney car park, PL23 1DG
Info wildrunning.net/204

Set off downhill from the start to join the South West Coast Path on Readymoney Road. Turn R and follow the road then the coast path south-west around St Catherine's Point and then to the prominent red and white Gribbin Tower (2.5 miles/4.1km). Continue on the coast path heading north-west to Little Gribbin, then north to a path junction on the hill above Polkerris (4.3 miles/7km). Leave the coast path and turn inland, bearing R at a road and joining the Saints' Way. Take the first L through Tregaminion and onto a footpath east across fields. Still on the Saints' Way pass Trenant Farm, go along another field edge, through woodland and then up to Lankelly Lane (5.6 miles/9km). Run along Lankelly Lane, turn R onto Polvillion Road then R through a gate onto a footpath going generally south and contouring around the hill until you reach Readymoney Road. Turn L and retrace your outbound steps back to the start.

5 BODMIN

Distance 5.5 miles/8.5km
Ascent 293 metres
Start Rough Tor car park, PL32 9QJ
Info wildrunning.net/205

Leave the car park on the obvious path south-east towards the rocky summit of Rough Tor (1 mile/1.5km). Run east downhill along rough paths and aiming for the De Lank River Bridge just upstream of the walled fields (1.5 miles/2.4km). Cross here and take the track uphill and trending R or south to the trig point on the summit of Brown Willy (2 miles/3.3km). Leave the summit going north on vague paths trending R to stay on the higher ground of High Moor and contouring around Roughtor Marsh to your L (3.4 miles/5.5km). At grid ref SX160821 near some small pools turn L onto paths around the head of the marsh to the end of Roughtor Plantation (3.9 miles/6.2km). Find the track that goes north-west through the middle of the woods and stay on this as it curves to the L, joining Lower Moor Plantation and emerging at the start.

6 THE HURLERS & CHEESEWRING

Distance 10.5 miles/16.5km
Ascent 383 metres
Start The Hurlers car park, PL14 5LE
Info wildrunning.net/206

Take the track north-west past the Hurlers stone circles, turning L at a three-way fork at 0.6 miles/1km and reaching an old flooded quarry (1.1 miles/1.8km). Keep to the track around the quarry then west to the end of a long stone row (1.7 miles/2.8km). Turn R here and follow the row north to reach a wall at 2.2 miles/3.5km, turn L along the wall and join a track near Siblyback Farm. Turn R at a track junction and take the track north-east to reach the edge of Smallacombe Woods (4 miles/6.4km). Join the track up the edge of the wood then R, crossing Withey Brook and picking up a bridleway east to the end of a road (6 miles/9.7km). Turn R onto a path to the trig point summit of Kilmar Tor. Drop down to the south and onto the path of the old railway around Langstone Downs and then R to the summit of the Cheesewring (9 miles/14.5km). Drop down to the L and go along the main path through the quarry and back to Minions, passing the old mine workings. Turn R onto the road to return to the start.

11 Black Hill

South Devon & Dartmoor

Devon's southern coastline runs westwards from Seaton on the Jurassic Coast, past the Exe Estuary and the cathedral city of Exeter and around the South Hams Peninsula, finally meeting Cornwall at the River Tamar just beyond Plymouth. The South West Coast Path winds along its length, the running varied and enjoyable, from sandy beaches and wooded trails to rugged, remote headlands and seaside promenades. The South Hams covers the large peninsula south of Dartmoor, bordered by Torbay to the east and Plymouth to the west. Inland you'll find proper Devon countryside: rolling hills, farmland, woodland and several sizeable rivers making their way from the high ground of Dartmoor to the English Channel. Many of the area's larger settlements, including Dartmouth, Kingsbridge and Salcombe, lie along the coast, making the most of the glorious sea views and numerous picturesque bays and harbours.

Dartmoor covers a total of 368 square miles, making it the largest and highest upland in Southern Britain. Its rough, peat-topped ground is dotted with rocky, granite tors, the exposed knuckles of the volcanic bedrock that stretches right down through Cornwall to the Isles of Scilly and beyond. Many of the larger tors are excellent for bouldering and even some gentle scrambling. More than 160 of Dartmoor's hills have the word 'tor' in their name and these distinctly shaped piles of rocks are a good guide to navigation once you learn to recognise them. Take care with route-finding in poor weather and check military firing times as there are several live firing ranges on the moors.

Dartmoor combines a great range of wildlife, including its famous wild ponies, with fascinating history from stone rows and circles to the ruined medieval village at Hound Tor. There are two official mountains here: High Willhays at 621 metres and Yes Tor at 619 metres. Cut Hill, Whitehorse and Hangingstone Hill are also all over 600 metres and a 'round' of all five hills, with about 20 miles of distance, makes up the Dartmoor 600 Challenge devised by Tamar Valley-based Run Venture, an

7

8

9

expert-staffed trail running hub, shop and café. Dartington Hall, just outside Totnes, is a Grade I listed building surrounded by a 1,200-acre estate of leafy woodland, parkland and riverside trails. The Dartington Hall Trust is a charity promoting the arts, sustainability and social justice and there are shops, cafés and holiday accommodation, including camping, on site. Our Dartington run (7) takes in a loop of the main estate and is a good introduction to the trails here; however, it's well worth taking some time to explore further; estate maps are available at the visitor centre.

Making for the coast, we visit the pretty twin villages of Newton Ferrers and Noss Mayo (run 8), set either side of a tidal creek. This is a perfect place to base yourself for a weekend's running on the coast path, with some of the best fish and chips around served at the Ship Inn, right by the water's edge. The route sets off from the village along a densely wooded creekside trail before joining the South West Coast Path and following this around the headland, passing Gara Point, Blackstone Point and Stoke Point, with the most spectacular views of this intricate section of coast. Turning inland on quiet, sunken lanes it heads back down to Newton Ferrers, crossing the creek to return to the start.

Heading eastwards along the coast, across the Kingsbridge estuary from bustling Salcombe, Prawle Point, the remote southernmost tip of Devon, reaches out into the sea. A glorious run (9) around the headland is rewarded with stunning views across Salcombe estuary to Bolt Head, with its dramatic rock formations and sandy bays edged with an improbably blue sea. Look out for flocks of rare cirl bunting, which can only be found in this part of the country, and, over the summer months, the wildflowers that decorate the sunny coastal cliffs. Starting at Prawle Point itself this run takes you past Gammon Head before climbing steeply to reach the village of East Prawle, home to the quirky Pig's Nose pub. From here it's an enjoyable descent back to the coast path, by way of peaceful Malcombe Sand, a great spot for a swim, before returning to the start.

Routes 7-10

7 DARTINGTON

Distance 5.5 miles/8.5km
Ascent 270 metres
Start Dartington Estate, TQ9 6EL
Info wildrunning.net/207

From the start turn L onto the riverside path and through woodland to the road near Staverton (2 miles/3.2km). Continue on the path trending L around North Wood reaching the road by Old Parsonage Farm (2.9 miles/4.6km). Turn R onto the road then L onto a track leading south to the corner of the shops' car park. Turn L here joining the signed cycle track south-east towards Totnes until you reach the estate road (4 miles/6.4km). Turn L onto the road then R onto a footpath following the River Dart north-east (4.8 miles/7.7km). Turn L away from the river and take the path uphill to the start.

8 NOSS MAYO & NEWTON FERRERS

Distance 10 miles/16km
Ascent 418 metres
Start Church Road car park, PL8 1EH
Info wildrunning.net/208

Head downhill from the start to the creek then follow Passage Road or the footpath in Ferry Wood west along Newton Creek to the Yealm estuary. Continue on the South West Coast Path around Gara Point, east past Warren Cottage and then curve north above Stoke Beach. Continue on the coast path past Beacon Hill and down the steep hill to Wadham Beach. At the top of the next hill turn L, leaving the coast path, and run along the track to the road (6.7 miles/10.8km). Turn R onto the road, take the next L and then R onto a byway. Follow this north, then turn L at the next junction to the road at Membland. Take the road back to Bridgend. At high tide, turn L back to the start, or at low tide turn R, crossing the tidal walkway back to the start.

9 PRAWLE POINT

Distance 6 miles/9.5km
Ascent 359 metres
Start Prawle Point car park, TQ7 2BY
Info wildrunning.net/209

Join the South West Coast Path and bear R, south-west, to a path junction at The Pig's Nose (1.2 miles/2km). Turn R away from the coast path and inland on a streamside path and join a bridleway, then a road at a sharp bend (2 miles/3.2km). Follow this south-east into East Prawle. Take the first R then the second L onto Town Road, until a bridleway at a sharp bend (2.7 miles/4.3km). Follow the bridleway east then around to the L and down to the coast at Woodcombe Sand. Turn R onto the coast path and south-west back to the start.

10 COLETON FISHACRE

Distance 6 miles/9.5km
Ascent 793 metres
Start Coleton Camp car park, TQ6 0EQ
Info wildrunning.net/210

Head east to reach the South West Coast Path at Scabbacombe Head. Turn R onto the coast path and follow it generally south-west to the old gun emplacements and lookout points at Inner Froward Point (3.3 miles/5.3km). Continue on the coast path now heading north-west towards Kingswear. Reach a track junction at 4.4 miles/7km and turn R, uphill and inland, past Home Farm and Higher Brownstone Farm before reaching the road at Coleton Barton Farm. Continue in the same direction past the entrance to Coleton Fishacre to return to the start.

11

11

13

Taking in an enjoyable, challenging loop around the National Trust's house and exotic gardens, our Coleton Fishacre run (10) manages to pack a lot of hill into a fairly short distance. Starting out across farmland it soon descends steeply to the coast path where exciting, undulating running eventually takes you all the way back up to the top of the headland.

The south-east of Dartmoor is one of its most popular, accessible and beautiful corners. The Haytor and Hound Tor run (11) discovers some of the very best bits, starting and finishing at the Visitor Centre, where you'll also find the mobile unit of the excellent Home Farm café from the National Trust's Parke estate, not far away. From here it's straight into the climbs, following the well-worn paths to the top of Haytor, from where the steep scramble to the rocky summit is well worth the effort for the views. A long descent past disused quarries plunges you into a wooded valley, crossing Becka Brook on a traditional Dartmoor clapper bridge before ascending to Hound Tor. Explore the weathered granite stacks and boulders before a fun, fast descent on good trails takes you through the ruined, 13th-century medieval village, back across Becka Brook and up the steep climb to the cairn-topped summit of Black Hill. The ridgeline from here makes for a breathtaking final run back to Hound Tor.

Our High Willhays run (12) visits Dartmoor's two mountain summits, starting with a crossing of the huge dam at Meldon Reservoir before running along the full length of the water's edge. Climbing up towards the summit of High Willhays takes you past Black a Tor Copse, once of the finest surviving examples of high-level sessile oak woodland in the country. An airy ridge path joins the two summits and from Yes Tor the long, slaloming descent on clear paths back to Meldon is pure joy.

Our final Dartmoor adventure explores the high, open land around Princetown (13). Starting in Princetown it takes in a loop of remote moorland on wonderfully clear, runnable trails. Climbing up and over South Hessary Tor, it follows moorland tracks past ancient settlements and stone circles – the remnants of the area's Bronze Age history. The return route takes you past the Crock of Gold, a cairn and kistvaen (Bronze Age grave), one of the best preserved of its kind on the moor.

Routes 11-13

11 HAYTOR & HOUND TOR

Distance 6.5 miles/10km
Ascent 402 metres
Start Haytor Visitor Centre, TQ13 9XT
info wildrunning.net/211

Climb to Haytor Rocks, turn R and take the path north-west past an old quarry to the old granite tramway. Cross and head downhill to the east of Holwell Tor to another tramway, turn L to Holwell Quarry (1.2 miles/1.9km). At the end of the quarry take a steep R downhill and into some woodland, cross Becka Brook on a new clapper bridge then run uphill, trending R to Hound Tor (2.2 miles/3.6km). Turn R and run down the path, past the old medieval village and then uphill to a gate. Follow the path steeply downhill, cross Becka Brook and up a rocky path to a junction. Turn L onto the bridleway down to Leighon then stay R up a byway to the road below Black Hill (4.1 miles/6.6km). Turn R and run up to Black Hill and along the ridge to Smallacombe Rocks. Continue south to the tramway then take paths south past Haytor Quarries to the start.

12 HIGH WILLHAYS

Distance 8 miles/12.5km
Ascent 541 metres
Start Meldon Dam car park, EX20 4LU
Info wildrunning.net/212

Cross the dam and turn R onto the Meldon Reservoir shore path to the far end and then up the West Okement River to the woodland (2.1 miles/3.4km). Turn L and, leaving the main paths, run uphill past Black Tor to the summit of High Willhays. Turn L here and take the ridge path to the more prominent summit of Yes Tor (3.9 miles/6.2km). Either run straight back to the start on the vaguely pathed north slope of Yes Tor, or follow the path north-east towards West Mill Tor but take the larger track L before the summit and run downhill to the track at Black Down (5.2 miles/8.4km). Turn L and run generally north-west back to the dam and the start.

13 PRINCETOWN

Distance 7.5 miles/11.5km
Ascent 205 metres
Start Plume of Feathers Inn, PL20 6QQ
Info wildrunning.net/213

Head south-east on the well surfaced path out of the Plume of Feathers car park, passing South Hessary Tor and continuing towards Nuns Cross Farm (1.7 miles/2.9km). Turn L leaving the main path and going east to a small road, turn R onto this and run to the end. Here it becomes a bridleway which you follow north-east across moorland to a path junction (4.2 miles/6.8km). Turn L and take the bridleway west past the Crock of Gold and back into Princetown.

Exmoor coast

North Devon & Exmoor

Exmoor National Park covers 267 square miles of unique and varied landscape, including open moors and farmland, lush woodland, fast-flowing streams and rivers winding their way through steep-sided valleys, and towering cliffs rising from the Bristol Channel. As a result, the running here is extraordinarily diverse, from tough, tussocky moorland and technically challenging coast path to gentler multi-user paths. Although no single place is particularly high, the regular undulations and steep gradients make for some challenging, but enjoyable, running.

Lundy lies in the Bristol Channel, 12 miles from the coast of North Devon. A solid lump of granite more than 50 million years old, the island measures just 3 miles in length and ¾ of a mile across. Rich in wildlife, it is home to thousands of seabirds, including the chatty, clown-like puffins which, it is suggested, give the island its name – 'lundi' being the old Norse word for puffin. Seals play in the surf and Soay sheep, Sika deer and wild goats graze all over the island. There are 23 buildings, all owned by the Landmark Trust, where visitors can stay, and a campsite near the only pub, the Marisco Tavern. There isn't a huge choice of run routes on Lundy, but there's lots to see and the unique feel and setting of the place makes it a special, and definitely wild, place to run.

The north Devon section of the South West Coast Path winds its way along high clifftops and up and down steep wooded gorges, past the towns of Lynton and Lynmouth with their resident goats, and out to the green and tranquil surrounds of Hartland. Autumn is a great time to visit, when the summer crowds have left, the hedges are laden with blackberries, and flocks of geese, skuas and shearwaters fill the air, migrating south. Hartland is well worth a visit for its incredible folded rock formations. These 320 million-year-old sedimentary rocks buckled under the forces of the two great continents of Laurasia and Pangaea colliding.

Managed by the South West Lakes Trust, the 730-acre reservoir of Roadford Lake lies in the Wolf Valley, north-west of Dartmoor, surrounded by wildlife-rich woodland, pasture, orchards and

15

16

16

rare Culm grasslands. Dormice, bats, waterbirds and buzzards all make their homes here and it's a peaceful and pleasant place to explore. Our run at Roadford Lake (14) is an enjoyably varied loop, taking in a nice stretch of the lakeside with views across the silvery water and long sections on forest tracks and through open countryside. Most of the running is on firm, clear paths but some of the route may be wet and boggy after heavy rain.

Hartland Point, the northernmost tip of Devon's Hartland Peninsula, reaches out into the sea at the point where the Bristol Channel meets the Atlantic Ocean. This run (15) begins at Hartland Quay, a former harbour destroyed by fierce storms, that dates back to the time of Henry VIII. Rising and falling with the huge sea cliffs, the South West Coast Path guides you around the peninsula with fine views across to Lundy, some 12 miles offshore. Look out for the Lundy helicopter over the winter months, which flies from Hartland Point. The coast path drops down into wooded Mouth Mill where our route turns inland, following the stream up a leafy cleft to cross the headland, passing Hartland village and the impressive, privately owned, Hartland Abbey. A final descent to sea level returns you to the Quay.

Our Lundy run (16) begins at the Marisco Tavern, the only pub on the island, where hearty breakfasts, simple but tasty lunches and evening feasts, boast plenty of local produce. From here it circumnavigates the island, following the winding coast path past sheer granite sea cliffs, remote cottages and grazing deer, with views out to the sparkling sea on one side and peaceful grassland to the other. There are no cars here, few permanent residents, wildlife that roams peacefully with no fear of humans, and many trails to explore. The feeling of being away from it all – a perfect, peaceful escape – makes running here an incredibly special experience. Regular departures on-board the MS Oldenburg take two hours from Ilfracombe over the summer months.

The deep, wooded valley at Heddon was a favourite haunt of Wordsworth, Coleridge and Shelley. There's a real drama about the place, from the narrow, winding, near-vertical country lanes that access the valley to the far-off glimpses of a bright blue sea framed by steep, rocky headlands. Our Heddon Valley run (17) begins at Hunters Inn, owned by the National Trust, and traces

Routes 14-16

14 ROADFORD LAKE

Distance 13.5 miles/21.5km
Ascent 425 metres
Start Headson car park, EX20 4JR
Info wildrunning.net/214

Turn R onto the road then L on a bridleway past Breazle Farm and north to a road. Cross this and follow footpaths across fields, through woodland and over the River Wolf then uphill to the road in Eworthy (3.2 miles/5.2km). Turn R onto the road then L, then R. Turn R at the crossroads onto this slightly busier road north to a forestry road junction (4.7 miles/7.6km). Turn L into Witherdon Plantation, R at the next T-junction and continue south-west through the woodland to the second R to reach the road at Thorn Barrow (6.5 miles/10.4km). Turn L onto the road to Ivyhouse Cross, turn L here then take the bridleway L past Westweek Barton and across a couple of fields to reach the road near Germansweek (6.5 miles/10.4km). Turn L onto the road then R into the village. At the church turn R, along a footpath south-west to the road. Cross the bridge then take the bridleway R along the lakeside back to the start.

15 HARTLAND

Distance 14 miles/22km
Ascent 1035 metres
Start Hartland Quay, EX39 6DU
Info wildrunning.net/215

From Hartland Quay join the South West Coast Path heading north around Hartland Point then east to Blackchurch Rock (SS 298265, 7.5 miles/12.1km). Leave the coast path and turn inland beside the stream through Snaxland Wood and R onto the bridleway going west through Brownsham Wood to the road and car park at Brownsham. Follow the road across Beckland Cross and then L onto a byway through Norton to another road. Turn L onto the road downhill and L to Pattard Bridge (10.6 miles/17km). Turn R just before the bridge then L onto a footpath leading west through Pattard Wood to the road near the entrance to Hartland Abbey. Turn R onto the road and go uphill, take a footpath L above the abbey to another road. Turn L and take the road into Stoke, turn R along the road back to the start.

16 LUNDY

Distance 6 miles/9km
Ascent 111 metres
Start Marisco Tavern, EX39 2EY
Info wildrunning.net/216

From the Marisco Tavern take the main track north to the north end of the island (2.5 miles/4km). Turn L and follow the path on the western clifftop back in a southerly direction until you reach the lighthouse at Beacon Hill. Turn L here along the track east back to the outbound route, then R to return to the start.

17

18

19

the wide track known as the Carriageway steeply uphill and along the edge of the headland to Woody Bay. Here it zigzags down through woodland, joining a lower path (also the South West Coast Path and the Tarka Trail) to return to Heddon Mouth, finally running along the valley upstream to return to Hunters Inn. Food, drink and accommodation are available at the inn.

Our Foreland Point run (18) is a gem, taking in a superb section of coast path, a glorious, high-level traverse across open moorland and a verdant stretch of the Doone Valley alongside Badgworthy Water. You get a lot of value for your miles here: ascents and descents, views, culture and fantastic running in unbeatable surroundings. From the start it climbs up and over Countisbury Hill before plunging down a fun descent into the wooded valley of the East Lyn River. Following the river upstream there are several excellent swimming spots to be found along the way. At Rockford a steep climb takes you right up onto the high moor, to Shilstone Hill at 403 metres, followed by a joyful section of moorland tracks and blissful views. Dropping back off the moor, this time into the beautiful Doone Valley, the run follows Badgworthy Water, past the campsite at Cloud Farm, making straight for the coast. Joining the South West Coast Path at Glenthorne, the final miles take you along dramatic, wooded cliffs right above the sea, and around Foreland Point, the northernmost spot in mainland Devon.

At 519 metres, Dunkery Beacon is the highest point on Exmoor. This run (19) makes the most of two waymarked trails: the Macmillan Way West, a 102-mile route from Castle Cary in Somerset to Barnstaple in Devon; and the Coleridge Way, a 50-mile route from Nether Stowey in Somerset to Lynmouth in Devon. The steepest section comes right at the start, ascending from the car park straight up to the summit cairn of Dunkery Beacon itself. A long, wonderful descent following the Macmillan Way down the sloping north-eastern flanks of Dunkery Hill brings you to the village of Brockwell, from where the Coleridge Way weaves through a series of wooded valleys to return to the start.

17 HEDDON VALLEY

Distance 6 miles/9.5km
Ascent 960 metres
Start The Hunters Inn, EX31 4PY
Info wildrunning.net/217

From the National Trust Hunters Inn strike north on the path, taking the R higher path which climbs slowly through woodland to the highest point of the route above Highveer Point. Follow the path as it turns R and hugs the coast east past the Beacon, then reaches a road above Woody Bay (2.5 miles/4.1km). Turn L onto the road downhill until you can turn L onto the South West Coast Path at SS 679487 (3 miles/4.9km). Take the coast path west below and in the opposite direction to the higher path you took on the outbound journey. It turns sharp L up the Heddon valley and back to the start.

18 FORELAND POINT

Distance 15.5 miles/24.5km
Ascent 1595 metres
Start Barna Barrow car park, EX35 6NE
Info wildrunning.net/218

Head west from the car park and L at the path junction to the road by the Blue Ball Inn. Cross and follow the path down to the East Lyn River. Turn L along the river path to the footbridge at Rockford (2.7 miles/4.4km). Cross and turn L onto the road then R up a footpath to the higher road. Turn L then R at a sharp bend onto a footpath leading up and over Shilstone Hill. Take the next L onto bridleways trending R down to Badgworthy Water (6.8 miles/10.9km). Turn L and run beside the river to cross the footbridge at Cloud Farm, then take the track to the road at Malmsmead. Turn R onto the road then L onto a path across Oare Water and L down the Coleridge Way. Turn L at SS 791484 uphill to County Gate car park on the A39. Cross and join paths down to the coast path, turn L back around Foreland Point and over Butter Hill to the start.

19 DUNKERY BEACON

Distance 6.5 miles/10km
Ascent 522 metres
Start Dunkery Bridge, TA24 7AT
Info wildrunning.net/219

Start on the obvious path north to the summit of Dunkery Beacon. Turn R and follow the Macmillan Way West, crossing the road and continuing in the same direction to a path junction at SS 924428 just south-west of Brockwell (3 miles/4.8km). Turn sharp R and take the Coleridge Way south-west and down to a stream in woodland at SS 909404. Turn R here, leaving the Coleridge Way and heading west uphill on a track back to the start.

Durdle Door

East Devon & Dorset

The 96 miles of the Jurassic Coast stretch between Old Harry Rocks near Swanage in Dorset and Exmouth in Devon. Documenting some 180 million years of the earth's history, this beautiful, varied and fascinating coastline is a UNESCO World Heritage Site.

Some of the Jurassic Coast's best known and most visually impressive features lie at its Dorset end: the great limestone arch of Durdle Door; the 15-mile stretch of shingle at Chesil Beach; the chalk stacks at Old Harry Rocks; and Golden Cap, a mini Matterhorn from its seaward side, the highest point on the south coast of England. Inland, some of the best running takes to the long chalk ridges where glorious views of the peaceful Dorset countryside are guaranteed. Corfe Castle, standing on the Purbeck Ridgeway, is an iconic reminder of the English Civil War, partially demolished in 1646 by the Parliamentarians.

The section of the South West Coast Path that links Devon and Dorset is known as the Undercliff: an inescapable 7-mile section of landslips overgrown with a tangled jungle of intriguing plants and trees through which the path cuts a clear tunnel. The Undercliff has inspired many, including author John Fowles, who based a scene from his novel The French Lieutenant's Woman here and lived in Lyme Regis, at its eastern end, and Elaine Franks whose intricately observed book on the area is almost as vivid as actually being there.

The East Devon section of the Jurassic Coast falls within an Area of Outstanding Natural Beauty, a landscape characterised by tranquil woodland, vast areas of heathland, rolling grassy hills, fertile river valleys, breathtaking coastal views and dramatic clifftops. From the peaceful pebble beaches at Budleigh Salterton and Branscombe to the sculpted old red sandstone sea stacks at Ladram Bay, this is a fascinating section to explore.

Inland, the Blackdown Hills cover much of the border between East Devon and Somerset, a serene and undiscovered landscape

20

21

22

characterised by steep ridges, high plateaus and wooded valleys, networked by quiet country lanes and meandering footpaths. Nearer to Exeter, Woodbury Common's 200 million-year-old Triassic pebblebeds are thought to be the remnants of a vast desert, which once stretched across to France where the Channel now lies.

The Exe Estuary Trail run (20) is a flat, traffic-free walking and cycling route that takes in the full length of the Exe Estuary between Exmouth and Starcross with glorious estuarine views throughout. There are regular train stations along the way, so you can run as much or as little of the trail as you like. A 3-mile detour at halfway takes you to Exeter Quay, not far from the city centre, where there's a good range of places to relax in the sunshine and refuel. Lutzy's Café by Haven Banks is one of our favourite spots and there's kayak and bike hire and an indoor climbing wall nearby, too. The trail is popular with families so it may get busy during summer weekends and school holidays.

Woodbury Common, part of the East Devon AONB, is a large area of heather-clad pebblebed heathland, networked by numerous inviting trails. This run (21) takes in a superb loop of the East Devon commons, starting at the pretty village of East Budleigh and ascending to the very top at Woodbury Castle. Don't forget to stop and take in the fine views from here before joining the East Devon Way for a scenic loop. An enjoyable, long descent takes you back off the commons to East Budleigh and the friendly 16th-century pub, the Sir Walter Raleigh.

Crossing the border into Dorset, the National Trust-owned, thousand-year-old ruined castle at Corfe stands on the long, chalk escarpment of the Purbeck Hills. Our Corfe Castle run (22) takes in a loop that links up the Purbeck Way – 15 waymarked miles between Wareham and Swanage – and the Hardy Way, a 217-mile loop taking in many of the classic Dorset landscapes beloved by Thomas Hardy and starting at his birthplace near Dorchester. This route also takes you around the Blue Pool at Furzebrook, a deep clay bowl filled with blue(ish) water and surrounded by 25 acres of heath and woodland (paid entry). Parking and a café is available at Corfe Castle's visitor centre and there are several excellent options for camping nearby.

Routes 20-22

20 EXE ESTUARY TRAIL

Distance 19 miles/30km
Ascent 241 metres
Start Exmouth Station, EX8 1BZ
Finish Starcross Station, EX6 8NY
Info wildrunning.net/220

From Exmouth Station head south along the road, R at the roundabout onto Imperial Road then R onto the East Devon Way. Follow this R and up the estuary path going north-west. At Lympstone either go slightly inland on the East Devon Way or stay closer to the estuary on the road. Continue on the trail crossing the River Clyst into Topsham and along roads L back to the river. Turn R onto the riverside path under the motorway and stay on the northern bank of the River Exe all the way into Exeter (10 miles/16km). Cross the suspension footbridge and skirt the southern shore, cross the first bridge L then run along the east bank of the canal to Countess Wear Bridge (12.1 miles/19.5km). Cross the canal using the road bridge and take the western shore path on the Exe Valley Way under the motorway to the Turf Locks pub. Cross the canal onto the riverside path south to Starcross Station.

21 WOODBURY COMMON

Distance 8.5 miles/13.5km
Ascent 329 metres
Start East Budleigh, EX9 7ED
Info wildrunning.net/221

Set off on Hayes Lane north-west uphill to the path junction at SY 051850 near Hayes Barton. Turn R and take the path north to the road at Yettington, turn R then L on the road and then R onto a bridleway at the edge of the woods (1.7 miles/2.8km). Follow this north then L at the fork and across the common to Woodbury Castle. Continue north then L onto the East Devon Way to reach the B3180. Cross and continue on the East Devon Way along a lane then bear L onto a track leading south through some woodland and back to the B3180 at Four Firs car park (4.9 miles/7.9km). Continue on the East Devon Way south-east to the next road, turn R then L, leaving the East Devon Way and taking a footpath south-east across East Budleigh Common. Join Hayeswood Lane back into East Budleigh. Turn L on High Street to return to the start.

22 CORFE CASTLE

Distance 6 miles/9km
Ascent 219 metres
Start Corfe Castle, BH20 5EZ
Info wildrunning.net/222

Turn R out of the car park onto the A351 north briefly then turn L onto the Purbeck Way heading west, go around a sharp R then L onto a bridleway. Stay on the Purbeck Way, turning R at the first junction and straight across at the next junction, trending L to join a road and the Hardy Way (2.4 miles/3.9km). Turn L onto the road and follow it south until you can turn L onto a footpath at SY 931822 straight onto Knowle Hill. Climb uphill then L up the ridge to the summit. Take the ridge path east then drop down to the southern edge of the hill just before the trig point. Run along the track east towards the castle and around the eastern end of the hill back to the Purbeck Way and the outbound route. Turn R and return to the start.

23

24

25

At 191 metres, Golden Cap is the highest point on England's south coast, named for the distinctive layer of golden greensand rock that forms its pointed summit. Our Golden Cap run (23) begins at Seatown, right at the foot of the hill, climbing up to loop around Langdon Hill – it's worth visiting in summer for the incredible display of bluebells in the woods here. A long, fast descent beside a stream through fields and St Gabriel's Wood brings you to the edge of the sea. From here it's a long climb on a dramatic clifftop section of the South West Coast Path all the way to the summit of Golden Cap, to be rewarded by the best views around. Staying on the coast path there's a steep but enjoyable descent back to Seatown, where the Anchor Inn comes recommended.

The Isle of Portland is 4 miles long by 1.7 miles wide, joined to the mainland by the shingle spit of Chesil Beach. An important feature of the Jurassic Coast, the north of the island is formed from sand and clay, whereas the south lies on hard limestone. Due to its prominent position, Portland bears the scars of many years of military presence and quarrying for its much sought-after white limestone, used to build St Paul's Cathedral and the UN headquarters. Yet despite this it retains many natural riches, from interesting wildlife to rugged cliffs and hidden coves. This run (24) circumnavigates the island, making the most of its diversity, including a stretch on the leg-sapping shingle to start and finish.

Durdle Door lies within the 12,000-acre Lulworth Estate, which is privately owned but open to the public, seeing around 200,000 visitors each year. Despite its popularity, out of season this is a peaceful yet awe-inspiring place, a great stone arch stepping out into the sea, improbably standing the test of time – for now at least. The coast around here is equally striking, from the perfect oval of neighbouring Lulworth Cove to the chalk cliffs at White Nothe to the west. Our Durdle Door run (25) takes in a delightful loop, much of which feels wonderfully wild and remote, starting along the grassy headland above the Door with great views in all directions, in particular across to the Isle of Portland. Just before Upton it dives downhill to reach the South West Coast Path at Ringstead, a peaceful bay that's perfect for a mid-run dip – there's a nudist beach 20 minutes' walk east of the main beach. From here it's an enjoyable run along the clifftops back to Durdle Door.

25

Routes 23-25

23 GOLDEN CAP

Distance 4.5 miles/7km
Ascent 406 metres
Start The Anchor Inn, DT6 6JU
Info wildrunning.net/223

Join the South West Coast Path west from Seatown, forking R at about ½ a mile uphill towards Langdon Hill Woods. Turn R at the south-west corner of woodland and follow the path uphill to a forest track, turn R onto this around to the Langdon Hill car park (1.3 miles/2.1km). Take the track through the top of the car park and around the northern end of the wood, turn R at SY 409930 and pick up a footpath south-west past Filcombe Farm then generally south-west to the coast path near St Gabriel's Mouth (2.7 miles/4.3km). Turn L onto the coast path and back to the start.

24 TOUR OF PORTLAND

Distance 13 miles/20.5km
Ascent 1285 metres
Start Chesil Beach Visitor Centre,
  DT4 9XE
Info wildrunning.net/224

Take the path by the A354 onto Portland but stay R on the coast path. Climb uphill at the southern end of Chesil Cove and leave the coast path to cross New Road towards the eastern coast. Join the footpath north-east joining Verne Hill Road then turn L onto Glacis Road which becomes the South West Coast Path. Follow the path south to Portland Bill (7.3 miles/11.8km). Now stay on the coast path north up the western coast until you join the outbound path above Chesil Cove. Turn L and retrace your steps to the start.

25 DURDLE DOOR

Distance 10 miles/16km
Ascent 472 metres
Start Durdle Door car park, BH20 5PU
Info wildrunning.net/225

Return from the car park along the road through the holiday park to the main road at Newlands Farm, turn L and join a footpath leading west roughly parallel to the coast. Follow this to a car park at the end of the road at SY 757824 (4 miles/6.5km). Run along the road until a footpath L passing Glebe Cottage and leading to the South West Coast Path at the village of Ringstead. Turn L onto the coast path east above Ringstead Bay to Durdle Door. Take the busy and obvious path inland and uphill back to the start.

Westbury White Horse

Somerset, Avon & Wiltshire

Its name meaning 'land of the summer people', Somerset is a county of great contrasts, from the wild moorland and wooded valleys of Exmoor through the Quantock Hills and open grasslands of the Somerset Levels to the Mendip Hills. The Mendips lie right across Somerset from Frome in the east to Brean Down in the west, with steep, snaking tracks and grassy summits interspersed with deep wooded gorges, of which Cheddar is perhaps the best known. Wiltshire, in contrast, is characterised by high downlands and wide valleys, dominated by the great chalk plateau of Salisbury Plain with its 2,300 prehistoric sites and long history of military use. The megalithic stone circle at Avebury is the finishing point of the 86-mile Ridgeway National Trail, which runs between here and Ivinghoe Beacon in the Chilterns.

The Quantock Hills run from the Vale of Taunton Deane in the south for about 15 miles to Quantoxhead on the Bristol Channel. This was England's first AONB and boasts incredibly diverse landscapes of heathland, oak woodlands, ancient parklands and agricultural land. On a clear day, from the highest point at Wills Neck, it is possible to see Glastonbury Tor to the east, the Gower Peninsula to the north, Exmoor to the west and the Blackdown Hills to the south.

The city of Bath, nestled in a sheltered valley surrounded by wooded hills and magnificent countryside, is a UNESCO World Heritage Site, rich in Roman and Georgian history and architecture. The Kennet and Avon Canal runs through the heart of the city, before windings its way past picturesque Cotswold villages to the small but perfectly formed town of Bradford-on-Avon; the towpath makes an enjoyable run, with several train stations along the way. The Cotswold Way enters its final miles as it approaches Bath, 102 miles after leaving Chipping Campden, taking in the spectacular high ground around Dyrham Park and Bath Racecourse before descending to finish at Bath Abbey in the city centre.

27

27

28

Bristol is the most populous city in the south-west, yet it has numerous green spaces and adventurous trails within easy reach. The dramatic Avon Gorge, which separates the large, grassy area of the Downs from the 850-acre Ashton Court estate, was carved by glacial meltwater at the end of the last ice age. Protected, for now, from future development, this western fringe of the city boasts some of the best opportunities for running adventures.

Crook Peak – its name deriving from the old English 'cruc' meaning 'peak' – rises temptingly within clear sight of the M5 motorway. On many occasions, before we ran there, we admired its perfect conical shape as we drove past and wondered whether it would make a good run. Our run here (26) takes in thoroughly enjoyable circuit of the summits of both Crook Peak and its neighbouring Wavering Down, with excellent running on grassy trails and fine views across the Mendips, the Somerset Levels and out across the Bristol Channel to Wales from the tops. It's a great place to stop a stretch your legs en route to the West Country – and there's even an annual Crook Peak Cake Race.

The Quantock Hills run north-west to south-east across west Somerset. The main ridgeline along the top is part of an old drovers' road and also the Macmillan Way West, with some sections that feel like a run through time, worn and sunken through thousands of years of footfall and lined with ancient beach trees. Well maintained and easy to follow, this is a great place to start exploring the hills, with most of the surrounding footpaths and bridleways extending from this central trail. The Quantocks run (27) begins near the pleasant village of Crowcombe and takes in a good section of the ridge path as far as the trig point-topped summit of Beacon Hill. Here it dives down the hillside into lush woodland, shadowing a series of streams along wooded combes. The final climb back up to the summit of Black Hill to finish is a good challenge for the legs and rewarded with glorious 360-degree views. An enjoyable out-and-back extension to Wills Neck, the highest point in the Quantocks, adds a couple of extra miles and another great vista.

At over 120 metres deep and 3 miles long, Cheddar is England's largest gorge: a truly spectacular sight with its sheer limestone

26 CROOK PEAK

Distance 7.5 miles/11.5km
Ascent 370 metres
Start Webbington Road layby, BH26 2HN
Info wildrunning.net/226

Take Webbington Road east to the junction with Rackley Lane where you turn L onto a footpath leading uphill. Take the R onto a byway to the road in Compton Bishop, turn L onto Butts Batch then R onto Church Lane. Go straight ahead onto a track where the road goes R. Stay on this footpath around a R bend and east across fields and above Compton Farm, then generally R to reach Old Coach Road in Cross (2.2 miles/3.6km). Turn L onto the road for 400 metres to a L onto a bridleway going north. Follow this to a junction with the West Mendip Way (3.5 miles/5.6km). Turn L onto the bridleway going west past the trig point on Wavering Down to the summit of Crook Peak. Turn L onto the path leading south-east down the ridge to reach Webbington Road and the outbound path, then bear R to return to the start.

27 QUANTOCKS

Distance 7 miles/11km
Ascent 295 metres
Start Crowcombe Park Gate, TA4 4AB
Info wildrunning.net/227

Join the Macmillan Way West in a north-westerly direction along the main Quantock ridge. After 1.9 miles/3km at ST 129398 stay R on the main track, leaving the Macmillan Way which bears L and downhill. Continue north past Bicknoller Post to the trig point on Beacon Hill. Drop down the northern side of this hill slightly and take the next sharp R onto a path going south-east to the ridge of Longstone Hill (4 miles/6.4km). Stay south here dropping down into the woods at Lady's Edge and following the stream L to the next path junction where you turn R and continue south uphill and back onto the open moorland. Turn L at the main track and then R over the hill and past the trig point back to the start.

28 CHEDDAR GORGE

Distance 8.5 miles/13.5km
Ascent 347 metres
Start Blackrock Gate layby, BA5 3BT
Info wildrunning.net/228

Follow the track east towards Black Rock, turn L uphill after the gate and around to the L up a long flight of steps and south-west to a path junction. Turn R onto a footpath leading across fields, to the L of Piney Sleight Farm and past Charterhouse Farm to the road (2.6 miles/4.2km). Turn R and then L onto a footpath north-east across fields to the open moorland below Beacon Batch. Skirt the eastern edge of the moorland to a path junction, turn L then after 0.6 miles/1km bear R onto the straight path to the trig point (4.4 miles/7.1km). Run south-east back to the track junction, turn L east to the wireless station masts. Fork R on the road downhill, turn R onto the next road then L onto a footpath to Blackmoor. Turn R at the next junction, then R onto a byway to cross a road. Take the path down Velvet Bottom to the start.

30

30

31

walls and rocky pinnacles. Our Cheddar run (28) takes in a stunning loop of the surrounding Mendip landscape, starting along the top of the gorge with vertiginous views into its cavernous depths. The climb up Black Down to the top of Beacon Batch, the highest point in the Mendip Hills at 320 metres, is rewarded with wonderful views and the knowledge that it's all downhill from now on. The final stretch along the gently meandering valley of Velvet Bottom provides outstanding running, bringing you back into the top end of the gorge.

Easily accessible from Bristol city centre, Ashton Court estate covers 850 acres of parkland and woodland. Our Ashton Court run (29) packs a bit of everything into just 3 miles, with a tough climb, woodland trails, open grassland and a fun, technical descent. Neighbouring Leigh Woods offers a good way to extend the run should you wish, or link up with the Downs on the opposite side of the Avon Gorge by way of the Clifton Suspension Bridge.

The River Avon rises in the Cotswold Hills of South Gloucestershire and makes its way through Wiltshire and Somerset to join the Severn Estuary at Avonmouth near Bristol, passing many picturesque towns, villages and stretches of countryside along its route. The historic town of Bradford-on-Avon is the starting point for our Two Valleys run (30), which follows the course of the river to its confluence with the River Frome before exploring a hidden valley and the beautiful village of Iford, with its honey-coloured manor. A peaceful stretch alongside the Kennet and Avon Canal brings you back into Bradford.

Cley Hill rises from the Wiltshire plains on the edge of the Longleat estate, a grass-covered chalk prominence, rich in wildlife. Known as a UFO hotspot, there are often crop circles in the surrounding fields and regular sightings of unexplained lights in the skies above the hill. Older legend has it that it was created by the devil who dropped a sack of earth that he had intended to use to bury the nearby town of Devizes. Its distinctive, sculpted shape is the result of erosion by ancient seas, prehistoric human activity and more recent farming and quarrying. Our Cley Hill run (31) takes to the inviting chalk trails that carve their way across the hill's steep sides, climbing to the very top for big, open skies and views across the surrounding countryside.

29 ASHTON COURT

Distance 3.5 miles/5.5km
Ascent 154 metres
Start Church Lodge car park, BS41 9JH
Info wildrunning.net/229

Set off north from the car park and turn L onto the open common area, taking paths north-west uphill to reach a track. Turn L, running south-west parallel to the road to a sharp corner at ST 541711 (1 mile/1.7km). Turn R then R at the next junction, trend L now to the main track along the edge of the golf course, turn R on this and follow it to the path junction at ST 554723 (2.4 miles/3.8km). Turn R onto the path to Ashton Court, stay R of the buildings and choose the smaller path through woodland to the open area at the beginning of the run. Turn L and return across it to the start.

30 TWO VALLEYS

Distance 7.5 miles/12km
Ascent 335 metres
Start Bradford-on-Avon Station, BA15 1EF
Info wildrunning.net/230

Join the path at the western end of the car park and turn L under the bridge. Turn R onto the towpath to the R of the tithe barn along to Avoncliff. Go under the aqueduct and continue west along the river to the road at Freshford (2.4 miles/3.9km). Turn R across the bridge then L into the field, stay R uphill then L downhill to the road. Turn R then L at Dunkirk Mill. Take the footpath uphill through woodland to the A36 (3.4 miles/5.5km). Turn L into the parking area, join the footpath and trend R through Friary Wood then continue east to the road at Iford (4.7 miles/7.6km). Turn L across the bridge then R past the house and uphill, L at the top and along the road for ¼ mile to a bridleway on your R. Follow this to Westwood. Turn R then L onto a footpath, and stay R to reach the outbound route at Avoncliff. Turn R and return to the start detouring through Barton Farm Country Park for a change.

31 CLEY HILL

Distance 6 miles/9.5km
Ascent 203 metres
Start Cley Hill car park, BA12 7RE
Route wildrunning.net/231

Take the main track towards Cley Hill but turn R onto the Mid Wilts Way after the farm buildings. Just before the A36 leave the Mid Wilts Way and turn L onto a bridleway leading north-west, past Cley Hill Farm to a road at Water Farm. Turn L onto the road then L onto a footpath to the road at Corsley (3.4 miles/5.4km). Turn L on the road past the church, then R onto a footpath leading south across fields to the road at Corsley House. Turn R onto the road to a junction with the A362 and cross it onto a footpath to a smaller road. Turn R then L onto a footpath going east, recrossing the A362 and passing Sturford Mead Farm before climbing to the summit of Cley Hill. Head south of the summit and along the track back to the start.

32

33

34

Salisbury Plain covers 300 square miles of chalk downland, mainly in the county of Wiltshire. Large areas of the sparsely populated plain are used for military training purposes; however, it's also rich in wildlife and archaeology and is a fascinating place to visit. Our Imber Perimeter run (32) tracks the Imber Range Perimeter Path, a waymarked route around the Imber military firing range. Starting and finishing on the Wessex Ridgeway and following the escarpment above the Westbury White Horse, the route passes through Warminster, Tilshead, Chitterne and Heytesbury. Between these settlements, however, there are some very remote sections – this is a challenging and lengthy run and reasonable navigation skills along with plenty of supplies are strongly recommended. Check www.gov.uk/government/publications/salisbury-plain-imber-range-perimeter-path for up-to-date live firing and access information before visiting.

Pewsey lies on the western fringes of the North Wessex Downs AONB, a pleasant and well-serviced village with a train station and excellent access to the surrounding countryside. The white horse here was cut into the hillside by volunteers from the local Fire Brigade in 1937, replacing a lost 18th century one. Our Pewsey White Horse run (33) follows the White Horse Trail out of Pewsey straight to the white horse and steeply up onto the escarpment. A long, enjoyable section runs along the chalk edges of Pewsey Hill and Fyfield Down before descending through fields and the village of Milton Lilbourne. The final section alongside the Kennet and Avon Canal is a peaceful way to finish.

The Bath Skyline is a National Trust-maintained waymarked trail that traces the open spaces above the city, its views extending to the rolling hills beyond. This run (34) winds its way through hidden limestone valleys, meadows carpeted with flowers and tranquil beech woodlands. At times the running is surprisingly challenging with some rough, steep ground, however on reaching those hard-won high points you are rewarded with breathtaking panoramas that open out beneath your feet. The route also passes an Iron Age hill fort, Sham Castle, on the outskirts of the University grounds, and Prior Park Landscape Garden with its rare Palladian Bridge, serpentine lake and paths and caves to explore (paid entry/NT membership).

Routes 32-34

32 IMBER PERIMETER

Distance 31 miles/49.5km
Ascent 854 metres
Start Warminster Station, BA12 9BP
Info wildrunning.net/232

Leaving the station turn L onto Copheap Lane then R onto Elm Hill, to a path junction. Turn L and join the Imber Range Perimeter Path, uphill initially and trending north-west to Upton Cow Down (2.9 miles/4.7km). Turn R and follow the path generally north-east to the trig point on Stoke Hill (9.4 miles/15.2km). Take the Imber Path south-east to the A360 junction (13.1 miles/21.1km). Turn R onto the road briefly then bear R onto a path leading south but detouring through Tilshead, then south-west to the B390 in Chitterne (20.4 miles/32.8km). Shortly turn R on the Imber path, going west on a byway to a road at East Hill Farm. Turn L towards Heytesbury. Turn R above Heytesbury onto a footpath heading north-west over Cotley Hill, Scratchbury Hill and Battlesbury Hill to Sack Hill Road. Take this south turning R onto Elm Hill and returning to the start.

33 PEWSEY WHITE HORSE

Distance 9.5 miles/15km
Ascent 248 metres
Start Pewsey Library, SN9 5EQ
Info wildrunning.net/233

From the start (or the station) turn R onto North Street then L onto High Street. Turn R onto Ball Road and fork L onto Southcott Road. Turn R onto a footpath through woodland then L to Green Drove Farm. Turn R here then L onto Green Drove which leads to the Pewsey White Horse. Climb the steep path beside the horse and trend L, on a footpath below Pewsey Hill and along Fyfield Down to a path junction at SU 188588 (3.7 miles/5.9km). Turn R going north-east then drop down the hill and run north across fields to the road at Priory Cottage (4.6 miles/7.4km). Turn L onto the road into Milton Lilbourne. Take the footpath R after the church and fork L, cross two roads and rejoin the road at New Mill. Turn R and cross the railway then bear L onto the canal path to Pains Bridge (8.1 miles/13km). Turn L and follow the path to Knowle then R onto a footpath parallel to the railway. Turn L onto North Street and return to the start.

34 BATH SKYLINE

Distance 6 miles/9km
Ascent 276 metres
Start Bathwick Hill, BA2 6JZ
Info wildrunning.net/234

From the route's crossing point on Bathwick Hill, bear south between houses and out onto the fields trending L and uphill to the road at Widcombe Hill. Turn L up to the bend where you cross and follow a track uphill. Turn R at the junction and bear south again before turning L onto the path parallel with Claverton Down Road. Turn L in Larch Wood and run north-east, crossing Claverton Down Road and joining The Avenue by the Bath Cats and Dogs Home (2.8 miles/4.5km). Turn R then L onto a path leading north across a large field and trending L above Hengrove Wood. Continue on the waymarked Skyline path which skirts the edge of the woodland around the golf course on Bathampton Down. Pass the communication masts at ST 768655 and continue south-west through woodland, detouring up to Sham Castle. Descend steeply to North Road, turn R then L onto a footpath down to Cleveland Walk, turn L on this to return to the start.

South & East

Southern and Eastern England is home to a diverse spectrum of landscapes, from London's grassy parks and riverside trails to the dramatic chalk cliffs at Beachy Head, and from Surrey's wooded hills and the rolling, grassy downland of the North and South Downs to the vast, sandy beaches, broads and heather-covered heaths of East Anglia.

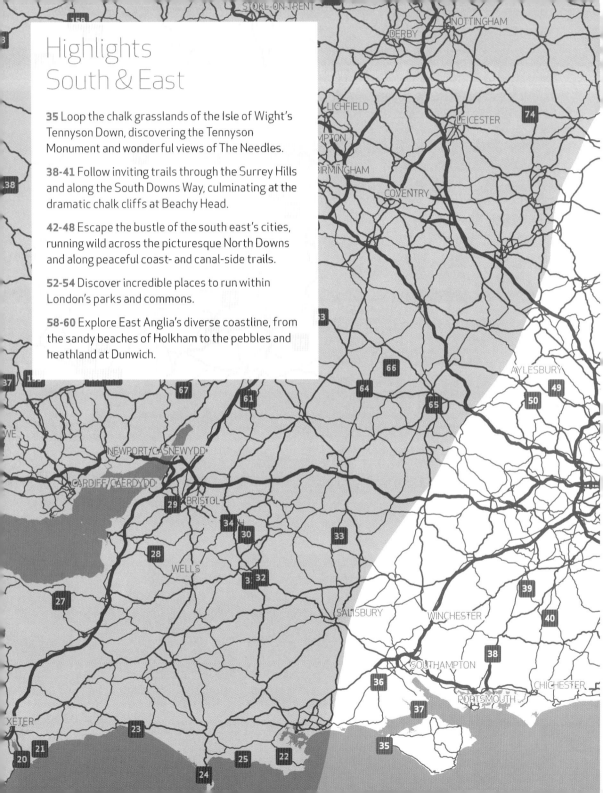

Highlights
South & East

35 Loop the chalk grasslands of the Isle of Wight's Tennyson Down, discovering the Tennyson Monument and wonderful views of The Needles.

38-41 Follow inviting trails through the Surrey Hills and along the South Downs Way, culminating at the dramatic chalk cliffs at Beachy Head.

42-48 Escape the bustle of the south east's cities, running wild across the picturesque North Downs and along peaceful coast- and canal-side trails.

52-54 Discover incredible places to run within London's parks and commons.

58-60 Explore East Anglia's diverse coastline, from the sandy beaches of Holkham to the pebbles and heathland at Dunwich.

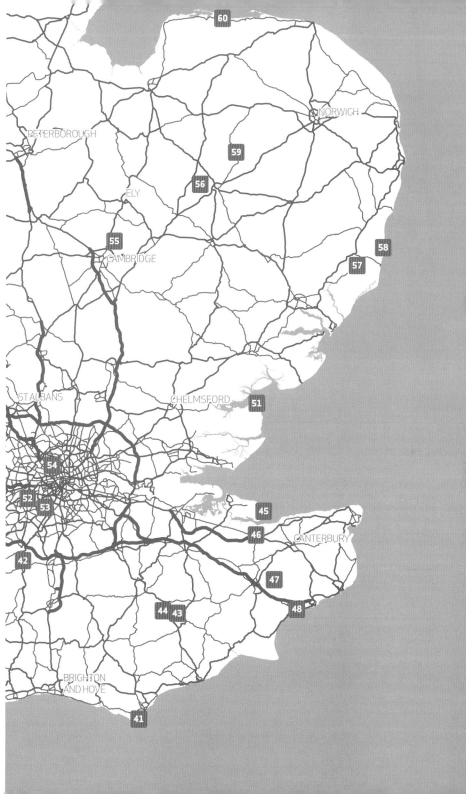

Frensham

Hampshire & the South Downs

Originally used for deer hunting by William I in the 11th century, the New Forest covers 150 square miles of broadleaved woodland, tree plantations, heath and pastureland. The National Park extends even further (218 square miles), making it the largest area of unsown vegetation in lowland Britain. It's an enjoyable place to run with over 140 miles of well-kept trails undulating their way through the varied landscape. Several rivers run through the forest and drain to the nearby sea and, in the south of the National Park where the New Forest meets the Solent, you'll find seabirds, pine-fringed meadows and glorious sea views.

The South Downs is a range of chalk hills that extends from Hampshire's Itchen valley in the west to Beachy Head, near Eastbourne, in the east. Rich in wildlife and archaeology, this is also a great place to run and the 100-mile South Downs Way, a route used by people for some 8,000 years, winds its way invitingly along the ridge between Winchester and Beachy Head. At its north-eastern end the South Downs merges with the Surrey Hills. With over 40 per cent of the landscape here being woodland, this is a perfect place to escape to run amongst the trees, just a short distance from London.

At 984 square miles, the Isle of Wight is England's largest island, with over half being a designated AONB. The wildest and most peaceful areas are in the west of the island, with its dramatic coastlines and chalk downland ridge that runs across the whole island, ending in the iconic Needles stacks. The Isle of Wight Marathon is Britain's oldest continuously held marathon, having been run every year since 1957.

Like so many islands, the Isle of Wight has a character all of its own. There's plenty to explore here and the area is rich in wildlife (including red squirrels), history and culture. Tennyson lived on the island for 40 years from 1853 and some of the best routes we've found pay homage to his name. The Tennyson Trail is a 14-mile undulating and adventurous run across the

35

36

37

island from Carisbrooke to The Needles, while Tennyson Down (run 35) provides a wonderfully scenic loop, taking in the wilder western edge of the island and heading right down to The Needles. Post-run tea and cake, complete with proper china and grand views, is served at the Old Battery Tearooms located in the former Port War Signal Station.

Heading across the water to the New Forest, our next route sets out from the pretty town of Lyndhurst (run 36), right in the centre of the National Park. A loop of wild-feeling open heathland takes in a rare road-crossing-free section of the forest, although it's hard to avoid the network of roads and train lines altogether here. The route passes Ashurst Station so if you're arriving by train begin here. For a pleasant extension to the run, cross the B3056 at Matley Passage and head down through Denny Wood towards Brockenhurst, following one of the many trails that wind back to Lyndhurst.

Lepe Country Park lies at the south-eastern corner of the New Forest, a popular but picturesque spot with fine views out across the Solent to the Isle of Wight. Admission is free but there are parking charges. The Lepe Loop (run 37) begins with a glorious mile or so of running right along the edge of the coast, reaching the Beaulieu Estuary where it heads inland following good trails through fields and woodland, eventually returning to the coast at Lepe. Note, the coastal footpath is liable to flooding at high tide.

The South Downs Way runs for an enticing 100 miles between Winchester and Beachy Head. There are many outstanding sections for running and it's a great route for fastpacking, with plenty of campsites to choose from along the way and train stations at either end. Our Butser Hill run (38) begins at Queen Elizabeth Country Park and heads straight for the summit of Butser Hill which, at 271 metres, is the highest point on the South Downs chalk ridge and the second-highest in the National Park. From here there's an amazing long descent down the less-steep north-west flank of the hill. Butser Hill fell race takes place here each September, with three ascents of the hill in just 5 miles.

Routes 35-37

35 TENNYSON DOWN ISLE OF WIGHT

Distance 6 miles/9.5km
Ascent 247 metres
Start High Down car park, PO39 0HY
Info wildrunning.net/235

Facing south turn L and follow the footpath east towards Freshwater Bay. Turn R at the end of the woodland and head towards the sea joining the coastal Tennyson Trail (1.1 miles/1.7km). Turn R and follow the trail west passing the Tennyson Monument where you leave the Tennyson Trail and stay L along the coast to the Old Battery at the western tip of the island (4 miles/6.7km). Head back east along the northern edge of the hill to the start.

36 LYNDHURST

Distance 6.5 miles/10km
Ascent 90 metres
Start Bolton's Bench car park, SO43 7BQ
Info wildrunning.net/236

Head south-east through Matley Wood to a path junction at SU 339079 (2.4 miles/3.9km). Turn L here past Ashurst Lodge and through Ashurst Wood to a path junction near the remains of Saltpetre House at 3.8 miles/6.1km. Turn L and head south-west, bear R at the next path junction then R where the path crosses Beaulieu River. Continue on the path around Foxhill Moor then trend L on paths heading south-west to intersect with the outbound path on White Moor. Turn R to return to the start.

37 THE LEPE LOOP

Distance 5 miles/8km
Ascent 72 metres
Start Lepe Country Park, SO45 1AD
Info wildrunning.net/237

Follow the path to the beach and turn R heading west along the coastal path towards the Beaulieu River estuary. Continue onto a road and take a R onto a footpath at a left-hand bend (1.7 miles/2.8km). Follow this footpath north away from the coast, staying L at the first path junction then turning R at the second (2.4 miles/3.8km). Follow this footpath to the road, crossing to join a bridleway heading north-east to Burnthays Copse and then east to a path junction just east of East Hill Farm (3.5 miles/5.6km). Turn R onto a footpath and follow this around a L corner then south back to Lepe beach. Turn L here to return to the start.

38

39

40

Frensham Common covers 922 metres of heathland rich in wildlife, including lizards, woodlarks, terns and nightjars, and dotted with ancient gnarled oak trees. There are two large lakes on the common – Frensham Great Pond and Frensham Little Pond – and a wide variety of landscape features that make for interesting and enjoyable running. The Frensham run (39) takes you around both ponds and through many different parts of the common. Swimming is permitted at Frensham Great Pond, perfect for a post-run dip on a warm day, or a spot of swimrun, and there's a National Trust café at the Little Pond for well-earned refreshments. Note, blue-green algae is sometimes present so avoid the water when signs are up.

The hidden trig point that stands at 280 metres on the wooded summit of Black Down is the highest point in Sussex and also in the whole of the South Downs National Park. The mixed landscape of grassland and woodland is scored through by ancient sunken lanes and drovers' roads, perfect for exploring at a run. Forage on the run for ripe blackberries and bilberries over the summer and autumn months. Our Black Down run (40) follows the Serpent Trail north to Haslemere, where you could also start the route if arriving by train, weaving through the outskirts of the town before heading back towards Black Down to join the Sussex Border Path. Winding woodland trails bring you to the Temple of the Winds, a favourite spot of Tennyson's, from where there are far-reaching views across the Sussex countryside.

The awe-inspiring white cliffs at Beachy Head and the surrounding coast are a fitting finale to the 100-mile South Downs Way, and as good a reason as any to choose to run it west-to-east. The Beachy Head & Seven Sisters run (41) starts and finishes on this National Trail, taking in dramatic Beachy Head, lush woodland at Friston Forest, a meandering stretch of the Cuckmere River and the incredible undulating clifftop trail over the Seven Sisters.

38 BUTSER HILL

Distance 6 miles/9.5km
Ascent 396 metres
Start Queen Elizabeth Country Park, PO8 0QE
Info wildrunning.net/238

Follow the South Downs Way under the A3 and through the overflow car park into the large field below Butser Hill. Take the clear path uphill then turn R and follow the track past the radio masts to the trig point (1.5 miles/2.4km). Follow the path north down Ramsdean Down ridge to join a byway heading north to the road at Twentyways Farm (2.7 miles/4.4km). Turn L and follow the road for ½ a mile then turn L down Limekiln Lane byway to the car park at Cross Dyke (4.6 miles/7.4km). Turn sharp L here and follow the South Downs Way back to the top of Butser Hill then back to the start.

39 FRENSHAM

Distance 5 miles/8km
Ascent 71 metres
Start Frensham Great Pond, GU10 3DX
Info wildrunning.net/239

From the start follow the bridleway north-east across Frensham Common, cross the A287 and then turn L, following the bridleway north to the edge of the common (1.1 miles/1.7km). Turn R and head east to Frensham Little Pond. Follow the footpath around its eastern shore, joining a track at the south-eastern corner and following this to a junction with a bridleway at SU 866407 (2.7 miles/4.3km). Turn R and follow the bridleway past the end of Sandy Lane and L at the junction after the footbridge. Follow this bridleway south-west to Pond Lane at the south-eastern tip of Frensham Great Pond. Follow Pond Lane to return to the start.

40 BLACK DOWN

Distance 7 miles/11km
Ascent 365 metres
Start Tennyson Lane car park, GU27 3BJ
Info wildrunning.net/240

Follow the waymarked Serpent Trail R from the car park and north along the road to a L turn after about ½ a mile. Follow this bridleway north-west past High Barn Farm and across the B2131 into Haslemere (2.4 miles/3.9km). Turn L off the Serpent Trail

back to the B2131, Turn L and then R after a short distance to another road. Turn L then R onto a byway uphill past Stedlands Farm. Turn L into Chase Wood heading south-east to the Sussex Border Path onto Black Down. Turn R onto the Serpent Trail to reach Temple of the Winds (5.6 miles/9km). Follow the main trail north back to the start.

41 BEACHY HEAD & SEVEN SISTERS

Distance 15.5 miles/24.5km
Ascent 1109 metres
Start Beachy Head Countryside Centre, BN20 7YA
Info wildrunning.net/241

Follow the South Downs Way north to the A259. Cross and continue north on the South Downs Way over Willingdon Hill crossing a road at Jevington. Leave the South Downs Way at the next junction (TQ 556017, 5.5 miles/8.8km). Turn L and follow the bridleway south-west through Friston Forest to Westdean (8 miles/13km). Turn L here to join the alternative South Downs Way south to the coast at Cuckmere Haven. Turn L and follow the coast path east back to the start.

Box Hill Circular

Kent & the North Downs

Kent is often referred to as the garden of England for its abundance of orchards and agriculture, thanks to its mild climate and fertile soil. Amongst its many borders, the county has some more unusual ones: with France, halfway through the Channel Tunnel, and with Essex in the middle of the Thames Estuary. The Weald Dome, centred around Tunbridge Wells, is formed from layers of limestone, sandstone and clay, whilst the North and South Downs that flank the Dome are of the chalk for which the area is famous, forming the iconic White Cliffs of Dover from which France can be seen on a clear day. The running here is greatly varied, from the green lushness of the forests and rolling hills in the west, to the vast solitude of the salt marshes in the east.

Parts of the North and South Downs Ways pass through the county, and there is an abundance of other waymarked trails for great running days out. The North Downs, much more easily accessible from the centre of London than their neighbouring South Downs, is a range of chalk hills that run from Farnham to the White Cliffs of Dover, passing through two Areas of Outstanding Natural Beauty: the Surrey Hills and the Kent Downs. The North Downs Way follows these hills for 153 miles, winding its way through areas rich in wildlife and history.

Although the channels which once made their separation more obvious are now silted up, the Isle (formerly isles) of Sheppey comprises three land masses: Sheppey itself, Harty and Elmley. Harty, with its vast views across the Swale Estuary to mainland Kent and out to sea past Whitstable Bay, lies at the south-eastern tip of the island and was once described by Sir John Betjeman as sitting in "splendid isolation, with seabirds wheeling by and the Thames so wide as to be open sea, and air so fresh as to be healthier than yoghurt (unflavoured)". This is a remote and almost strangely quiet place, with just a few buildings dotted about and the pub – the Ferry Inn – with its gardens sloping right down to the water's edge. Vast numbers of birds fill the land, sky and sea, and by night the chilling shriek of a barn owl echoes

42

43

44

through the stillness. Across the Swale lie the Oare Marshes, a nature reserve and home to abundant wildlife and thousands of seabirds. Thames sailing barges, with their great red-brown sails, can often be seen at the mouth of the Swale, awaiting the tides that will allow them passage.

Box Hill lies within the Surrey Hills region of the North Downs. Taking its name from the ancient box woodland that grows on the slopes surrounding the hill, this is a fascinating place to explore. The Box Hill Circular (run 42) takes you on a tour of the wooded hills and valleys of this part of the country, whose beautiful and diverse landscapes often feel a million miles from the busy south-east. There are also a number of waymarked walks around Box Hill, great for running or wildlife spotting. Refuel at the National Trust café at the visitor centre.

One of our most enjoyable projects since writing the first edition of Wild Running has been working with the Forestry Commission to bring self-navigated 10km Wild Running routes to a number of its sites, which balance commercial timber production, wildlife conservation and outdoor recreation outstandingly well. Bedgebury, situated in the High Weald AONB, is home to the National Pinetum and has many excellent trails for running and cycling. Our Bedgebury run (43) takes in our favourite loop, with a fun selection of forest roads and technical trails.

Lying at the heart of the High Weald AONB, Bewl Water is the largest inland stretch of open water in the south-east, holding up to 31 million litres of water. It's free to visit, although there is a charge for parking. The 12.5-mile Bewl Water trail (run 44) all the way around the reservoir is an enjoyable challenge, and includes a variety of forest paths, all-weather track and quiet country lanes. It's suitable for bikes and running buggies, too.

Routes 42-44

42 BOX HILL CIRCULAR

Distance 10 miles/16km
Ascent 495 metres
Start Westhumble station, RH5 6BT
Info wildrunning.net/242

Follow Crabtree Lane north-west to the Beechy Wood car park. Turn R here onto a bridleway heading north to a path junction (1.6 miles/2.5km). Turn R and follow a bridleway east and cross the A24 into Mickleham. Turn L and at a track junction (TQ 173540, 3 miles/4.9km) turn R. Follow the footpath uphill across a byway and onto a bridleway running north-east to a path junction in Cherkley Wood. Turn R and run downhill to Lodgebottom Road. Cross and continue on the bridleway, forking L and crossing Headley Heath. Turn R before reaching Headley Common Road and follow the path south then south-west around the common to a junction at the edge of the houses in Box Hill (6.7 miles/10.8km). Turn L following the track south, crossing Boxhill Road and bear R onto the North Downs Way. Follow this over Box Hill then turn R, following the high ground to the north before dropping down to Burford Bridge.

Follow the path south and under the A24 then follow Westhumble Street back to the start.

43 BEDGEBURY

Distance 7 miles/11km
Ascent 198 metres
Start Bedgebury Park, TN17 2SJ
Info wildrunning.net/243

Bedgebury Forest is dotted with walking and cycle trails and most junctions have a numbered finger post – carrying a forestry map will allow you to easily locate yourself. Start by the bike hire centre and head south uphill to the radio masts. Continue around to the L and downhill past the old sawmill to a big track junction at marker 56 (1.1 miles/1.8km). Turn R and follow the main trail L to Louisa Lake. Continue uphill past the lake trending R to a main path junction with a gate at TQ 734334 (2.7 miles/4.4km). Turn R then L at Louisa Lodge and follow the track around Sugarloaf Hill to a junction called Iron latch at TQ 733341 with a marker post labelled T (3.7 miles/6km). Turn L and follow this track past Brick Kiln Cottages, then fork R onto a track which leads downhill to the Forestry Commission offices (4.6

miles/7.4km). Turn L and follow the track south back to the main junction near the sawmill (5.5 miles/8.9km). Turn R here and return to the start along the outbound route.

44 BEWL WATER

Distance 12.5 miles/20km
Ascent 428 metres
Start Bewl Water visitor centre, TN3 8JH
Info wildrunning.net/244

Leave the car park and cross the dam following the lakeside path clockwise around Bewl Water. The path, initially also the Sussex Border Path, stays close to the shore until midway along the southern edge on the promontory near Borders Farm at TQ 679318 (7.3 miles/11.8km). Leave the lake shore and follow Lower Hazelhurst Road south, continuing in the same direction onto Burnt Lodge Lane and turning R onto a footpath at 8 miles/13km. Follow this across a field and join Birchetts Green Lane until you can turn R towards Chessons Farm (9.5 miles/15.3km). Follow this track east past the farm to regain the shore of Bewl Water. Turn L and follow the shore path all the way back to the start.

45

47

48

At just 36 square miles the Isle of Sheppey, separated from mainland Kent by the Swale Estuary, has plenty of great trails to explore. The Harty run (45) loops around the former island of Harty, the southernmost tip of the Isle of Sheppey. Remote and wild, with far-reaching views out to sea, this sparsely populated corner is alive with birds, from avocets to barn owls, many of which can be spotted at the Swale Nature Reserve. Almost completely flat, the land is a mixture of marshes and agriculture, with rounded hillocks that are the remains of medieval saltworks. Earthy tracks run in straight lines around the edges of vast fields and along the shallowly shelving coastline. Refuel at the 16th-century Ferry House Inn, which sits alone under big skies right at the edge of the estuary.

Following the opposite shore of the Swale estuary from the Isle of Sheppey, our intriguing Oare and the Swale run (46) tours the peninsula around the Oare Marshes Nature Reserve, enjoying views across wide open marshland and farmland from the centre of Faversham. A longer run of around 10 miles starts in Oare itself, following the Swale Heritage Trail to Conyer before branching right onto the Saxon Shore Way to return to Oare.

The Wye Downs run (47) is a tour of quintessential English countryside, starting above the Devil's Kneading Trough and heading through farmland to the pretty village of Wye in the Stour Valley. From here it follows the North Downs Way along the chalk downland ridge that rises steeply from the surrounding Kent Weald. There's plenty of excellent running to be discovered here, including challenging ascents and fast descents of the Wye Downs, with their looping, steep-sided valleys carved by 2.5 million years of freezing and thawing of the underlying chalk.

Our next route follows the Royal Military Canal path for 28 miles along the length of the old Royal Military Canal (run 48) from Seabrook, Kent to Cliff End in East Sussex. The route takes in the vast wilderness of Romney Marsh and the old cliffline that runs past wooded hills and quiet villages. Once the site of intense military activity it is now a peaceful, wildlife-rich place. At just over a marathon in distance it's a decent undertaking in one go, or you could spread it over a weekend with a stop along the way.

Routes 45-48

45 HARTY

Distance 6.5 miles/10km
Ascent 29 metres
Start Leysdown Coastal Park, ME12 4RJ
Info wildrunning.net/245

Follow the beachside path south-east past to Shell Ness. Turn R here to follow the Swale Estuary inland along the marsh edge to reach a track near Sayes Court at 3.5 miles/5.6km. Turn R and follow this track north to Elliotts Farm where you turn R and follow a path north-east across marsh and farmland back to the start.

46 OARE & THE SWALE

Distance 8 miles/13km
Ascent 120 metres
Start Faversham Station, ME13 8EA
Info wildrunning.net/246

From the station wind generally north-west through Faversham to Oare, going over the bridge and through Oare, taking a footpath on the L (1.8 miles/2.9km). Follow the footpath to Luddenham Court. Turn R on the road then continue onto a footpath heading north-east across fields, crossing a road

near Little Uplees and continuing on a byway to the Swale Estuary (4.2 miles/6.7km). Turn R and follow the coast path past the Harty Ferry visitor centre. Turn R at the headland following Oare Creek inland on the Saxon Shore Way. Turn L in Oare and reverse the outbound run to the start.

47 WYE DOWNS

Distance 5 miles/7.5km
Ascent 219 metres
Start Coldharbour Lane car park, TN25 5HE
Info wildrunning.net/247

Leave the car park heading north around the valley then bear L on the path down the ridge to a road at Pickesdane Farm. Cross the road and follow the footpath north-west across fields and into Wye on Cherry Garden Lane. Fork L onto Bridge Street then R onto Church Street. Follow the footpath by the church and turn R on the North Downs Way, heading east along Occupation Road and out into fields. Continue on the North Downs Way across a road and curving R uphill past the Wye Crown then head south-east down the Wye Downs ridge and back to the start.

48 ROYAL MILITARY CANAL

Distance 29 miles/46.5km
Ascent 115 metres
Start West Hythe, CT21 5NN
Finish Cliff End, TN35 4HF
Info wildrunning.net/248

Start on the southern bank and follow the canal west to a footbridge in Pennypot (3.2 miles/5.1km). Cross and follow the north bank to a small road bridge near Ruckinge (10.5 miles/16.9km). Cross and follow the south bank to the A2070 bridge (12.4 miles/19.9km). Cross and follow the north bank to a lock near Bosney Farm (19.5 miles/31.4km). Cross and follow the eastern bank of the River Rother and the Sussex Border Path south into Rye (22.2 miles/35.7km). Cross with the A259 and stay L along the River Brede, cross again on the road and stay L still following the Royal Military canal path then turn L, crossing to the east bank at Brede Sluice. Follow the path south from here, briefly joining Sea Road near Winchelsea and staying on the eastern bank and canal path to the end of the canal at Cliff End.

Ivinghoe Beacon

In & around London

Away from – or sometimes even hidden within – the hustle and bustle of the city, the potential for escape to beautiful and runnable places from London and its surrounds is surprisingly great. Almost half of London is green space, with hundreds of parks and gardens filled with unexpected flora and fauna, ancient woodlands, salt marshes and historical intrigue, most of which lie within an hour's journey of the centre. Wildlife-rich Hampstead Heath is home to more than 30 spring-fed ponds, three of which allow swimming. A well-timed visit, avoiding the commuting and sightseeing masses, opens up a whole new world of exciting places to run.

The Chiltern Hills rise above the Vale of Aylesbury in Buckinghamshire, networked by well-worn trails that make for extensive and excellent quality running. The Chilterns form part of a system of chalk downs that run throughout Eastern and Southern England, formed between 65 and 95 million years ago. This 'chalk group' runs through Salisbury Plain, Cranborne Chase, the South Downs and the Isle of Wight in the south, whilst continuing north-eastward across north Hertfordshire, Norfolk and the Lincolnshire Wolds, finally arriving in a prominent escarpment at the Yorkshire Wolds.

One of the most heavily wooded parts of England, the area is also home to stunning open heath and commons and picturesque gardens and parkland, making for a great variety of running experiences. There are some challenging ascents and enjoyably fast descents but nothing too steep – it's a good run up to the stone monument on the wooded summit of Haddington Hill, the highest point of the Chilterns at 267 metres. Ivinghoe Beacon, at the northern end of the Chiltern Hills, is the start (or finish) point of both the Ridgeway and Icknield Way National Trails. The Ridgeway runs westwards, passing through the Wessex Downs and finishing at the World Heritage Site of Avebury 87 miles later, while the Icknield Way travels east 112 miles along an ancient trackway to Knettishall Heath in Suffolk.

49

49

51

Its distinctive shape rising straight out of the flat lands of the surrounding Vale of Aylesbury, Ivinghoe Beacon is a great summit run or a start/finish point for exploring the inviting chalk trails that lead from here across the long, grassy ridges. Our run to Ivinghoe Beacon (49) takes in a great loop of classic Chilterns countryside from Tring train station. Starting with a stretch of the Ridgeway, it takes you over the steep-sided Pitstone Hill to reach the summit of Ivinghoe Beacon before linking with the Icknield Way to return through woodland to Tring.

Our Wendover Woods run (50) takes to the trees, following winding trails through delightful mixed woodland. Starting at Wendover station and heading out of town there's a good climb to the top of Boddington Hill, site of an Iron Age hill fort. From here there's an enjoyable loop of the woods, descending to finish back at the station. Runs 49 and 50 make a great weekend for anyone based near London.

East of London, on Essex's Dengie Peninsula, there's a degree of wildness that's a surprise to find hidden in this corner of the busy south-east. Bradwell Cockle Spit nature reserve covers 30 acres of shell bank and mudflats along a remote stretch of Essex coastline, an internationally important area for its vast numbers of seabirds. Our run here (51) loops around the end of the peninsula, at the mouth of the Blackwater river, a place of far-reaching views, wild trails and the less romantic Bradwell Power Station, which ceased production in 2002.

Routes 49-51

49 IVINGHOE BEACON

Distance 10 miles/15.5km
Ascent 331 metres
Start Tring Station, HP23 5QR
Info wildrunning.net/249

Head north-east on the road then turn L onto the Hertfordshire Way and L again onto the Ridgeway, heading north-west. Follow this trail along Grim's Ditch and across a road. Cross the next field then follow the trail north uphill and across another road at a sharp bend. Continue on the trail north to the trig point on Ivinghoe Beacon (3.5 miles/5.7km). Turn R and follow the ridge east to the obvious R turn into the fields below, follow this path around to the R and back uphill to join the Icknield Way. Turn L and follow the trail south-east, continuing in the same direction but leaving the Icknield Way at Ward's Hurst Farm to reach a path junction by some waterworks (6.3 miles/10.7km). Turn R on the footpath across Beacon Road and south-west along paths through Sallow Copse to a byway at SP 974129 (7.6 miles/12.2km). Turn R onto the byway, following it west past the visitor centre and downhill to the road in Aldbury.

Follow Station Road then turn R onto the Hertfordshire Way, take the next L and stay on this path back to the road and Station.

50 WENDOVER WOODS

Distance 6.5 miles/10.5km
Ascent 241 metres
Start Wendover Station, HP22 6BT
Info wildrunning.net/250

Follow Station Approach south-east and L onto Pound Street, then onto High Street, R onto Tring Road and R on Honey Banks. Turn R on Colet Road and L on Barlow Road, continue onto Beechwood Lane then R up Boddington Hill to a junction with the outer Aylesbury Ring trail (1.4 miles/2.3km). Turn L and follow the trail north-east in Wendover Woods, passing the car park and Go Ape, then trending R to follow a trail south. Join a larger trail at the south-eastern corner of woodland and cross the road at SP 897074 near Milesfield (3.4 miles/5.4km). Continue on the path, trending R through Hale Wood and Barn Wood to a path junction south of Boswells Farm. Turn R and follow the Ridgeway north-west into Wendover and onto Pound Street, turn L to return to the start.

51 BRADWELL COCKLE SPIT

Distance 6.5 miles/10km
Ascent 34 metres
Start Eastland Country Park, CM0 7PP
Info wildrunning.net/251

Follow the track east to the coast, L along the coast path then west along the River Blackwater to the power station. Pass the power station and continue on the coast to the end of Waterside Road in Bradwell Waterside (3.9 miles/6.2km). Follow the road inland and onto a footpath at the sharp bend. Follow the path south-east across fields to a road junction at Down Hall. Turn R and follow the road south into Bradwell-on-Sea. Turn L onto East End Road and follow this back to the start.

52

53

54

Created by Charles I as a deer park in the 17th century, Richmond Park covers 2,500 acres of grassland, woodland, lakes and trails in South-West London. The Tamsin Trail (run 52) is a great introduction to the park, being a wide, surfaced loop around the perimeter, accessible from any of the main gates. We'd highly recommend exploring further, though, in particular the Isabella Plantation, a 40-acre woodland garden with ponds and streams set within a Victorian woodland plantation planted in the 1830s. The evergreen azaleas here mean it's a peaceful, leafy sanctuary at any time of the year.

Diving under the A3 from Richmond Park, our next route takes in neighbouring Wimbledon Common (53), which actually comprises three areas: Wimbledon Common, Putney Heath, and Putney Lower Common. Made famous by The Wombles, this is a great place to escape for a run and easily accessible from several train stations. Our run passes the Iron Age hill fort at Caesar's Camp and the Grade II listed Wimbledon windmill. It can easily be combined with the Tamsin Trail for a longer route, or a weekend's running adventures all within easy reach of the capital.

Run, swim, or combine the two in our Hampstead Heath swimrun (54), which explores the Heath's rambling hills, trails and ponds. Covering nearly 800 acres of open space just a few miles from the centre of London, Hampstead Heath is a deservedly popular place and its three swimming ponds (women's, men's and mixed) offer an enjoyable way to cool down after a run.

52 TAMSIN TRAIL

Distance 7.5 miles/11.5km
Ascent 130 metres
Start Richmond Gate, TW10 6RP
Info wildrunning.net/252

This route takes a clockwise lap of Richmond Park described from Richmond Gate. The other main entrances are Roehampton Gate to the north-east, Robin Hood Gate in the south-east and the Queen's Road entrance in the south-west. Deviating our route from Robin Hood gate and turning R into the park will allow you to run through the Isabella Plantation and Hamcross Plantation before regaining the Tamsin Trail to the west. Or exit Richmond path at the Robin Hood Gate and extend the run by looping Wimbledon Common as well. We'd also recommend running one or more of the cross-park paths which are often quieter; Roehampton Gate to the central Pen Ponds and then along the Capital Ring path to Richmond Gate is enjoyable.

53 WIMBLEDON COMMON

Distance 8 miles/12.5km
Ascent 113 metres
Start Wimbledon Station, SW19 7NL
Info wildrunning.net/253

Follow the path next to the railway turning R to cross Worple Road into Malcolm Road. At its end take the path joining you to Sunnyside, turn R onto Ridgeway then L on Lingfield Road to the eastern corner of Wimbledon Common (0.9 mile/1.4km). Enter the common and follow the path west to the R of Rushmere and across Cannizaro Road to the junction. Turn L on Camp Road and follow it to the end (1.7 miles/2.7km). Follow the path in the same direction across Caesar's Camp and slightly south to a path junction and footbridge over the Beverley Brook. Don't cross the bridge, turn R and follow the path north to footbridge in the north-west corner (you can turn L here and join the run up with Richmond Park). Turn R and follow the path between Wimbledon Common and Putney Vale Cemetery to Kings Mere. Turn R following the path south near the eastern edge of the common to intersect with the outbound path. Turn L and return the same way to the start.

54 HAMPSTEAD HEATH SWIMRUN

Distance 4 miles/6.5km
Ascent 139 metres
Start Hampstead Heath Station, NW3 2QD
Info wildrunning.net/254

Follow South End Road north and turn R on a cycleway across East Heath, crossing between the ponds and swimming in the mixed pond if you fancy it. Continue running, curving L to Viaduct Pond. Turn L and follow the path around the southern end of the pond and to the R to Vale of Health Pond. Turn R and follow paths north-east to Kenwood House. Turn R and follow paths south-east between the Highgate Chain ponds and then L to Millfield Lane, turn R onto this and follow it past the Kenwood Ladies' Pond. Turn R away from the lane and along the eastern bank of the boating pond, turn R after this and then L past the south-western bank of the men's pond. Turn R after the last pond and cross the heath to reach the edge near houses, turn L and follow these south. Turn R and follow the road west back to the start.

East Anglia

The relentless erosion of the soft chalk and clay earth of the East Anglia coast by the North Sea has sculpted a landscape that is unique and fragile. Since the North Sea flood of 1953, millions of pounds have been spent on building flood defences to keep the people and land along this stretch of the coast safe. The specific conditions here – an expansive network of rivers and lakes, grazing marshes, reed beds and wet woodlands – have also created the Broads, a beautiful, protected area abundant in wildlife. Once thought to be natural features, the Broads were in fact created as a result of medieval peat excavations by the local monasteries, the cathedral alone taking some 320,000 tons of peat per year. Many of the coastal trails take you right out into the marshlands, utterly peaceful with just the calls of the seabirds and your footsteps to keep you company. This is a place that, in its own way, feels uniquely wild.

Suffolk's quiet lanes, dotted with honesty boxes selling produce from its fertile land, wind their way through its gently rolling green hills, a subtle change from the flat lands of Norfolk. Suffolk has some wonderful beaches, many relatively undiscovered, from the pebbles of Dunwich to sandy Claremont, on the Sunrise Coast. The Suffolk Coast Path has some outstanding running and stretches from Felixstowe in the south to Lowestoft in the north, near to Hopton-on-Sea, the starting point of the Norfolk Coast Path, which then joins with the Peddars Way.

The Brecks covers an area of 392 square miles of open, gorse-covered sandy heathland and tranquil forest in the north of Suffolk and across the border into Norfolk. A haven for wildlife and a place whose heritage stretches back to the Stone Age, it is also a geologically fascinating area. There is a wealth of trails to explore on the Brecks, with several waymarked long-distance routes crossing the area, including the Icknield Way, the Angles Way and the Iceni Way. There are many circular routes, descriptions for which are available in a booklet from the Brecks

55

56

57

Countryside Project. Or, spend an enjoyable day simply exploring the many trails, paths and tearooms the area has to offer.

North of Cambridge, the Fens are a low-lying coastal plain, a former marshland drained by dykes and channels. The Waterbeach Fens run (55) is a loop of classic fenland, starting at the station in Waterbeach and following the Harcamlow Way across to the village of Lode. From here it follows Bottisham Lode, also National Cycle Network route 11, to reach the River Cam at Bottisham Lock, following the Fen Rivers Way back to Waterbeach.

Covering 47,000 acres of pine, broadleaf and heathland across the Norfolk/Suffolk border, Thetford Forest is Britain's largest man-made lowland forest. It was created after the First World War to replenish trees used across the country during the conflicts. The forest provides open access to runners, walkers and mountain bikers – so many trails just waiting to be explored… Our Thetford run (56) takes in the High Lodge area of the forest on gently winding trails with nature-inspired sculptures hidden among the trees. Passing a magnificent sculpture of a goshawk the open trails lead you down wide breaks through dense forestry. Look out for wildlife – including real goshawks – and the 15th-century Thetford Warren Lodge.

Managed by the Suffolk Wildlife Trust, Blaxhall Common is a fascinating landscape with an Iron Age burial mound and ditches dug during the Second World War to prevent enemy gliders from landing. Rich in wildlife, there are many species of butterfly plus rare birds, lizards and adders to be spotted here. The Tunstall and Blaxhall run (57) begins at the heart of the common, following the waymarked Sandlings Walk until it reaches the coast. From here it takes to the Suffolk Coast Path, following the tidal waters of Long Reach before heading into the trees at Tunstall Forest. Leaving the coast path at Chillesford it rejoins Sandlings Walk, following forest and then heathland trails back to the start.

55 WATERBEACH FENS

Distance	8 miles/12.5km
Ascent	25 metres
Start	Waterbeach station, CB25 9HS
Info	wildrunning.net/255

Follow Clayhithe Road south-east and across the River Cam to Clayhithe. Turn L off the road onto the riverside path and then immediately R away from the river on the Fen Rivers Way. Turn R at the junction and follow the path south-west to a path junction near Horningsea (1.5 miles/2.4km). Turn L onto the Harcamlow Way, follow this path around the intriguingly named Stow-Cum-Quy Fen until you reach Fen Road north of Lode (4.2 miles/6.7km). Turn L onto the road and follow it north-west to a sharp bend at Vicarage Farm. Leave the road and continue straight ahead on a path in the direction of the River Cam. Turn L and follow the riverside path back to Clayhithe. Turn R to return to the start.

56 THETFORD

Distance	6.5 miles/10km)
Ascent	47 metres
Start	Thetford Forrest Park, IP27 0AF
Info	wildrunning.net/256

The Forestry Commission walking and cycling trails are available on a map from the visitor centre and can be helpful for further exploring the forest. Our route heads south from the start past the woodland sculptures and the mountain bike skills area to a large forest crossroads (0.9 miles/1.4km). Turn L and follow the track to a sharp R, take the next L and follow this track, taking the fourth main L at TL 832831 (2.7 miles/4.4km). Follow this north-east to the boundary between the managed forest and the golf course. Turn L and follow this path north past Thetford Warren Lodge. Continue around to the L following the Beach Walking Trail across the exit road, then bear L to cross the exit road again (5 miles/8km). Continue south but turn R at the next main track. Follow this west back to the playing fields in front of the visitor centre and run across these back to the start.

57 TUNSTALL & BLAXHALL

Distance	4.5 miles/7km
Ascent	27 metres
Start	Blaxhall Common, IP12 2EJ
Info	wildrunning.net/257

Follow Sandlings Walk south-east from the start, crossing a road then leaving the Sandlings trail to continue ahead on a footpath to Heath Cottages. Turn R here and run west through woodland and across Tunstall Common, turning R on a path 100 metres before reaching the road at Tunstall village (2 miles/3.3km). Follow the path north, turning L at the next junction and then reaching the road. Follow this past Walk Farm and continue around a sharp R corner north to the B1069 at White Cross Farm (2.8 miles/4.6km). Cross the B1069 and follow a bridleway north to a junction with a byway at the corner of Tunstall Forest (3.5 miles/5.7km). Turn R and follow the track back to the start.

58

59

60

Our Dunwich Beach run (58) takes in the varied landscape and scenery around Dunwich, from heather- and gorse-clad heathland to wave-washed beach. It starts with an intriguing section of the coast path that passes the two Sizewell nuclear power stations (a third is due to be completed in 2031) and Minsmere bird reserve. The run then heads inland across the beautiful expanse of Dunwich Heath and through woodland into Eastbridge village, then crosses Sizewell Belts and Leiston Common. A final stretch of woodland returns you to Dunwich. Refuel at the National Trust café, or picnic on the beach.

Pingos are shallow depressions found in the Brecklands of Norfolk and Suffolk. They were formed during the last ice age by bubbles of underground ice which expanded, forcing the soil upwards. Centuries of weathering created craters, now filled with water to create pools that teem with wildlife. The Great Eastern Pingo Trail (run 59) discovers the weird and wonderful pingos on a peaceful route through the wooded sandy brecks around Thompson Water and the nature reserve.

A spectacular alternative to the coast path run between Holkham and Wells-next-the-Sea, our Holkham Beach run (60) follows the broad white, sandy beach inland from where you emerge from tall pine trees on a boardwalk leading from Lady Anne's Drive, all the way to Wells. The return trip follows winding streets through Wells to the Holkham estate, running through peaceful woodland and past the Hall, ice house and lake to the main entrance, before returning to the start. Or simply turn around and head back on the beach, right at the water's edge.

Routes 58-60

58 DUNWICH BEACH

Distance	9 miles/14.5km
Ascent	118 metres
Start	Sizewell, IP16 4UD
Info	wildrunning.net/258

Head out towards the sea and turn L, running along the beach or the Suffolk Coast Path in front of the power station north until you reach the National Trust café and visitor centre (3.1 miles/5km). Turn L inland and trend L across heath to the end of a road (5.3 miles/8.6km). Turn L and follow the road south through Eastbridge where you fork L and continue on the road to a L turn to the Round House (6.3 miles/10.1km). Take this L and follow the track to the R and then south to a junction just north of the radio mast and car park on Lover's Lane. Turn L and follow the path R across the Sizewell Belts and Leiston Common to a junction on Sandy Lane. Turn R and follow the lane south-east to reach the road to the R of the power station, turn L here to return to the start.

59 GREAT EASTERN PINGO TRAIL

Distance	7.5 miles/11.5km
Ascent	39 metres
Start	Pingo Trail car park, NR17 1DP
Info	wildrunning.net/259

Follow the main path which was once the route of a railway south-west through woodland and past lots of pingos. Leave the woodland behind but continue on the same path passing Crow's Farm and more pingos in the Sandpit Plantation. Continue across Breckles Heath and then move south through the managed woodland to reach the road at Hockham Heath (2.7 miles/4.4km). Turn R and follow the road which joins the Peddars Way on the course of an old Roman road. Fork R off the road but follow the Peddars Way north-west to a path junction beside Thompson Water (4.6 miles/7.4km). Turn R leaving the Peddars Way and following a footpath passing many more pingos before joining a small road at Butter's Lodge. Follow the road in the same direction but turn R onto a footpath before the road junction. Follow the footpath east through woodland back to the start.

60 HOLKHAM BEACH

Distance	8 miles/13km
Ascent	97 metres
Start	Lady Anne's Drive, NR23 1RG
Info	wildrunning.net/260

Run north onto the beach and turn R either on the coast path or on the sand and continue to the lifeboat station and the end of Beach Road (2.1 miles/3.4km). Turn R and follow the path on the marsh side of the road south to the Quay Road. Turn L onto this and then R onto Staithe Street. Follow this then L onto Station Road and R on High Street which turns into Church Plain. Turn R on Church Street then L up Market Lane past the school and out onto a track which you follow to the junction on Gallow Hill (4.9 miles/7.9km). Turn R and follow the track across the B1105 at a junction and through Golden Gates into the Holkham estate. Follow Golden Gates Drive north-west towards Holkham Hall but turn R at a junction on the edge of the small belt of woodland to the east of the house. Follow this path north past the old almshouses in Holkham and across the A149 onto Lady Ann's Drive, and stay on this back to the start.

Froggatt & Curbar Edge

Central

There's a great variety of landscapes to explore across Central England, from the rolling countryside of the Cotswolds and the Welsh Borders, to nature reserves and parkland near the Midlands' busy cities, through to the Peak District's craggy edges and remote moorland.

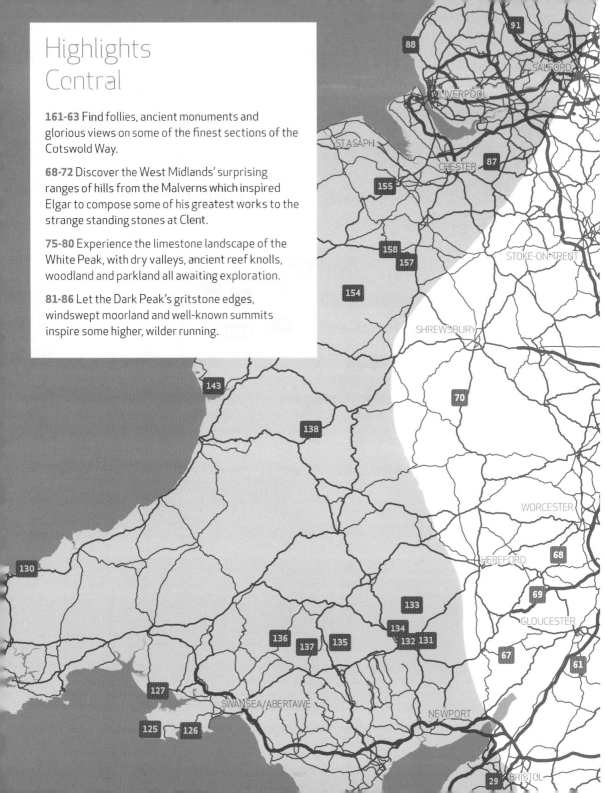

Highlights
Central

161-63 Find follies, ancient monuments and glorious views on some of the finest sections of the Cotswold Way.

68-72 Discover the West Midlands' surprising ranges of hills from the Malverns which inspired Elgar to compose some of his greatest works to the strange standing stones at Clent.

75-80 Experience the limestone landscape of the White Peak, with dry valleys, ancient reef knolls, woodland and parkland all awaiting exploration.

81-86 Let the Dark Peak's gritstone edges, windswept moorland and well-known summits inspire some higher, wilder running.

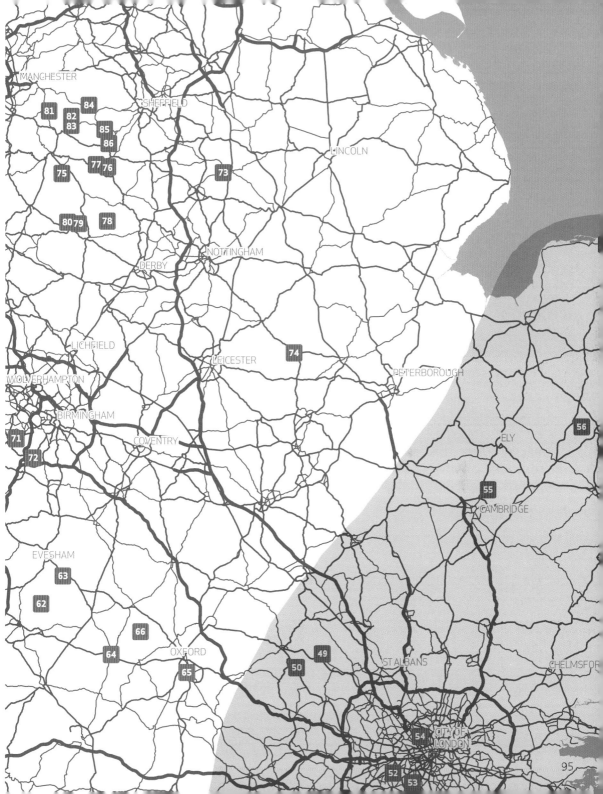

MANCHESTER

SHEFFIELD

LINCOLN

81

84

82
83

85
86

77 76

75

80 79

78

73

NOTTINGHAM

DERBY

LICHFIELD

LEICESTER

74

PETERBOROUGH

WOLVERHAMPTON

BIRMINGHAM

COVENTRY

71

72

ELY

56

55

CAMBRIDGE

EVESHAM

63

62

66

64

OXFORD

65

49

50

ST ALBANS

CHELMSFOR

54

CITY OF
LONDON

52
53

Broadway Tower

Oxfordshire & the Cotswolds

The Cotswold hills run south-west to north-east through 6 counties including Gloucestershire, Oxfordshire and Warwickshire. They cover an area 25 miles across and 90 miles long, with the highest point being Cleeve Hill at 330 metres, just outside Cheltenham. The northern and western edges of the Cotswolds are marked by the steep, limestone escarpments of the Cotswold Edge down to the Severn Valley and the Warwickshire Avon. The eastern edge is bounded by Oxford, and the west by Stroud. To the south-east, the upper reaches of the Thames Valley are often considered to mark the limit of this region, whilst to the south the Cotswolds reach to the World Heritage City of Bath.

The area is deservedly designated an Area of Outstanding Natural Beauty and this, along with the striking limestone landscape, provides varied and exciting running along exposed ridges, through lush green fields and wildflower meadows and along country lanes and through the attractive towns and villages built of the Cotswold stone, a golden, oolitic limestone. The Cotswold Way runs along the Cotswold escarpment for 102 miles between picturesque Chipping Campden and Bath. The running is varied, from quiet lanes through honey-coloured villages to steep climbs and inviting trails. The Cotswold Way is well signposted and can be run in sections or used as part of circular routes, many of which are also waymarked, or even run in its entirety.

Oxfordshire boasts a lengthy network of footpaths and bridleways, winding through the pretty countryside to connect its populated areas. These paths are the result of an interesting history, from trade and industry links to a legal requirement in the past for all residents to have access to churches. There is plenty to discover here, from the open vistas of the Vale of the White Horse to leafy beech woodlands and dense forested areas.

61

62

63

The Haresfield Estate lies high on the Cotswold escarpment, an intriguing landscape of rolling hills, steep edges, dense woodland and hidden rocky crags. The Cotswold Way carves its way through the estate, one of the most scenic sections of its 102-mile length, with views out across the Severn Estuary to the Forest of Dean and the Brecon Beacons. The Haresfield Beacon run (61) follows the Cotswold Way around a stunning series of wooded curves in the escarpment before plunging off the viewpoint down a gloriously long ridge. Reaching the valley floor it rejoins the Cotswold Way, running right through pretty Standish Wood to finish.

Belas Knap is a fascinating site – a Neolithic long barrow some 5000 years old that was excavated in the 19th century. It lies not far from the summit of Cleeve Hill in Gloucestershire, the highest point in the Cotswold Hills. Our Winchcombe and Belas Knap run (62) begins in the historic town of Winchcombe, passing 15th-century Sudeley Castle before joining a section of the Windrush Way, a 14-mile waymarked route ending in Bourton-on-the-Water. Climbing steeply up onto the Cotswold escarpment there's a loop around Belas Knap before a stretch of the Cotswold Way returns you to Winchcombe.

The Broadway Tower run (63) follows a short, challenging but enjoyable route, starting in the pretty village of Broadway and making its way unrelentingly up the Cotswold Way across a series of fields to the 18th-century Capability Brown folly of Broadway Tower at the very top. On reaching the summit it's hard not to turn around and run as fast as you can back down again – flying across the grassy hillside is pure joy, with good conditions underfoot and stunning views all the way. As an alternative, you can follow paths and tracks to Coneygree Lane before making your way through fields to Broadway.

Routes 61-63

61 HARESFIELD BEACON

Distance 7.5 miles/11.5km
Ascent 462 metres
Start Standish Wood car park, GL6 6PP
Info wildrunning.net/261

Turn R onto the road and follow until a L turn onto a footpath, head downhill through the woods, fork L at the path junction and continue to the Cotswold Way at the edge of the woodland. Turn L onto this and follow it, curving towards the north where it joins and follows a road. Turn L off the road but still on the Cotswold Way running through Cliff Wood to another road (2.2 miles/3.6km). Turn L briefly on the road, then R following the Cotswold Way up to Haresfield Beacon. Turn L here and follow the Cotswold Way around Bunker's Bank close to the road then curving R to the topograph at SO 826083 (3.5 miles/5.6km). Leave the Cotswold Way and continue downhill to the road at Tudor House Farm. Turn L and follow the road to Standish Park Farm then R onto a footpath. Follow this south across fields then trend L through woodland to rejoin the Cotswold Way near Randwick. Turn L and follow this trail through Standish Wood back to start.

62 WINCHCOMBE & BELAS KNAP

Distance 7 miles (11km)
Ascent 281 metres
Start Winchcombe, GL54 5PZ
Info wildrunning.net/262

Turn R out of the library car park, then R onto Cowl Lane, L on High Street then R onto Castle Street. Follow this to a R turn off the road onto a footpath heading south-east across parkland and joining the waymarked Windrush Way. Follow this past Sudeley Castle and south roughly following the Beesmoor Brook to a junction with a byway at SP 034258 (1.9 miles/3.1km). Turn R on the byway to Newmeadow Farm then L onto a track, turn R at the junction then L by Humblebee Cottages to a road. Turn R on the road and follow it to a L onto the Cotswold Way. Follow this through woodland then uphill across a field to Belas Knap (4 miles/6.4km). Follow the path R then turn R at the junction with a track, leave the Cotswold Way and follow the track north past Hill Barn Farm joining a road to a T junction at SP 019262 (5.2 miles/8.3km). Turn L at the junction onto the Cotswold Way and head north across fields to Winchcombe and the start.

63 BROADWAY TOWER

Distance 5 miles (7.5km)
Ascent 240 metres
Start Broadway Village car park, WR12 7AH
Info wildrunning.net/263

Follow Church Close back to Church Street, turn R and then R onto High Street and run through Broadway on the Cotswold Way. Follow the waymarked trail turning R off the road and between houses then up the obvious path across fields and through several gates to Broadway Tower. If you don't just turn around and run back down, turn R behind the tower leaving the Cotswold way and heading south along the ridge. Turn R and follow the path downhill around Broadway Tower Country Park and onto Coneygree Lane. Turn R on the road at Broadway Court and then R again onto a track heading north across fields and between houses to get back onto Broadway village High Street.

64

65

66

The Windrush Valley run (64) follows a delightful loop from the Cotswold town of Burford, whose honey-coloured buildings cascade down its elegant, sweeping high street. Our outward route, along the northern banks of the river, rises and falls with the rolling countryside, while the return trip follows a stretch of the National Cycle Network route 57 and tranquil riverside trails through pretty villages back to Burford.

Port Meadow covers some 440 acres of riverside meadow along the Thames in Oxford. An open area of grazing land with rights protecting it from ploughing or development dating back 4,000 years, there's a long history of human activity here, from Bronze and Iron Age sites through 17th-century English Civil War fortifications to the raves of the 1980s. Today it is mostly a peaceful place, popular with runners, dog walkers and picnickers. Our Port Meadow run (65) takes a tour of the meadows – a post-run swim is highly recommended.

The Oxfordshire Way traverses the county for 67 miles from the Cotswolds to the Chilterns, linking with several other long-distance trails en route. The Charlbury run (66), starting at the station in this pretty village, takes in a section of the Way, making use of the area's great network of bridleways to join this to the nearby Shakespeare Way. Enjoyable running on clear, well-maintained paths, trails and tracks brings you back into Charlbury. The Oxfordshire Way in this part of the county also makes an excellent station-to-station run, following the River Evenlode as it meanders between picturesque Cotswold stone settlements.

64 WINDRUSH VALLEY

Distance 8.5 miles/13.5km
Ascent 114 metres
Start Burford car park, OX18 4DN
Info wildrunning.net/264

Run back along Church Lane then L onto Guildenford and L again onto Witney Street. Follow this out of Burford to a L onto a footpath following the River Windrush to the road at Widford. Turn L and cross the bridge then R on a footpath to Swinbrook. Turn R and follow the road through the village then L onto a footpath opposite the pub. Cross the next couple of fields and a road to reach another road at Stonefold (3.6 miles/5.8km). Turn R and follow the road south and across a bridge at Worsham. Turn R and follow the river path on the southern shore of the Windrush to the road in Asthall (5.3 miles/8.5km). Turn L on the road then R past the church and R onto a road out of Asthall. Follow this back to Widford where you join the outbound route, return along the river and through Burford to the start.

65 PORT MEADOW

Distance 6.5 miles/10km
Ascent 12 metres
Start Oxford Station, OX1 1HS
Info wildrunning.net/265

From the station turn R onto Botley Road then R onto the Thames Path on the east bank of the River Thames and follow north along the river. Cross a footbridge near Medley Manor Farm and continue on the path, following the west bank to Godstow Road (2.5 miles/4.1km). Turn R and follow the road past the Trout Inn (turning R and running south onto Port Meadow here leads you to a good stretch of river for swimming, which tends to be a bit quieter then the area closer to Oxford). Otherwise stay on the road through Wolvercote to a R onto a bridleway across Port Meadow before Godstow Road Bridge. Follow this south to the R of the trees in the nature park and past Round Hill. Follow the edge of the railway to the car park at the end of Walton Well Road (5.1 miles/8.2km). Follow the road over the railway then turn R onto the Oxford Canal Walk, follow this to the A4144, turn R and head back to the start.

66 CHARLBURY

Distance 7.5 miles/12km
Ascent 151 metres
Start Charlbury Station, OX7 3HH
Info wildrunning.net/266

Follow Forest Road from the station into Charlbury, join Dyres Hill then turn R onto Market Street. Follow this onto Sheep Street then Hixet Wood, heading south. Turn L onto Woodstock Road and continue onto Stonesfield Lane. Continue at the end onto a track, following the Oxfordshire Way south-east along the edge of several fields past Hill Barn Cottages to a path junction at Highfield Farm (2.8 miles/4.5km). Turn L and follow the bridleway north to a junction by Newbarn Farm, turn L here and follow the Wychwood Way north-west across a road and past the end of Ditchley Road to a junction at SP 377210 (5.3 miles/8.6km). Turn L onto Hundley Way until you reach the B4022 into Charlbury. Follow Enstone Road to join the outbound route on Sheep Street, turn R to return to the start.

Sutton Park

The Midlands & Welsh Borders

The West Midlands is a landlocked county bordered by Warwickshire to the east, Staffordshire to the north and west and Worcestershire to the south. It is a heavily populated area, second in the UK only to London. However, exploring outside its cities brings unexpected glimpses of wilderness, carefully preserved in its parks and green spaces, and an abundance of natural habitats in the form of 23 SSSIs (Sites of Special Scientific Interest). To the east lie the forests of Sherwood and Charnwood and the wolds and limewoods of Lincolnshire.

The Malvern Hills are formed from some of the most ancient rocks in England, some 680 million years old, with their highest point being the Worcestershire Beacon (425 metres). Their distinctive shape, a 9-mile undulating ridge with 15 distinct summits, is visible from many miles around. This is both a designated AONB (Area of Outstanding Natural Beauty) and an SSSI, with open grassland and heathland on higher areas whilst the lower hillsides and valleys are wooded with ancient broadleaf. The Malverns are fascinating to explore, with many iconic features such as the distinctive Iron Age earthworks of British Camp. Many tracks and trails offer great running with spectacular views, both on the hills themselves and in the surrounding countryside. The ridge of the hills, with views in every direction, is a wonderful place to watch the sun set of an evening.

Herefordshire and Shropshire form much of the border between England and Wales, often referred to locally as the Marches. These sparsely populated counties are characterised by thriving market towns, rolling agricultural land, river valleys, woodland, ridges and hills. The abundant natural features make this a fantastic place to run, with a network of green lanes, bridleways, footpaths and quiet lanes to explore, contrasting with the wilder, open landscapes of the rugged uplands.

69

70

70

The Forest of Dean covers 42 square miles of west Gloucestershire, a rare area of mixed ancient woodland. There are many trails through the forest, some waymarked, others to be linked up as you see fit. Our Forest of Dean run (67) explores the central forest, starting along a section of the 94-mile Gloucestershire Way and linking with National Cycle Network route 42. Ending at the sculpture trail and visitor centre, there's plenty of information available on local trails and other activities.

The Malvern Hills are great to explore at a run, with many different options from enjoyable circuits to an epic full traverse. Our run here (68) explores the northernmost hills that rise majestically above Great Malvern, taking in the peaks of North Hill and the Worcestershire Beacon with fine views out across the neighbouring counties of Herefordshire and Worcestershire.

The River Wye flows 134 miles from the high ground of Plynlimon in mid Wales to its confluence with the Severn Estuary. The Wye Valley is a place of great contrasts, at times bordered by high, dramatic crags and at others peaceful and verdant. The Daffodil Way (run 69) is a gently adventurous waymarked route around a serene corner of the Wye Valley that links up wooded copses and open countryside with quiet, winding country lanes.

The Shropshire Hills AONB covers 310 square miles of glorious, undulating borderland. Surprisingly wild feeling, with steep-sided valleys and high tops crisscrossed by inviting paths and trails, this is a great place for an adventure that's also brilliantly accessible; Church Stretton, right in the heart of the hills, has a well-serviced train station. Our Shropshire Hills run (70) explores some of the highlights of the area, starting deep in Carding Mill Valley and following ancient tracks and trails up to the highest point of the Long Mynd from where you're handsomely rewarded with fine views and a long downhill.

Routes 67-70

67 THE FOREST OF DEAN

Distance	6.5 miles/10.5km
Ascent	182 metres
Start	Speech House Rd car park, GL16 7EG
Info	wildrunning.net/267

Head north from the visitor centre and R at the first main forest track. Follow this generally east to join the waymarked Gloucestershire Way, trending L through woodland to a disused railway path (2.5 miles/4km). Cross and turn L, following the Wysis Way west to reach a second railway path. Turn L onto this to a junction. Turn R and continue to SO 610123 (6 miles/9.6km) where you leave the railway path and turn L to return to the start via the sculpture trail.

68 MALVERN HILLS

Distance	4 miles/6.5km
Ascent	445 metres
Start	Beacon Road car park, WR14 4EH
Info	wildrunning.net/268

Head north from the car park along the main trail, sticking roughly to the ridge up Summer Hill and then up to the trig point on the Worcestershire Beacon. Continue north on the high ground trending slightly L to the summit of Table Hill (1.6 miles/2.5km). Follow paths R or east around the northern side and then up to the top of North Hill. Head south, dropping down L into Green valley and passing St Ann's Well before contouring uphill below the Worcestershire Beacon and back over Summer Hill to the start.

69 THE DAFFODIL WAY

Distance	9 miles/14.5km
Ascent	151 metres
Start	Dymock, GL18 2AQ
Info	wildrunning.net/269

Follow waymarkers through the village, crossing the B4215 at Shakesfield. Follow the Daffodil Way south-west across fields, past Allums Farm to the road. Turn R and follow the road to a R onto a footpath before some woodland. Follow this north then L through Allums Grove to a road (2.9 miles/4.6km). Turn L on the road to a T-junction near Kempley Court. Cross onto the footpath opposite and follow this south to the road near Hill Brook Farm. Turn L following the road then forking left onto a track passing Brick House Farm to Kempley Green. Turn R othen L onto a path heading south-east through Dymock Wood then crossing the motorway on a road bridge. Turn L after the bridge following the road through Four Oaks. Turn L onto a footpath at SO 696284 and take it north under the motorway and north-east across fields along a stream past Boyce Court to finish.

70 SHROPSHIRE HILLS

Distance	6 miles/9km
Ascent	345 metres
Start	Carding Mill Valley, SY6 6JG
Info	wildrunning.net/270

From the highest car park follow the obvious path upstream, fork R at the confluence onto the Jack Mytton Way up the valley to the junction with the Shropshire Way at the top. Turn L and follow this and cross a road to the trig point on Pole Bank. Turn L here and follow the path east, crossing the road at Boiling Well Spring and following the path south-east roughly parallel to the road to the head of Townbrook Valley. Follow the path down this and L after the small reservoir into Carding Mill Valley. Turn L in the valley to return to the start.

71

72

73

The Clent Hills lie 10 miles south west of Birmingham city centre, networked by many miles of footpaths and bridleways and with breathtaking panoramic views over the Cotswolds, Shropshire Hills and Welsh Borders. The Clent Hills run (71) climbs to the Four Stones, erected by Lord Lyttelton of Hagley Hall in the 18th century, and over the summit of Walton Hill which, at 316 metres, is the highest point in these hills. Early morning is the best time to run here, watching the sun rise with the world to yourself.

A great weekend's running when combined with the previous route, our Lickey Hills run (72) takes in a long loop of the forested ridge on runnable, tree-lined trails through the Lickey Hills Country Park. Covering over 500 acres of woodland, grassland and heath, this wildlife-rich natural haven is a perfect escape from the busy West Midlands cities.

Heading east, the village of Edwinstowe lies in the Heart of the Forest area of Sherwood Forest. Home to the legend of Robin Hood and the Sherwood Forest visitor centre this makes a great place to begin an exploration of the forest. Our Sherwood Forest run (73) explores some of the best of the local area, including an enjoyable stretch along the Robin Hood Way and a detour to visit the awe-inspiring 800-year-old 'Major Oak'.

The Rutland Water run (74) circumnavigates a reservoir managed by Anglian Water set in peaceful countryside between Oakham and Stamford. It's a popular place for water sports and cycling and rich in wildlife, particularly water birds. The surfaced trail around the lake makes a fantastic longer run, perfect for marathon training or a good challenge to complete in its own right. The full circuit is 23 miles, but if you miss out Hambleton Peninsula it reduces the distance to 17 miles. The peninsula on its own is 15 miles.

Routes 71-74

71 CLENT HILLS

Distance 4 miles/6km
Ascent 289 metres
Start Nimmings Wood visitor centre, DY9 9JR
Info wildrunning.net/271

Follow the obvious track uphill and along the ridge to the Four Stones, bearing L through woodland to the road by the church in Clent. Cross and follow the footpath up into the Clent Hills. Bear L over the top of Walton Hill to reach a road, crossing and following the footpath to St Kenelm's Road. Turn L and L again onto Chapel Lane. Turn R onto a footpath then L heading north-west across fields to a path junction in the nature reserve, and turn L here to return to the start.

72 LICKEY HILLS

Distance 5.5 miles/8.5km
Ascent 273 metres
Start Lickey Hills Country Park, B45 8ER
Info wildrunning.net/272

Head south over Cofton Hill, turning R at the base and following a path across a footbridge. Bear L, skirting the eastern edge of Pinfields Wood, behind some houses

and up its western edge to SO 994750 (2.1 miles/3.4km) crossing Twatling Road. Follow the footpath opposite to Old Birmingham Road. Cross and run past the obelisk to Monument Lane. Turn L on a footpath and bear R over Beacon Hill, bearing R at the base around the golf course to reach a track by Hillside House. Turn R then L and then R onto a footpath heading south down to Rose Hill Road. Turn R on this road then L onto a path over Bilberry Hill and back to the start.

73 SHERWOOD FOREST

Distance 7.5 miles/11.5km
Ascent 114 metres
Start Edwinstowe Youth Hostel, NG21 9RN
Info wildrunning.net/273

Follow the southern edge of the forest L from the start and bear L at the next junction. Continue in the same direction across the Blackpool Plantation and past the Black Pool to a junction with the Robin Hood Way at Vals Hill. Turn R and follow this trail north and to the L of Hanger Hill onto Hanger Hill Drive to a path junction in the Boundary Plantation. Turn R here and follow the edge of the forest east, forking R and heading south-east on

a bridleway across Budby South Forest. Follow this trail south back into Sherwood Forest Country Park but detouring off R to visit the Major oak. Return to the same path and follow it south back to the start.

74 RUTLAND WATER

Distance 15.5 miles/25km
Ascent 237 metres
Start Oakham Station, LE15 6RE
Info wildrunning.net/274

Follow Station Road south and fork L onto Melton Road, follow this onto High Street then Catmos Street. For a clockwise route, turn left onto Stamford Road joining the Macmillan Way and follow the north shore to Barnsdale Hotel, where you fork R on the path away from the road. From here follow the lakeside path past Whitwell to the dam in the north-east corner. Follow the eastern shore past Edith Weston and then along the southern shore to the A6003 at Manton. Turn R and follow the western shore north past the birdwatching centre and through Egleton, leaving the lake and trending L on a path across the A6003 and onto the B641. Turn R here to return to the start.

The Peak District
– The White Peak

The Peak District is an upland area, lying mainly in northern Derbyshire but also reaching into Cheshire, Greater Manchester, Staffordshire and Yorkshire. An area of striking contrasts, it is split by its geology into the northern Dark Peak, a place of open moorland and gritstone crags and quarries, and the southern, White Peak with its rolling, limestone valleys and hills. The weather dictates the mood in this part of the country, with heavy cloud making the grey of the gritstone even greyer, the walls and stony tracks reflected and magnified by gunmetal skies. Yet on a clear, sunny day, the mood is light and the fells are welcoming, with bright colours standing out in brilliant juxtaposition to the rock. Orchids and cowslips line the paths across pastureland where cattle swish their tails and skylarks chatter overhead. At each turn a new view opens out below: patterned, stone-walled fields, gritstone edges or high moorland stretching off into the distance.

Most of the villages in the Peak District National Park are within the White Peak, making it popular with tourists, particularly in the summer months. Access to the spectacular countryside in this part of the Peaks is particularly easy, with footpaths, bridleways and green lanes forming a vast network of runnable trails to explore. Half an hour's run from any of the busier areas will take you to beautiful wild places where few others go, from remote high moorland overlooking patchworks of medieval strip fields to grassy, tussocky hillsides and picturesque limestone valleys filled with wildflowers, such as those found on Chrome Hill and neighbouring Parkhouse Hill.

The Chatsworth estate is a runners' playground of winding country lanes, peaceful trails alongside the sparkling River Derwent and pleasant running through lush deer parks bounded by swathes of mixed forest. It's worth the long climb up to the wooded hilltops for some exploring in the tree-lined valleys beyond and, of course, the return trip down the wide, grassy hillside – fast, exhilarating and joyous – as the magnificent Chatsworth House and gardens appear below. Payment is

76

76

77

required to visit the house and gardens, but the 1,000-acre park is free to enter. Passing right through the estate, the Derwent Valley Heritage Way is 55 waymarked miles of enjoyable and varied running along the Derwent Valley, from the silver expanse of Ladybower Reservoir through the Derwent Valley Mills World Heritage Site to the historic inland port of Shardlow, ending at Derwent Mouth at its confluence with the River Trent.

Chrome Hill and its neighbouring Parkhouse Hill are 'atolls' – limestone reef knolls, the remains of 340 million-year-old coral reefs that once edged a shallow pool of water. These intriguingly sculpted hills, which rise to a high point of 425 metres straight from the relatively flat surrounds, are great to explore and always make for a good photo, too. Our Chrome Hill run (75) begins in the nearby village of Earl Sterndale, taking in a pleasant loop of the surrounding limestone countryside before heading up and over the dragon's back spines of first Chrome Hill and then Parkhouse Hill, with plenty of steep ascents and descents along the way. Aside from the great running there are other reasons to visit: the hills are a Site of Special Scientific Interest for their wide range of limestone flora, and, if you're lucky, a mysterious double sunset can be viewed from nearby Glutton Bridge, over the River Dove.

The pretty town of Bakewell is a jumble of cafés, outdoor shops and Bakewell pudding outlets arranged around the beautiful River Wye. It's a great base for exploring the local countryside, with many well-maintained trails leading out into the hills all around. The Bakewell and Chatsworth Loop (run 76) begins in Bakewell and heads steeply up and across Carlton Pastures and onto the hillside above the Chatsworth estate. Winding through woodland it emerges at the top of the deer park, where an awesome descent brings you down to the River Derwent, whose wide meanders pass right past the grand house. Following the Derwent Valley Heritage Trail, there's a short section on quiet lanes through the village of Baslow before a steep climb up a rough track brings you onto the wide open spaces of Longstone Moor for fabulous views of the White Peak. Descending steeply off Longstone Edge the run passes through the village of Great Longstone before joining the surfaced Monsal Trail to return to Bakewell.

Routes 75-77

75 CHROME HILL & PARKHOUSE HILL

Distance	5 miles/8km
Ascent	554 metres
Start	Earl Sterndale, SK17 0BU
Info	wildrunning.net/275

Follow the path west from the village, crossing the B5053 and turning R at the next two junctions, through Glutton Grange and north to a path junction at SK 082677 (1.2 miles/2km). Turn L and follow the path to join the road up Dowel Dale. Continue on the road then turn L on a track to Stoop Farm, crossing fields and ascending the ridge of Chrome Hill. Continue along the ridge, descending the steep side and crossing another field and lane. Continue over Parkhouse Hill to the path near Glutton Grange, turning R then L and recross the road to return on the outbound route to Earl Sterndale.

76 BAKEWELL & CHATSWORTH

Distance	12.5 miles/20km
Ascent	661 metres
Start	Bakewell station car park, DE45 1GE
Info	wildrunning.net/276

Follow the road uphill, fork R on a bridleway across the golf course then uphill to the road. Turn R and follow the path generally east but staying L to the lodge in the north-eastern corner of Calton Plantations. Turn L through New Piece Wood and follow the path downhill to the road R of Edensor, cross and then follow the path to Chatsworth Bridge. Cross and turn L following the Derwent Way north to the A619 in Baslow (4.6 miles/7.4km). Cross onto Ealon Hill then L onto School Lane, R on Calver Road then L across the bridge. Turn R and follow Bubnell Road along the river, curving L away from the river and uphill to Hassop Road (6.7 miles/10.7km). Cross and follow the byway uphill above the quarries then down to the top of Moor Lane (8.8 miles/14.2km). Turn L and follow the initially steep path downhill and out across fields, trend R down a dry valley and join a track to the road in Great Longstone. Turn R and follow the road into the village, turn L onto Main Street, R on Croft Road then L to the end of Edge View Drive. At the end turn L down a footpath and out into the field. Cross this in the same direction to reach the Monsal Trail. Turn L to follow this back to the start.

77 LONGSTONE MOOR

Distance	12.5 miles/19.5km
Ascent	722 metres
Start	Holme Lane, Bakewell, DE45 1GF
Info	wildrunning.net/277

Turn R off Holme Lane, following a track north over open hillside. Turn L onto the Monsal Trail through Headstone tunnel and over the viaduct. Turn R, descending to cross a footbridge and the road. Follow lane up Hay Dale, straight on at crossroads then R onto footpath (5.5 miles/8.8km). Continue through fields and over a road heading east to a track junction. Turn R then L, through a field and then Bleaklow Farm. Cross fields trending R and crossing a track at SK 215731 (8.1 miles/13.1km). Continue downhill to Hardrake Lane. Cross a stile then cross fields to Great Longstone. Turn R into the village, turning L onto Main Street, R on Croft Road then L to the end of Edge View Drive. At the end turn L down a footpath, crossing fields to reach the Monsal Trail. Turn L to return to Bakewell.

78

79

80

The Longstone Moor run (77) makes a perfect second day to our Bakewell and Chatsworth Loop. It takes in the Monsal Trail, an 8.5-mile surfaced, traffic-free trail between Bakewell and Chee Dale, crossing the much-photographed Headstone Viaduct. A challenging ascent through leafy Hay Dale brings you to Longstone Moor and breathtaking views of the White Peak from Longstone Edge.

Lying near to Wirksworth in the very south of the Peak District, 2-mile-long Carsington Water is a reservoir operated by Severn Trent as an emergency water supply for the surrounding area. Set in a scenic valley surrounded by rolling, grassy hills and woodland, it's a popular spot for water sports, with boat hire and instruction available. The Carsington Water run (78) follows the trail all the way around the reservoir, an enjoyable 8 miles that's also suitable for running buggies and cycling.

CAUTION There is a short stretch along the B5035 which doesn't have a verge – please take extra care or run through Carsington village to avoid. Bike hire is available at the visitor centre.

The River Dove carves its way through the south-western Peak District for 45 miles from near Buxton to its confluence with the River Trent. The deep valleys of Dovedale (run 79) make for some wonderful explorations and the route alternates between these and the high, grassy fells that surround the river. Don't forget to hop across the famous stepping stones not far from the start of the run.

The Ilam Park run (80) takes a challenging but scenic loop on either side of the River Manifold between the National Trust Ilam Park, a 158-acre country park and part of the White Peak estate, and the village of Wetton. Starting out across fields surrounded by glorious limestone landscapes, it joins the Manifold Way and follows this until it reaches Thor's Cave, a natural limestone cavern some 80 metres up a steep crag from the base of the valley. Steps on the Manifold Way lead up to the cave, a very worthwhile diversion. Leaving the cave our run passes through Wetton before heading back to Ilam, this time on the eastern side of the river.

Routes 78-80

78 AROUND CARSINGTON WATER

Distance 7.5 miles/12km
Ascent 188 metres
Start Carsington Water visitor centre, DE6 1ST
Info wildrunning.net/278

We describe this route in a clockwise direction from the visitor centre but you could join at any point and run in either direction, just keep the water on the same side until you get back to where you started. From the visitor centre follow the shore trail north initially and around to the R until you reach the B5035 (1.7 miles/2.8km). Either continue along the road until you can turn sharp R at the north-east tip of the lake or detour through Carsington to avoid the busier road. Then follow the eastern shore south-west through Hall Wood and Upperfield Farm to reach the road and parking at the south-western tip of the lake (6.2 miles/10km). Turn R following the path up the western shore and back to the start.

79 DOVE DALE

Distance 9 miles/14km
Ascent 1065 metres
Start Dovedale car park, DE6 2AY
Info wildrunning.net/279

From the car park follow the main path north-east up into Dove Dale, passing the caves and stepping stones and following the valley to the bridge at Milldale (3 miles/4.8km). Turn R here climbing away from the river and following the path over Shining Tor before descending steeply L to the road. Turn L and take the road back to Milldale to a L turn onto a footpath. Follow the path uphill to join Pasture Lane. Fork L then turn L onto a path heading south-east down Hall Dale and back to the River Dove. Turn R and follow this south to Ilam Rock, where you follow the path R uphill to the fields at the top of the dale. Turn L here and skirt the edge of Dovedale Wood south then R and head west to Ilamtops Farm. Turn L and follow the path south around Bunster Hill and back to the start.

80 ILAM PARK

Distance 10 miles/15.5km
Ascent 741 metres
Start Ilam Park, DE6 2AZ
Info wildrunning.net/280

Follow the path north out of the car park and then L onto a bridleway downhill to the River Manifold, crossing a footbridge and ascending to Rushley. Join the road and follow it north-west to Throwley Hall. Leave the road and continue on the Manifold Trail across fields descending to the river at Beeston Tor Farm. Turn L and follow the River Manifold around a long R bend and past Thor's Cave. Cross the river and follow the footpath east away from the river up to Leek Road at Wetton (4.9 miles/7.9km). Turn R off the road on a short footpath cutting the corner, to turn R onto Ashbourne Road, then take the footpath R at the junction with Carr Lane. Follow this south, forking L and crossing Larkstone Lane. Continue in the same direction along the rim of the river valley then around to the L, then turn R and head south past Castern Hall down to the river and road where you rejoin the Manifold Trail. Follow this south along the river and back to Ilam.

Crowden Clough

The Peak District – The Dark Peak

The Dark Peak – sometimes also called the High Peak, although the areas differ slightly – forms the higher, wilder northern part of the Peak District, lying mainly in Derbyshire and South Yorkshire. On these high moorland plateaus, the underlying limestone is covered by a cap of millstone grit, resulting in a dark and brooding landscape, often peaty and waterlogged underfoot. The famous gritstone outcrops, fantastic for climbing and bouldering, form an inverted horseshoe shape around the lower limestone White Peak. The highest points of the Dark Peak include Kinder Scout at 636 metres and Bleaklow (610 metres), separated by the steep, winding road of Snake Pass, and Black Hill at 582 metres.

Perhaps the best known of the National Trails, the Pennine Way begins in Edale, nestled deep in the Hope valley, making its way northwards along England's rugged backbone to Kirk Yetholm, just over the Scottish border, some 268 miles later. This is a trail steeped in running history, from the annual winter Spine Race to the epic battles for the Pennine Way record between rivals Mike Cudahy and Mike Hartley. At the time of writing Mike Hartley still holds the record, which he set in 1989 – an incredible 2 days 17 hours 20 minutes and 15 seconds. Right along its length there are many outstanding sections to run and many great circular routes based around the trail.

The Dark Peak's unmistakable gritstone edges make for some incredible running, with many good trails winding along the tops of the escarpments and great views throughout. The annual Nine Edges Endurance Challenge takes in a 21-mile route from Ladybower Reservoir to Baslow, ticking off nine edges along the way and raising money for Edale Mountain Rescue Team. As well as a fell running race there's also one for climbers (one route on each edge) and mountain bikers.

In 1932, 500 men and women took to the slopes of the Peak District's highest point, Kinder Scout, to demand access to the open moors and hills which, at that time, were the sole province of

81

81

82

the grouse-shooting gentry. Five men were jailed for their part in the Kinder mass trespass but their efforts were not in vain. Three weeks later 10,000 ramblers marched in protest and access for all was finally granted, paving the way for future generations of walkers and runners to explore the wilds of the Peak District. Our Kinder Trespass run (81) follows the route of the trespass from the banks of the River Kinder at Hayfield up through dramatic scenery to reach the Pennine Way at Ashop Head.

Crowden Clough, rising enticingly from the Vale of Edale, is a classic Grade 1 scramble that takes you right up to the Kinder Plateau. Thoroughly enjoyable on a dry, sunny day but slippery in the wet, there's a path that runs all the way up the side of the brook, regularly changing sides as it climbs, so you can easily miss out any sections you don't feel like tackling. The Crowden Clough run/scramble (82) begins in Edale, where there's a station and café, and follows the Pennine Way to Upper Booth. Leaving the Pennine Way it follows Crowden Brook, from a gentle start through woodland and drystone-walled fields to the steep, rocky end section that tops out at Crowden Tower – look out for peregrine falcons which can sometimes be spotted here. The descent is via Grindsbrook, an easier scramble and a good route up if you'd prefer to avoid the steeper ground, straight back down into Edale.

On the opposite side of the Vale of Edale from Kinder, a long, beautiful ridgeline runs from Lord's Seat in the west to Lose Hill in the east, summiting the peaks of Mam Tor and Hollins Cross in between. This is, in our opinion, one of the best ridgeline runs in the country, being at once brilliantly runnable, easily accessible and set within the most stunning Peak District scenery. Making a perfect weekend's running when combined with the Crowden Clough run, our Mam Tor Ridge run (83) also follows the Pennine Way out of Edale, only this time it heads north from Upper Booth and climbs steeply to Rushup Edge to gain the ridge. A long and lovely trail leads all the way to the other end, where a fun, fast descent brings you back down to the River Noe. The final stretch follows the horseshoe of the valley back around to Edale.

Routes 81-83

81 KINDER TRESPASS

Distance   9 miles/14km
Ascent   906 metres
Start   Bowden Bridge car park, SK22 2LH
Info   wildrunning.net/281

From the campsite or car park, take the road up the valley and onto the path at the end running north-east to the L off the Kinder Reservoir and up William Clough to a path junction with the Pennine Way (2.4 miles/3.9km). Turn R and follow the Pennine Way to the top of the Kinder Downfall. Continue on the Pennine Way running south on the western edge of the Kinder Plateau, past the trig point on Kinder Low and down to a path junction at SK 080861 (5.8 miles/9.4km). Turn R away from the Pennine Way and west on a stony bridleway downhill into Coldwell Clough. Turn R and follow this valley back to the start.

82 CROWDEN CLOUGH

Distance   6.5 miles/10km
Ascent   663 metres
Start   Edale Station, S33 7ZP
Info   wildrunning.net/282

Follow the road north, turn L at the start of the Pennine Way and follow it west across fields to Upper Booth. Turn R onto the track then R again after the bridge onto a small footpath following the Crowden Brook north up Crowden Clough. Some parts are scrambly if you stay in the brook's bed but can be avoided by using higher paths to the sides. Reach the top of the clough at SK 094872 (3.4 miles/5.5km) and join a path to the R (Crowden Tower is a short detour to the R from here). Follow this path east and then down into Grindsbrook Clough. The path follows the Grinds Brook back to Edale and the start of this route.

83 MAM TOR

Distance   14 miles/22km
Ascent   1092 metres
Start   Edale Station, S33 7ZP
Info   wildrunning.net/283

Follow the road north and turn L onto the Pennine Way, following this to the road at Upper Booth. Cross here, following the footpath on the other side heading south and uphill to the col at SK 099829 (3.5 miles/5.6km). Turn L here and follow the path over Rushup Edge to the road that passes over the col at Mam Tor. Cross the road and follow the paved path to the trig point on Mam Tor. Continue along the ridge past Hollins Cross and up to the summit of Lose Hill (7.5 miles/12km). Turn R and follow the path downhill to Townhead, turn R and follow the path parallel to the road and railway north, crossing both on Bagshaw Bridge. Continue in the same direction past Upper Fulwood Farm and L along Backside Wood to Jaggers Clough. Turn L and follow the edge of the high ground south-west past Clough Farm and along the road through Nether Booth. Turn R onto a path and follow this back to Edale via Ollerbrook Booth.

86

86

86

Our Win Hill and Ladybower run (84) really does have a bit of everything. This outstanding route begins on a gentle trail along the shores of the Upper Derwent Reservoir, a good warm-up for the climb to 538 metres at the top of Back Tor. Then a long, lovely ridge run takes you along Derwent Edge before an enjoyable, winding descent returns you to the water at Ladybower. Another steep ascent brings you to the shapely summit of Win Hill, from where the views out across the dramatic Dark Peak landscape are second to none. Follow the ridge – a former Roman road – across the high ground that descends at first gradually and then plunges into the tree-lined Woodlands valley. A final hill brings you back to the start.

Our Stanage (85) and Froggatt and Curbar Edge (86) routes take in some of the most famous of the Peak District's gritstone edges. The running is outstanding, with clear paths and glorious views throughout. These areas may get busy on a summer weekend, particularly with rock climbers, however on a breezy spring morning you'll very likely have the place to yourself. The Stanage run takes in a loop from the bustling village of Hathersage, easily accessed by train, up through drystone-walled fields onto Stanage Edge for a superb stretch of high-level trail. The final miles take you to the summit of Higger Tor and then all the way back down to Hathersage. The Froggatt and Curbar Edge run stays high throughout: a loop of the two edges and the wide open moorland of White Edge.

Routes 84-86

84 WIN HILL & LADYBOWER

Distance 16 miles/25.5km
Ascent 1440 metres
Start Fairholmes visitor centre, S33 0AQ
Info wildrunning.net/284

Run north to Derwent Reservoir dam, skirting to its R and turning L on the wide track at the top to Abbey Tip. Turn R here on the path up Abbey Brook and then up Sheepfold Clough to the summit cairn on Lost Lad. Follow this past Back Tor trig point, tracing the ridge around to the R over Dovestone Tor and along Derwent Edge all the way to Whinstone Lee Tor (7.6 miles/12.3km). Join the bridleway and follow it downhill and L around Lead Hill to the A57. Turn R and follow this then turn L on the A6013 down Ladybower Reservoir. Turn R across the dam then L down to the base of Parkin Clough. Turn R and follow the steep path to the summit of Win Hill (11 miles/17.7km). Continue over the back of Win Hill and then skirt around to the R onto the old Roman road. Turn R at a path junction skirting the wood down to and across Haggwater Bridge. Continue on the path crossing the A57 and passing Hagg Farm then heading downhill and bearing R back to the start.

85 STANAGE

Distance 8 miles/12.5km
Ascent 532 metres
Start Hathersage Station, S32 1DR
Info wildrunning.net/285

Begin on Station Road, turning R onto Oddfellows Road and continuing to Main Road. Turn L then R onto Baulk Lane, following footpaths across fields to the road at North Lees. Turn R on the road then L onto a footpath heading north-east uphill to the road below Stanage Edge. Turn L onto the road then R onto a bridleway running uphill through the Stanage Plantation and go through a gap in the rocky edge to the wide path along the top (2.8 miles/4.5km). Turn R and follow the Sheffield Country Walk south-east along the edge to the road at Upper Burbage Bridge. Cross and follow the path R to Higger Tor (5.3 miles/8.5km). Turn R and follow the path back to and across the road then follow the footpath opposite around to the L and downhill, trending L to Hathersage. Cross the A6187 and follow it L for a short distance before turning R down a track to Back lane. Turn L on this and then L on Station Road back to the start.

86 FROGGATT & CURBAR EDGE

Distance 10.5 miles/16.5km
Ascent 302 metres
Start Hay Wood car park, S32 3ZJ
Info wildrunning.net/286

Ascend steps to the road and cross carefully, following the path opposite through woodland and out onto open moorland along Froggatt Edge and then Curbar Edge. Cross at the road and continue on a path along Baslow Edge to a path junction. Turn L and follow this path past Wellington's Monument to the road. Cross and follow a path around to the L to a path junction at the corner of a wall near Swine Sty. Continue on the path north-west across Big Moor, past a trig point and curving to the R along White Edge to the road junction between the B6054 and the A625. Cross the A625 and follow the path onto Longshaw estate, passing Little John's Well and reaching the visitor centre and café. Turn L in front of the café and follow the path south-west through the estate and back to the A625. Turn R and follow the road briefly then take the path R past the Grouse Inn. Turn L at the junction in Hay Wood back to the start.

Langdale Pikes

North

The north of England has some of the best running terrain to be found anywhere in the world, along with a vibrant fell running scene. Explore a brilliantly diverse range of spectacular landscapes, from the open moorlands of the North Pennines to the deserted beaches of Northumberland and the rugged peaks and mountain tarns of the Lake District.

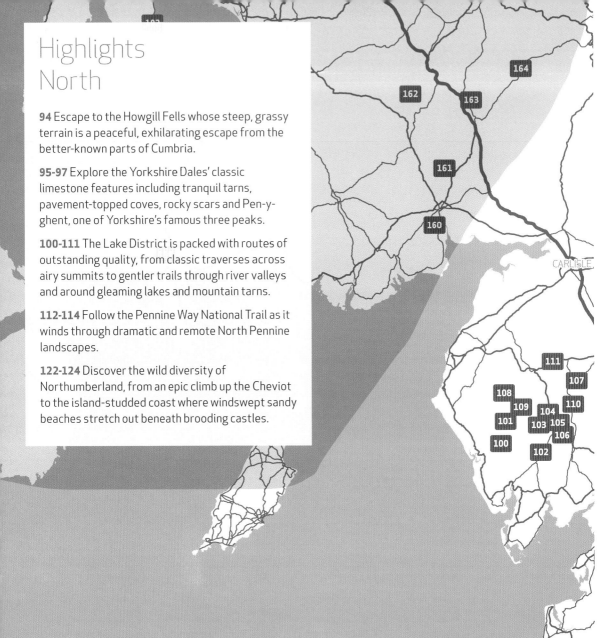

Highlights
North

94 Escape to the Howgill Fells whose steep, grassy terrain is a peaceful, exhilarating escape from the better-known parts of Cumbria.

95-97 Explore the Yorkshire Dales' classic limestone features including tranquil tarns, pavement-topped coves, rocky scars and Pen-y-ghent, one of Yorkshire's famous three peaks.

100-111 The Lake District is packed with routes of outstanding quality, from classic traverses across airy summits to gentler trails through river valleys and around gleaming lakes and mountain tarns.

112-114 Follow the Pennine Way National Trail as it winds through dramatic and remote North Pennine landscapes.

122-124 Discover the wild diversity of Northumberland, from an epic climb up the Cheviot to the island-studded coast where windswept sandy beaches stretch out beneath brooding castles.

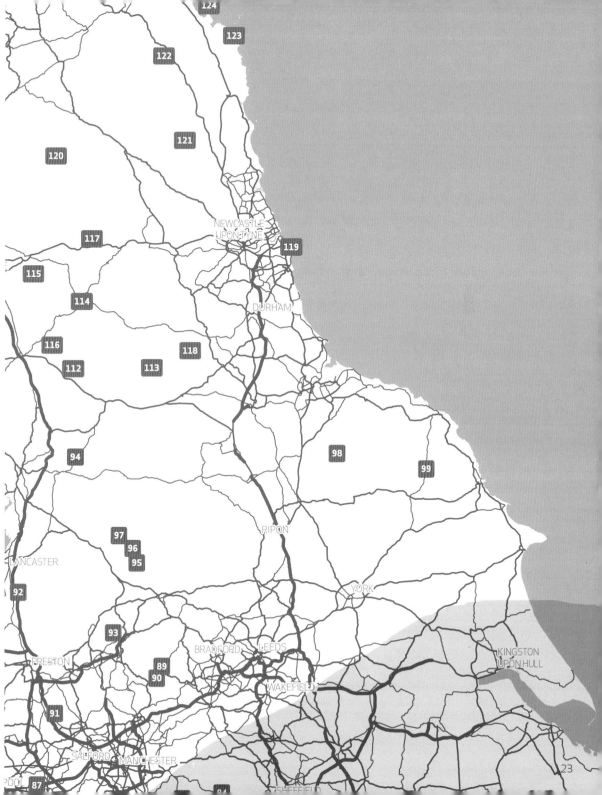

Mary Towneley Loop

South Pennines & Bowland Fells

The Pennines, often described as the backbone of England, stretch from the Peak District in Derbyshire northwards through Lancashire, Greater Manchester, the Yorkshire Dales and past the Cumbrian Fells to the Cheviot Hills on the Anglo-Scottish border. North of the Aire Gap, the Pennines' western spur into North Lancashire forms the Bowland Fells, and south of the gap is a spur into east Lancashire, comprising the Rossendale Fells and West Pennine Moors.

The South Pennines lie hidden between the better known Yorkshire Dales to the north and the Peak District to the south, with the city sprawl of Greater Manchester to the west. This is a unique landscape which has inspired many great writers and poets, including the Brontës and Ted Hughes. It is a vast, open area of sweeping, high moorland intersected by steep-sided narrow valleys dotted with settlements built from the local gritstone. The hillsides and drystone-wall-enclosed pastures bear the scars of a long history of industry and human use, from Mesolithic, Bronze Age and Iron Age findings to Roman roads and forts, and the mills and factories of the Industrial Revolution, powered by the area's fast-flowing streams.

The Bowland Fells, also known as the Forest of Bowland, is an Area of Outstanding Natural Beauty (AONB) characterised by gritstone hills, deep valleys and windswept moorland. One of the best known local landmarks is Pendle Hill, rising to a height of 557 metres and separated from the main fells by the River Ribble. A sombre and atmospheric place, perhaps in part due to its role in the witch trials of the 17th century, local legend has it that 'if you can see Pendle it's about to rain, if you can't, it's already started'. The Forest of Bowland is the sole north-western remnant of the ancient forest that once stretched right across England, also encompassing Sherwood Forest in Nottinghamshire, the New Forest in Hampshire and Savernake Forest in Wiltshire.

87

88

89

A remnant of the medieval Forests of Mara and Mondrem, the 2,400-acre Delamere Forest Park stands surrounded by Cheshire countryside. Managed by the Forestry Commission, there's a range of things to do here, with waymarked walking, running and mountain biking trails, plus a café and visitor centre. The Delamere Forest run (87) heads to a peaceful and less-explored corner of the forest, climbing up and over the summit of Pale Heights before following a section of the 32-mile Sandstone Trail. Contouring around the Iron Age hill fort at Eddisbury, the final stretch passes Delamere Station, where you can also begin the run.

The wide sweep of the beach backed by sandy dunes and dense woodland mean Formby (run 88) is a great place to explore on foot. This route takes in a varied loop with a bit of everything; it can easily be extended northwards where a network of inviting trails twists around the trees and dunes and the coast path runs the length of the beach. Look out for red squirrels and fossilised prehistoric footprints.

Hardcastle Crags covers 400 acres of steep-sided valleys, clear streams, waterfalls and lush woodland, studded with towering stacks of gritstone. At its heart is Gibson Mill, an off-grid eco building owned by the National Trust where you'll also find a café. Our next run, Hebden Dale (89), explores this fascinating area with an enjoyable loop around the dale, passing the crags on both the out and back stretches. Hebden Bridge Station isn't far away and works well as a start point, adding a couple of miles extra in each direction.

Routes 87-89

87 DELAMERE FOREST

Distance 5 miles/8km
Ascent 214 metres
Start Delamere Forest Park, CW8 2JD
Info wildrunning.net/287

Run back along the road and past the FC offices, turn R through the overflow car park and join the path through Eddisbury Wood. Turn L around the edge of the forest, then R along the eastern edge up Eddisbury Hill. Turn R onto a track near the top, trending L to reach the masts at Pale Heights (1.7 miles/2.8km). Turn L here and cross the meadow then follow the small path trending L join the old Roman road in the SE corner of the wood. Turn R and follow this back into the woods (3 miles/4.8km). Turn R up a steep path past the King's Chair then back down L to the path. Turn L past the wild boar sculpture then R onto a small path that curves R over some wooden walkways and north to the main path. Turn R here then L onto the Sandstone Way, follow this to the edge of the wood and take a small path R uphill and back to the masts at Pale Heights (4 miles/6.4km). Turn L and follow the main path north, downhill around a couple of bends and back to the start.

88 FORMBY

Distance 4 miles/6km
Ascent 42 metres
Start Formby Beach, L37 1LJ
Info wildrunning.net/288

Leave the car park and follow the road inland to the toilets, turn L here onto a footpath running north past the caravan site before trending L to the beach (1 mile/1.7km). You can continue north here in the dunes as far as Ainsdale-on-Sea if you wish and return to this route back along the beach. Our route turns L onto the beach and runs south on the sand for a mile, passing the start of the route and continuing to a path inland at approximately SD 270074 (2 miles/3.2km). Turn L inland and follow the path through woodland and along the field boundary to the north of Sandfield Farm. Continue east skirting the edge of the fields and trending R or north-east back to the road by the toilets. Turn L and return along the road to the start.

89 HEBDEN DALE

Distance 6.5 miles/10km
Ascent 514 metres
Start Midgehole Road car park, HX7 7AP
Info wildrunning.net/289

From New Bridge take the main path west in the woodland to the north of Hebden Water, following the river valley to the National Trust owned Gibson Mill (1.1 miles/1.8km). Stay on the same bank and continue on the path up Hebden Dale, passing Hardcastle Crags and following the valley L through Walshaw Wood to reach a footbridge at SD 959314 (2.9 miles/4.6km). Cross the bridge over Alcomden Water and turn L onto the road crossing Graining Water then climb the hill to a footpath heading left before Widdop Gate (3.2 miles/5.2km). Follow this footpath back down the river valley, hugging the south-western bank and dropping down to the riverside opposite Hardcastle Crags. Continue south past the footbridge to Gibson Mill and through Hebden Wood, across a small bridge and back to the start.

90

91

93

Named after Lady Mary Towneley, a campaigner for better bridleways in the 1980s and 90s, the Mary Towneley Loop (run 90) is a 47-mile waymarked circular route that includes a section of the 205-mile Pennine Bridleway, open to horses, cyclists and pedestrians. This is an enjoyable ultra- or multi-day challenge that takes you to some remote and exposed parts of the Pennines, linking up towns and villages along the way.

Standing at 363 metres, Rivington Pike rises from the slopes Winter Hill in the West Pennine Moors. Despite being close to the M61, this is a place that feels wild and remote, and the surrounding area has a great network of trails to explore. Our Rivington Pike run (91) follows clear paths up through Rivington Country Park to reach the wilds of Rivington Moor, climbing steeply over Rivington Pike before taking in a long sweep of open moorland. A thrilling descent off Winter Hill brings you around the edge of the hillside and down to the long, gleaming stretch of Rivington Reservoir to finish.

The River Wyre rises in the Forest of Bowland and flows for 28 miles through Lancashire to reach the Irish Sea at Fleetwood. The Wyre Way follows the meandering course of the river for 45 miles in total, split into three sections. Our Wyre Way run (92) takes in a peaceful, waymarked loop of the easternmost part of the Wyre Way, following the river through fields, woodland and moors in the foothills of the Bowland Fells.

The Pendle Way makes a 45-mile circular journey around Lancashire, an excellent ultra or multi-day run. There are several shorter variations, including the Pendle Three Peaks, taking in the three highest hills around Pendle: Weets Hill (6-mile loop), Boulsworth Hill (8-mile loop) and Pendle Hill (5-mile loop); there's also the 7.5-mile Witches Walking Trail. Our Pendle Hill run (93) traces the section of the Pendle Way that loops up and over Pendle Hill itself, a steep climb to the summit right from the start for glorious views across Lancashire on a clear day.

90 MARY TOWNELEY LOOP

Distance	44.5 miles/71.5km
Ascent	2428 metres
Start	Halifax Road, OL14 6ED
Info	wildrunning.net/290

This circular route can be started at any point, picking up the regular waymarkers. From our start point the route is described in an anticlockwise direction passing the following points: Widdop Reservoir, SD 936328 (7.2 miles/11.6km), Hurstwood Reservoir, SD 891320 (10.6 miles/17km), A646 at Holme Chapel (14.2 miles/22.8km), A681 in Waterfoot (21.6 miles/34.8km), A671 north of Rochdale (28.6 miles/46.1km), A6603 south of Walsden (37.3 miles/60km). The final section passes the Stoodley Pike Monument before descending to the start.

91 RIVINGTON PIKE

Distance	8 miles/13km
Ascent	425 metres
Start	Rivington Country Park, BL6 7SB
Info	wildrunning.net/291

Follow Rivington Lane uphill for about ½ mile then turn L and follow the zigzagging paths up the wooded hillside and past the gardens to the tower and summit of Rivington Pike (2.3 miles/3.7km). Follow the footpath south, turning L at the junction below Brown Hill and L onto the Rotary Way at Pike Cottage, crossing the moor past the masts to the trig point on Winter Hill (4.4 miles/7.1km). Continue on the path descending north to Rivington Road. Turn L on the road then L onto Belmont Road, following this around Noon Hill to the path below Rivington Pike. Turn R here to return to the start.

92 THE WYRE WAY

Distance	14 miles/22km
Ascent	493 metres
Start	Dolphinholme, LA2 9AQ
Info	wildrunning.net/292

Run east on footpath and turn R onto Wagon Road and join the waymarked Wyre Way. Follow this along the road, turning L onto the drive of Dolphinholme House but staying on the footpath heading east and following the course of the River Wyre. Continue on this path keeping L and crossing the river at Long Bridge, then follow the northern shore to a footbridge just west of Abbeystead Reservoir (2.6 miles/4.2km). Cross the bridge and take the path around the south side of the reservoir to a road. Turn L onto the road and cross a bridge then turn R on the Wyre Way, following the course of the Marshaw Wyre to a road at Well Brook. Follow this to Tower Lodge and turn L on the Wyre Way north to Tarnbrook. Turn L and follow the path south-west across the road at Emmetts and along the northern edge of the Abbeystead Reservoir to the outbound path. Turn R and follow this back to the start.

93 PENDLE HILL

Distance	5 miles/8km
Ascent	372 metres
Start	Barley car park, BB12 9JX
Info	wildrunning.net/293

Join the Pendle Way and follow it north-west through Barley and up to the R or north of Pendle Hill, passing Ings End, Brown House and Pendle House before reaching the ridge path just north of the summit. Turn L and follow the path past the trig point and south down Boar Clough into Ogden Clough. Turn L and follow the valley down past Upper and then Lower Ogden reservoirs and back into Barley.

Yorkshire Moors & Dales

Within the borders of the historic county of Yorkshire are areas widely considered to be among the greenest in England, with vast stretches of unspoilt countryside in the Yorkshire Dales and North York Moors providing mile upon mile of outstanding running. The county has a fine sporting pedigree to match, with its athletes winning seven golds, two silvers and three bronze medals in the 2012 Olympics which, if it were a country, would have placed it twelfth in the world medals table.

The Yorkshire Dales lie mostly within the National Park of the same name, with Nidderdale just outside the Park on its eastern edge. The Dales are a collection of valleys scored through by tumbling becks that make their way through the limestone geology, giving the area its characteristic green hilltops and boulder-strewn scree slopes that plunge into deep clefts. The great scoop of limestone forming Malham Cove was, some 50,000 years ago, a huge, glacier-fed waterfall which sent meltwater crashing down to the valley floor. A vast limestone pavement tops the cove, a great jigsaw of flat-topped boulders. On the western edge of the National Park, separated from the Lake District by the M6 and just over the Cumbrian border, the Howgill Fells provide a peaceful and less visited running destination with many outstanding routes. The features of the landscape here, with its leg-sappingly steep gradients, cascading waterfalls and wild plateaus, bridges the two National Parks perfectly.

The North York Moors National Park is one of the largest expanses of heather moorland in the UK. The running here is varied and exhilarating, from open moorland to woodland trails and windswept coastal paths. To the east the area is edged by the impressive cliffs of the North Sea coast, providing enjoyable and interesting coast path running along the Cleveland Way at Robin Hood's Bay. The northern and western boundaries are defined by the steep scarp slopes of the Cleveland Hills edging the Tees lowlands and the Hambleton Hills above the Vale of Mowbray.

131

94

95

96

Our Howgills run (94) explores the relatively undiscovered Howgill Fells, with a long, steep climb past the stepped cascades of Cautley Spout to the very summit of the range – the Calf at 676 metres. From here there's a long, flowing section of ridgeline running on the Dales High Way before a steep descent brings you into Bowderdale. The final miles follow Bowderdale Beck down the valley, joining your outward route back to Low Haygarth.

Our next run, the Malham Classic (95), follows one of the classic Yorkshire walking routes, taking in some of the very best bits of this part of the Dales. Starting in Malham village it climbs alongside Malham Cove to reach the limestone pavement at the top. Following the Pennine Way up a long, limestone valley and emerging onto open fell brings you to peaceful Malham Tarn. From here a tricky descent of Gordale Scar (CAUTION) brings you to the waterfalls and pools at Janet's Foss and the final run back into Malham.

A perfect partner to this Malham run if you're basing yourself in this part of the Yorkshire Dales for a weekend, the Fountains Fell run (96) takes in the remote and less visited Fountains Fell, high above Malham Tarn. It begins by following the Pennine Way up a long stretch of hillside to reach Fountains Fell Tarn and the summit plateau at just over 660 metres. From here there's a glorious ridge run out to Knowe Fell before you drop steeply from the hills to reach the shores of Malham Tarn.

Routes 94-96

94 THE HOWGILLS

Distance 6 miles/9.5km
Ascent 605 metres
Start A683 layby, near the Cross Keys Inn, LA10 5NE
Info wildrunning.net/294

Follow the obvious path north-west up Cautley Holme Beck, bearing L to pass Cautley Spout waterfall and climbing up Swere Gill to the trig point on the summit of the Calf (2.2 miles/3.6km). Turn R and follow the Dales High Way along the ridge towards Hazelgill Knott. Turn R at SD 673987 before you reach Hazelgill Knott and follow the path down next to Ram's Gill into Bowderdale (3.8 miles/6.1km). Turn R and follow Bowderdale Beck upstream, past Bowderdale Head and over the small col before descending to the path junction below Cautley Spout. Join the outbound path and follow it back down Cautley Holme Beck to the start.

95 MALHAM CLASSIC

Distance 7.5 miles/12km
Ascent 493 metres
Start Malham village, BD23 4DG
Info wildrunning.net/295

Follow Cove Road north through Malham then R onto the Pennine Way, bearing L at Malham Cove up the steps and across the limestone pavement to the head of the dry valley. Turn L up the valley to a gate. Turn R and continue on the Pennine Way up a dry valley out onto the moorland beyond, to a road. Cross and follow the path to the Lings Plantation on the south-eastern shore of Malham Tarn (3.2 miles/5.1km). Turn R off the Pennine Way to a junction with a bridleway, turning R and following it south to the road end at Street Gate. Continue in the same direction bearing L at the next junction and heading away from the road into the valley above Gordale Scar. Follow the scrambly path carefully down the scar into the valley below. Follow the path through the campsite to Hawthorns Lane. Turn R onto the road and then L onto a footpath past Janet's Foss waterfall and along Gordale Beck to the Pennine Way. Turn R onto this and follow it back to Malham.

96 FOUNTAINS FELL

Distance 9 miles/14km
Ascent 480m
Start Malham Tarn, BD24 9PT
Info wildrunning.net/296

Follow the driveway towards the field centre but turn L onto the Pennine Way after the smiley barn on the L. Go through the gate and follow the Pennine Way north along the edges of fields to the road. Turn R onto the road then L on the track up to Tennant Gill Farm. Head to the L of the farm and uphill to the col, cairn and mine workings to the north-east of Fountains Fell (3.9 miles/6.3km). Turn L off the Pennine Way and follow the path marked by finger posts over the high point and down slightly to a wall. Turn L along the wall over Fountains Fell summit and south. At the wall's end continue following finger posts and the line of an old fence to the second wall that comes up from the valley on your L (6.1 miles/9.8km). Turn L and follow the wall downhill to a junction with a bridleway. Turn R on this and across the next two fields, turn L on Knowe Fell following the wall south-east back to the road. Turn R and follow it to a sharp L onto a track back to the start.

98

98

99

At 694 metres, Pen-y-ghent is the lowest of the Yorkshire Three Peaks, the other two being Ingleborough (723 metres) and Whernside (736 metres). Our Pen-y-ghent run (97) follows the Pennine Way steeply up to its summit, before descending along the magnificent ridgeline that forms the mountain's northern slopes to reach its neighbouring summit, Plover Hill. Descending to join the Pennine Journey, followed by a stretch along Pen-y-ghent Ghyll, this route finishes along a second section of the Pennine Way.

On the north-western fringes of the North York Moors National Park lie the Cleveland Hills, home to the distinctive mini-mountain of Roseberry Topping and the 110-mile Cleveland Way National Trail. The Wainstones run (98) crosses the wilds of Cold Moor to reach the Cleveland Way, following it past the towering sandstone blocks of the Wainstones, a popular rock climbing venue, and up to Urra Moor, the highest point in the North York Moors at 454 metres. There's a final long downhill stretch bringing you back down from the wilds of the moors to the finish.

Staying in the North York Moors National Park, our Hole of Horcum run (99) begins with a traverse around this awe-inspiring 120-metre-deep by 1.2km-wide natural amphitheatre, sunk into the valley of the Levisham Beck. Legend has it the hollow was made by a giant scooping up a handful of earth; however, it's actually the result of 'spring sapping' – erosion of the bedrocks by underground water – a process which continues today. Following clear paths across the high, wild moorland there's an out-and-back to the viewpoint at Skelton Tower before you dive into the depths of the valley, then climb out steeply to return to the start.

Routes 97-99

97 PEN-Y-GHENT

Distance	10 miles/16km
Ascent	634 metres
Start	Dale Head, BD24 9PW
Info	wildrunning.net/297

Head off down the Pennine Way past Dale Head Farm and fork R at the junction, staying on the Pennine Way, across the moorland and up the steep climb to the summit of Pen-y-ghent (1.6 miles/2.6km). Continue in the same direction staying R of the wall and following the path north then around to the R over Plover Hill to intersect with the Pennine Journey bridleway on Foxup Moor. Turn R and follow this until you start curving L and descending more steeply, where you turn R onto a smaller path heading south-east to the road at Hesleden Bergh (6.5 miles/10.5km). Turn R on this road and join a footpath on the L after a cattle grid, then follow Pen-y-ghent Gill back to the same road near the Giant's Grave cairn. Cross the road and continue on the path to Blishmire House, turn L and follow its drive back to the road. Turn R and follow the road back to the start.

98 THE WAINSTONES

Distance	9.5 miles/15km
Ascent	671 metres
Start	Chop Gate car park, TS9 7JW
Info	wildrunning.net/298

Follow the road north to the junction then turn L onto a path uphill onto the ridge at Three Howes. Follow the ridge north to join the Cleveland Way at the 402m high point (2.7 miles/4.4km). Turn R on the Cleveland Way through Garfit Gap and up to Wainstones. Continue along the ridge over White Hill then curve R and descend to the B1257, Clay Bank. Cross the road and, still on the Cleveland Way, climb up onto Carr Ridge and follow this south-east to the trig point on Round Hill (6.2 miles/10km). Turn back on yourself then turn L, leaving the Cleveland Way and joining a bridleway heading west downhill. Cross the path junction near Medd Crag and continue down to the road at Bilsdale Hall. Turn L and follow the road, staying L at the next two junctions to return to the start.

99 HOLE OF HORCUM

Distance	7.5 miles/12km
Ascent	397 metres
Start	Saltergate car park, YO18 7NR
Info	wildrunning.net/299

Head along the path north parallel to the road to Gallows Dike above the Hole of Horcum. Stay high following the Tabular Hills Walk around the hole and south across Levisham Moor to Dundale Pond (2.5 miles/4.1km). Turn R here and follow an out and back path to visit the Skelton Tower and return to this spot. Then continue in the same direction down Dundale Griff to Levisham Beck (5.2 miles/8.4km). Turn L and follow the path north into the Hole of Horcum. Take the steep path up to Gallows Dike and turn R onto the outbound path and back to the start.

Coniston Fells

Lake District South

The Lake District's rugged fells, deep valleys, vast lakes and hidden mountain tarns make it one of the most exciting and awe-inspiring places for running. This inspiring landscape is also brilliantly accessible, with recent work on footpaths and cycleways meaning many of the different areas can be linked up without needing to run on the road. Every adventure in the Lakes is set in spine-tinglingly beautiful scenery, whether you're exploring the winding, green valleys and looking up at the surrounding peaks, or running across the fell tops with a bird's-eye view of everything that lies below. Designated a UNESCO World Heritage Site in 2017, the Lake District is home to all the land in England higher than 3,000 feet (914 metres) above sea level, including Scafell Pike, the highest mountain in England at 978 metres. It also contains the deepest (Wast Water) and the longest (Windermere) bodies of water in England.

For the purposes of the chapters in this book we have divided the Lake District into two sections, drawing an east-west line approximately through Scafell Pike. The south Lakes chapter begins with a tour of Eskdale, a peaceful corner of the western Lakes where the River Esk meanders its way through dramatic mountain scenery. Next there's a loop of the fells that edge the southern shores of Wast Water, also a good starting point for an ascent of Scafell Pike. Wasdale is the lifelong home of fell running legend Joss Naylor, whose epic peak-bagging attempts based around the Bob Graham Round (the original challenge is 42 peaks in 24 hours, however in 1975 Joss ticked off an astounding 72 peaks – a distance of around 100 miles – in 23 hours and 20 minutes) are still unachievable by most today.

On the opposite side of Scafell from Wasdale lies the curving, glacial valley of Great Langdale and a run around the classic horseshoe of peaks that ring the head of the valley. The Cumbria Way weaves alongside Great Langdale Beck to Chapel Stile, from where it's a short hop over Loughrigg Fell down to pretty Grasmere village, with its shingle-edged lake, perfect for a post-run dip.

100

101

102

Our Eskdale run (100) explores this broad green valley, starting out along the banks of the pretty River Esk, bordered by high crags down which waterfalls embroider a network of long, white veils. Crossing the river and running through the grounds of the friendly Woolpack Inn, there's a good climb up onto the fells to Eel Tarn. Great Barrow rises to your left here and makes an excellent out-and-back detour with fantastic views from the top, should your legs be up for an extra challenge. Otherwise, there's a clear path that descends enjoyably all the way back to the start. Eel Tarn and neighbouring Blea Tarn are both wonderfully peaceful swimming spots.

Remote and removed from the main Lakes tourist hotspots, many runners only visit beautiful Wasdale in a hurry during the England leg of the National Three Peaks Challenge – a shame as there's so much to keep you here for longer. Our Wast Water run (101) begins with a long stretch along the lake's southern shore before heading steeply up into the fells. From the top of Whin Rigg there's a glorious ridge run across to Illgill Head with incredible panoramic Lakeland views. A long, steep descent skirts Fence Wood before bringing you back to Wasdale Head. Stay at the National Trust campsite, right in the heart of the fells, or at the Wasdale Head Inn where you can enjoy a well-earned beer by a roaring fire.

The Coniston Fells run (102) follows a challenging and exhilarating high-level horseshoe of the summits and ridges that encircle Levers Water, overlooking the lake and village at Coniston. Starting with a gentle warm-up through the village outskirts and up through the valley, there's a long, steep climb past Low Water and straight to the summit of the Old Man of Coniston, at just over 800 metres. From here an awe-inspiring airy ridgeline takes you to Swirl How and then Wetherlam via the narrow ridge of the Prison Band. The running becomes easier here, following obvious paths down the grassy hillside and back to Coniston.

Routes 100-102

100 ESKDALE

Distance	5 miles/7.5km
Ascent	317 metres
Start	Dalegarth Station, CA19 1TF
Info	wildrunning.net/2100

Head along the road towards Boot and turn R opposite the pub down a track, past Eskview Farm and the church to the River Esk. Cross and turn L following the riverside path up the valley and slightly south to Low Birker. Turn R here and follow the track to the road at Doctor Bridge. Cross and follow this road north then R onto the valley road to the Woolpack Inn (2 miles/3.2km). Turn L following the footpath between the pub and the outdoor centre up the fell to Eel Tarn. Pass this to the west then turn L at the path junction. A nice detour here is to climb the scrambly Great Barrow to your L, otherwise follow this path south-west and down the Whillan Beck into Boot. Turn R on the valley road to return to the start.

101 WAST WATER

Distance	11 miles/17km
Ascent	1341 metres
Start	Wasdale Head, CA20 1EX
Info	wildrunning.net/2101

Take the road south to the bend, where you continue onto a bridleway heading south-west to the head of Wast Water. Turn L and then R onto the lakeside path, which follows the southern side of Wast Water all the way to the mouth of the River Irt by Low Wood. Turn L and follow the path up to Greathall Gill (4.7 miles/7.5km). Turn L again up the gill to the ridge path at the top. Turn L onto this and follow it north-east over Whin Rigg and along the ridge to Illgill Head. Continue on the path trending R and downhill to a path junction at NY 183055 near Maiden Castle Cairn (8.1 miles/13.1km). Turn L and follow the bridleway downhill to join the outbound path in the north-eastern corner of Wast Water. Turn R here away from the outbound route and follow the path up Lingmell Gill. Turn L at the next path junction and follow a path around the base of Lingmell to a footbridge over Lingmell Beck, cross this to return to the start.

102 CONISTON FELLS

Distance	8.5 miles/13.5km
Ascent	1105 metres
Start	Sun Hotel, Coniston LA21 8HQ
Info	wildrunning.net/2102

Set off on the footpath beside the pub to the bridge over Church Beck. Don't cross but stay on the path following the beck, which then bears to the L west to the path junction with the Walna Scar route at Crowberry Haws. Continue up the path through old mine workings and to the south of Low Water to reach the summit and trig point on the Old Man of Coniston (2.4 miles/3.9km). Take the path north along the ridge over the 796m cairn, above Little and then Great How Crags and onto the Swirl Band to the summit of Swirl How. Turn R and follow the Prison Band north-east down to Swirl Hawse then up, and trending R, to Wetherlam. Head south-east above Hen Tor and Hen Crag and down to a small tarn then continue south down the fell to join the bigger path in Hole Rake. Turn R and follow it down past the old mining works to the large track in the Church Beck Valley. Turn L onto this down then across the bridge to join the outbound route. Turn L to return.

103

104

105

The Great Langdale valley is a runners' paradise, surrounded by inviting peaks but with a network of lower-level trails that means there's something to suit everyone. If you're an experienced mountain runner the Langdale Horseshoe, following the course of the classic fell race, is a fantastic loop, taking in all the peaks that ring the valley. But a great place to start is with the Langdale Pikes (run 103), whose jagged tops form the distinctive skyline on the northern side of Great Langdale. Starting at Sticklebarn, a National Trust-run pub that's a very welcoming place for post-run refuelling, it heads up Stickle Ghyll to peaceful Stickle Tarn, then ticks off the first summit of Pavey Ark via its east ridge. From here the paths are intermittent and some navigation is required to guide you around the remaining summits of Thunacar Knott, Pike of Stickle, Loft Crag, Thorn Crag and Harrison Stickle.

Grasmere is another fantastic outdoor adventure base, with easy access to the higher fells as well as plenty of easier options. The lake is a wonderful swimming spot, along with nearby Rydal Water which is much quieter over the popular summer months. Our High Raise run (104) starts in the heart of Grasmere and makes its way alongside Easedale Beck up the valley to Sourmilk Gill. A steep climb alongside the waterfall brings you to Easedale Tarn and onwards, climbing steeply to the cairn and trig point summit of High Raise at 762 metres. After a short section across the wide plateau, with fine views of the surrounding fells, there's a steep drop down into Far Easedale and a gentle run back into Grasmere.

Loughrigg Fell's distinctive form with its stepped terraces, wooded lower slopes and rough outline stands proud between Ambleside and Grasmere at the entrance to the Great Langdale valley. At just 335 metres it's only a mini-mountain, but the views from the trig point-topped summit are outstanding. Our Loughrigg Fell run (105) starts along the shores of Rydal Water, looping around the eastern flanks of the fell to reach Loughrigg Tarn. From here there's a good climb to the summit before a fun, fast, zigzagging descent down the paved terrace paths brings you back to Rydal.

Routes 103-105

103 LANGDALE PIKES

Distance 6 miles/9.5km
Ascent 1087m
Start Sticklebarn car park, LA22 9JU
Info wildrunning.net/2103

Follow the path around the back of the pub and up the Stickle Ghyll valley to a bridge over the new hydroelectric dam. Cross and turn L uphill to the south-east corner of Stickle Tarn. Follow the path around to the R then north up to the top of Pavey Ark. Turn R and navigate along vague paths north to Thunacar Knott (or continue north for the amazing views from High Raise). Turn L and head towards Harrison Stickle but turn R before the steep climb to the summit and head west to the rocky spike of the Pike of Stickle. Climb back down the same way and then bear R to Loft Crag before heading north-east over Harrison Stickle and down to the south-western shore of Stickle Tarn. For a change, take the path down the western shore of Stickle Ghyll, turning L onto the Cumbria Way at the bottom and returning to the start.

104 HIGH RAISE

Distance 10 miles/15.5km
Ascent 988 metres
Start Red Bank Road car park, LA22 9PU
Info wildrunning.net/210

Follow Broadgate Road through Grasmere then turn L onto Easedale Road until a L onto a bridleway at a sharp R bend in the road. Follow the bridleway across Easedale Beck and up onto the fell. Climb up beside Sourmilk Gill then bear L around the southern shore of Easedale Tarn. Continue to ascend between Eagle Crag and Belles Knott to a path junction, turn R and head north-west over Sergeant Man to the trig point and shelter on High Raise (4.5 miles/7.3km). Turn slightly R and return to the path running north past Low White Stones to a path junction on Greenup Edge. Turn R following the bridleway east downhill over a low col and then down across Grasmere Common and beside Far Easedale Gill to intersect Easedale Road. Follow the road back to Grasmere, joining the outbound route and returning to the start.

105 LOUGHRIGG FELL

Distance 6.5 miles/10.5km
Ascent 797 metres
Start Rydal Water car park, LA22 9SE
Info wildrunning.net/2016

Carefully cross the A591 and follow the path R to cross the footbridge over the river. Turn L on the path through woodland and along the southern shore of Rydal Water to the road at Pelter Bridge (1.6 miles/2.6km). Turn R on the road for about ½ a mile to a footpath on the R. Take this path up Fox Ghyll and continue south-west to a path junction below Ivy Crag. Turn R here and stay R at the next junctions, passing to the north-east of Loughrigg Tarn (4 miles/6.4km). At the northern tip of the tarn stay R and follow the paths to the beck coming down to the corner of Intake Wood. Turn R here and take the steeper path up the beck to the summit on Loughrigg Fell. Turn L and follow the path back down to reach the western end of Loughrigg Terrace above Grasmere (5.1 miles/8.2km). Turn R along the terraces to a sharp L which brings you back to the beach at Grasmere. Turn R and follow the riverside path back to the start.

Great Gable via Sour Milk Gill

Lake District North

Our northern Lake District trails take on some of the big mountain challenges to be found in this part of the country – a mixture of classic circuits that lend themselves particularly well to running and our own favourite discoveries. This is a chapter packed with knife-edge ridgelines, leg-sapping ascents, eye-watering descents and summits with views that make it all worthwhile.

Named after the Roman road that once ran across it from Brougham, near Penrith, to Ambleside, High Street's summit is a wide, grassy plateau that has been used in the past for fairs and even for horse racing, hence its local name of Racecourse Hill. At 828 metres this is the highest point of the easternmost fells of the National Park. It's a long climb to reach the top, but if you're lucky enough to find yourself up there in good weather, and with not too much company, it's almost impossible not to run the well-defined, snaking trail with out-of-control childlike abandon. Parallel to High Street, to the west of the steeply winding Kirkstone Pass, the Helvellyn range runs north-south for nearly 7 miles, a glorious, rising and falling mountain ridge with no point along its entire length below 600 metres. The summit crown of the mighty Helvellyn itself, the third-highest mountain in England, is flanked by the two knife-edge buttresses of Swirral Edge and Striding Edge, with Red Tarn nestled between them.

One of the furthest north of the Lakeland fells, Blencathra's summit is formed from six distinct tops, the highest of which is Hallsfell Top at 868 metres. Documenting people and place beautifully in his film 'Life of a Mountain', Terry Abraham follows the story of Blencathra through the course of a full year, an enlightening and stirring journey. The mountain's awe-inspiring outline, inviting on a warm, summer's day but dark and terrifying in a storm, appears almost symmetrical when seen from the south-east, its flat-topped summit and sloping sides giving it its alternative name of Saddleback.

106

107

108

The Fairfield Horseshoe is a classic walking route that also makes a challenging and spectacular run. The annual Fairfield Horseshoe fell race was first organised by the Lake District Mountain Trial Association in 1966, with 9 miles of mountainous running and over 900 metres of ascent. Our Fairfield Horseshoe run (106) begins in bustling Ambleside, heading through Rydal village and straight up into the fells, climbing to the summit of Heron Pike at 612 metres and the main ridge, which rises steadily to run over Great Rigg and continues to the summit of Fairfield itself at 873 metres. From here the magnificent ridge heads gradually downhill, with several smaller rises to the summits of Hart Crag, Dove Crag, High Pike and Low Pike, before the final descent into Ambleside.

At 9 miles long by 0.75 miles wide, Ullswater is the second-largest body of water in the Lake District. The 20-mile waymarked Ullswater Way circumnavigates the lake, for the most part staying well away from roads and exploring the rugged fells within which it is set. Aira Force, owned by the National Trust and at the edge of Ullswater, is one of the most popular waterfalls in the National Park, and with good reason as its craggy woodland backdrop is utterly magical. Our Aira Force & Gowbarrow Fell run (107) loops around peaceful Gowbarrow Fell, adjacent to Aira Force, taking in fine views across the lake from its summit before visiting the famous falls as a fitting finale.

The two picturesque lakes of Buttermere and Crummock Water nestle together in the steep-sided Buttermere Valley, surrounded by towering fells. A deeply tranquil place, particularly if you're able to visit out of season, the lakeside trails here are some of the best in the National Park for running. The Buttermere run (108) circumnavigates Crummock Water, the larger of the two lakes, however if you'd like an additional 4.5 miles you can also run around Buttermere. The zigzagging ascent to the summit of Rannerdale Knotts is well worth the effort for its great running and outstanding views, but you can miss out this section if you prefer and stay on the lower path. Note, the permissive path along the north end of Buttermere is closed 1st April – 30th June for the sandpiper nesting season.

Routes 106-108

106 FAIRFIELD HORSESHOE

Distance 11 miles/17.5km
Ascent 1203 metres
Start Rydal Road car park, LA22 9AN
Info wildrunning.net/2106

Turn L and follow Rydal Road out of Ambleside, turn R onto a footpath shortly after crossing Scandale Bridge. Head alongside Scandale Beck before bearing L away from the beck on a good path across Rydal Park and past Rydal Hall. Turn R, passing Hart Head Farm and climbing onto the fells above Nab Scar. Follow the path up the ridge to Heron Pike at 612m, then Great Rigg at 766m and finally Fairfield at 873m (5.4 miles/8.7km). Turn R and, staying on the horseshoe ridge, start descending over Hart Crag at 822m and Dove Crag at 792m. Keep R tracing the ridge south over High Pike at 656m then Low Pike at 508m before dropping down towards Ambleside and joining the end of Nook Lane at Nook End Farm. Take the lane south into Ambleside, turning R onto Smithy Brow then R onto Rydal Road to return to the start.

107 AIRA FORCE & GOWBARROW FELL

Distance 4.5 miles/7km
Ascent 630 metres
Start Aira Force car park, CA11 0JS
Info wildrunning.net/2017

From the car park take the main path initially then turn R crossing Aira Beck on a footbridge and follow the path east. Turn R at the first junction then fork L ascending under Hind Crag and following the path L around Gowbarrow Park. Stay L past the shooting lodge and then climb to the trig point on Gowbarrow Fell (2.6 miles/4.1km). Continue on the path, descending west into the Aira Beck Valley. Turn L at the path junction and head down the beck and past the smaller waterfalls upstream of Aira Force. Join the tourists at the bridge over Aira Force and follow the well-used paths past the various viewpoints before returning down the main path to the start.

108 BUTTERMERE

Distance 10 miles/15.5km
Ascent 920 metres
Start Buttermere, CA13 9XA
Info wildrunning.net/2108

Head west out of the village to the L of the pub and across the fields between Crummock Water and Buttermere. Turn R onto the path on the far side and follow it north-west along the western shore of Crummock Water to the northern tip. Cross both bridges and turn R into the small wood below Scale Hill before running south-east along the eastern shore. You can follow this straight back to the start but we suggest turning L at Rannerdale Bridge and running up Squat Beck; the bluebells can be amazing here. Turn sharp R at the path junction at NY 179177, almost turning back on yourself then running out along the ridge to Rannerdale Knotts (8.4 miles/13.5km). Turn L and follow the steep path downhill to a path junction below. Turn L and follow this above the road and lake back towards Buttermere, joining the road. When you reach the National Trust car park on the R, turn R onto a path through woodland and down to cross a footbridge, then L to finish.

109

111

111

Great Gable lies at the heart of the Lake District National Park, rising to just under 900 metres between Wasdale and Borrowdale, two contrasting valleys connected by the Sty Head Pass. Our Great Gable via Sourmilk Gill run (109) starts in the remote hamlet of Seathwaite on the River Derwent at the southernmost reaches of Borrowdale. From here it climbs up alongside Sourmilk Gill, an outstanding scramble up slabby boulders that, while not being difficult, is engaging and a lot of fun. Emerging over the top into the great scoop of Gillercomb is wonderful, and on a hot day the plunge pools here are a perfect way to cool down after your climb. From here there's a long ascent to the summit of Great Gable followed by an exhilarating descent to Styhead Tarn. The final stretch follows a bridleway down the valley alongside the stream, passing the waterfall of Taylorgill Force before returning to Seathwaite.

The long, clear path that marches over the top of High Street (run 110) along the original route of the Roman road makes for a truly exceptional high-level trail run. You can simply follow the bridleway from Hartsop up Hayeswater Gill to the Knot, gaining the ridge and running to the summit of High Street and back. Alternatively, for an enjoyable loop, our route begins by following Pasture Beck to Thornthwaite Crag, joining the Roman road here and running the full length of High Street before descending back to Hartsop.

Our final Lake District route takes on the mighty Blencathra (run 111), but avoids the tricky ways to the top and sticks to the clearest and most runnable trails. Starting with a long but not too steep climb up the lower slopes of Scales Fell, following the River Glenderamackin, you'll eventually meet a fork in the path. Right takes you up to precipitous Sharp Edge, a fantastic and classic scramble if you have sure feet and a steady nerve, however our route bears left, following Scales Beck up into the coombe that holds Scales Tarn. From here there's a steep ascent to the summit at 868 metres, followed by a long and lovely (in good weather, at least) descent along the ridge of Scales Fell back down to the finish.

109 GREAT GABLE VIA SOURMILK GILL

Distance 5.5 miles/8.5km
Ascent 887 metres
Start Seathwaite Farm, CA12 5XJ
Info wildrunning.net/2109

Note: please park considerately and in the farmer's field car park to avoid access issue for tractors and the emergency services.

Take the path to the R of the farm, across the footbridge and up the scrambly path to the L of Sourmilk Gill. Follow the path bearing L in Gillercomb and up to Green Gable at 801m. Continue south-west through Windy Gap to Great Gable at 899m (2.1 miles/3.4km). Turn L and follow the obvious path south-east and downhill to the path junction at Sty Head. Turn L and follow the bridleway down the valley, to the west of Styhead Tarn and down Styhead Gill, crossing on a footbridge and turning R over Greenhow Knott to Stockley Bridge over Grains Gill. Cross then turn L on the path and head north back to the start.

110 HIGH STREET

Distance 6.5 miles/10.5km
Ascent 745 metres
Start Hartsop, CA11 0NZ
Info wildrunning.net/2110

From the end of the road in Hartsop turn R and cross Pasture Beck before following the path south-east up the valley. Climb the steep hillside at the head of the valley, turning L at the path junction at Threshthwaite Mouth and continuing up to the beacon at 784m. Bear L here onto High Street and follow this north-east past the trig point on Racecourse Hill. (A challenging extra loop can be added here by turning R onto the path over Mardale III Bell and then down past Small Water to Haweswater. Turn L and cross Mardale Beck then return to High Street on the path past Blea Water.) Back on the suggested route, continue along High Street keeping L along the ridge to The Knott at 739m. Turn L and follow the path steeply down to the northern end of Hayeswater. Turn R to head down Hayeswater Gill back to the start.

111 BLENCATHRA

Distance 4.5 miles/7km
Ascent 773 metres
Start Comb Beck bridge, NE of Scales Farm, CA12 4SY
Info wildrunning.net/2111

Take the path up Comb Beck into Mousthwaite Comb, curving R uphill to the path junction on the col at NY 346278. Turn L and follow the path, staying R above the Glenderamackin River to Scales Beck. Turn L to ascend the steep-stepped path to the track junction to the east of Scales Tarn. Our route turns L here along the steep path to the south of Scales Tarn and up to the summit of Blencathra. The other option is to turn R and climb the classic grade 1 scramble Sharp Edge – it's an enjoyable challenge but requires care and a cool head, especially if it's wet or windy. Turn L at the top of the scramble and follow the path to the summit (2.4 miles/3.9km). From the summit turn around and head east along the ridge then down the zig-zags to Scales Fell. Continue downhill trending L to join the outbound path in Mousthwaite Comb, and turn R to return to the start.

North Pennines & Hadrian's Wall

The North Pennines was designated an Area of Outstanding Natural Beauty in 1988 for its unique landscape of open heather moors edged by deep dales, upland rivers, hay meadows and stone-built villages, many of which echo the legacies of a mining and industrial past. This is a place of great contrasts where, away from the scars of its industrial history, there is a wild and rugged beauty to the landscape and many outstanding trails to be found. From the strange barren moonscape of Cross Fell to the wildflower meadows of Upper Teesdale and the breathtaking scenery of the Pennine Way, the running here is varied and enticing.

Hadrian's Wall marches across the north of England from Bowness-on-Solway, ½ a mile from the Scottish border, to Wallsend near Newcastle, 68 miles from the border. This huge, imposing structure with its many gateways, milecastles and turrets was built as a defensive fortification in Roman Britain. It marked the northernmost part of the then-vast empire of Rome, and building began in AD 122 under the rule of the emperor Hadrian. The 84-mile National Trail that traces the path of the wall runs along the river in Tyneside and through a swathe of agricultural land before heading up and onto the remote and spectacular upland section, dominated by the great dolerite escarpment of Whin Sill. Passing Crag Lough and the meeting point with the Pennine Way, the trail then gradually descends to the rich, rolling green pastures of Cumbria and finally the salt marshes of the Solway Estuary.

There is concern over erosion and damage to the wall and a 'User Code of Respect' asks visitors to keep to signed paths, particularly in poor weather. Circular routes enable you to appreciate the unique landscape and heritage of the area while minimising the impact upon the wall itself. The Moss Troopers' Trail is another alternative to the main path along the Wall. "This is a route for dreamers, drovers, revivers and rogues" suggests its creator, eco-walker and author Mark Richards. It takes in the

112

113

114

spectacular countryside and scenery to the north of Hadrian's Wall, avoiding the tourist trails and offering excellent and varied running terrain. The route is linear but can be linked up with the Hadrian's Wall Path at several points to create a shorter, circular run.

High Cup Gill runs down the middle of a vast, U-shaped, glaciated valley. At its northern end is High Cup Nick with its high, dolerite crags, exposed sections of the Whin Sill. The Pennine Way runs along the northern edge of the valley, a stunning section with superb views. Our High Cup run (112) starts in the pretty village of Dufton, where you'll also find a pub and café. It follows the Pennine Way up to the high ground above the valley to reach the nick, where there's a great descent to follow the gill all the way back to Dufton. The annual fell race here is a classic on the calendar, organised by fell racing legend Morgan Donnelly.

Starting in Middleton-in-Teesdale, and again following the Pennine Way, the Harter Fell & Lune Moor run (113) makes straight for open hillside, reaching the 481-metre summit of Harter Fell within the first couple of miles. On a clear day the view across the surrounding moors, rivers and reservoirs is well worth the effort. A less steep climb takes you over the remote wilds of Lune Moor then down and over the steep edge of Holwick Scar, another exposure of the mighty Whin Sill and part of the Upper Teesdale SSSI (Site of Special Scientific Interest). The final, flatter miles follow the Pennine Way along the many bends of the River Tees, passing several good swimming spots, before returning to Middleton.

Our Whitley Castle run (114) explores the area of the North Pennines around this Roman fort, also known as Epiacum, and the highest stone-built Roman fort in Britain. Situated on a private working farm and only partially excavated, the site is a Scheduled Ancient Monument dating back to the 2nd century. The Pennine Way passes to the south of the fort and it's a steep but enjoyable climb from the trail to the top, rewarded with fine views of the surrounding hills. In the valley below, the South Tynedale Railway is England's highest narrow-gauge railway, and offers an enjoyable scenic excursion – or a handy shortcut.

Routes 112-114

112 HIGH CUP

Distance 8.5 miles/13.5km
Ascent 570 metres
Start Billysbeck Bridge, CA16 6DB
Info wildrunning.net/2112

Pick up the Pennine Way east out of Dufton and past Bow Hall before climbing up south of Dod Hill to reach the steep ground on the ridge north of High Cup Gill. Follow the edge of this along Narrow Gate to High Cup Nick at the top of the gill (3.6 miles/5.8km). Turn R and enjoy the descent down High Cup Gill to the road at Harbour Flatt. Turn R and stay on the road back to Dufton and the start of the route. This route is also excellent and quite different in reverse – turn around at the road by Harbour Flatt to reverse it for a 12.5-mile/20km day.

113 HARTER FELL & LUNE MOOR

Distance 9.5 miles/15km
Ascent 372 metres
Start Middleton-in-Teeside, DL12 0SN
Info wildrunning.net/2113

Follow Bridge Street south up to the road junction. Continue straight to join the Pennine Way, heading south up Intake Hill and onto Crossthwaite Common. Keep L at the path junction, leaving the Pennine Way and following the edge of the open moor to the walled summit of Kirkcarrion. Stay beside the wall behind Kirkcarrion to cross the wall with the Pennine Way and fork R to the trig point of Harter Fell at 481 metres (2 miles/3.1km). Keep alongside the wall past the summit and cross the next two fields, then join the track in Rake Gill which meets the bridleway at Brown Dod. Turn R and follow this north-west then north across Green Fell and Holwick Fell, passing old buildings and dropping steeply into the valley below Holwick Scar. Turn R along the track to the road and continue to a L onto a footpath, descending through two fields to the Pennine Way beside the River Tees. Turn R and follow this back to the road and the outbound route, turn L to return.

114 WHITLEY CASTLE

Distance 6.5 miles/10.5km
Ascent 302 metres
Start Alston station, CA9 3JB
Info wildrunning.net/2114

Follow the A686 south through Alston and across the River South Tyne. Turn R onto the Pennine Way and follow it north along the river past Harbut Lodge to the A689. Turn R and then L, still on the Pennine Way, uphill behind Harbut Law. This section of path is also Isaac's Tea Trail. Stay on the path as it curves R and heads north-west across fields and over Gilderdale Burn to a bench by Whitley Castle (3 miles/4.8km). Detour off the Pennine Way to explore the castle, then rejoin the Pennine Way descending to the A689 at Castle Nook Farm. Follow the path across the road then turn R (off the Pennine Way but still on Isaac's Tea Trail), passing Kirkhaugh Station before crossing the river on Kirkhaugh Bridge and continuing R to the road. Turn R and follow the road south-east past Kirkside Wood and across Randalholm Bridge to reach a signed footpath heading R along the riverbank. Follow this south, joining the railway path to return to the start.

115

116

117

Deep within the North Pennines AONB, Geltsdale is a hidden, verdant valley where the River Gelt makes its way in stepped falls, wide meanders and spiralling rapids from its source on the Cumbria/Northumberland border to its confluence with the River Irthing, near Carlisle. Our Geltsdale run (115) begins through leafy woodland and fields alongside the river before heading up onto Talkin Fell for stunning views across the surrounding landscape. The rows of cairns along the summit ridge, visible from many miles away, have been built over the years by visitors from the leftover stones from former quarries, which also shaped the hillside with its many sinkholes and mounds. The final stretch down a long, clear track returns you to the valley.

At 890 metres, the summit of Cross Fell is the highest point in the Pennine Hills and also in England, outside the Lake District. It is a wild and remote place whose lonely beauty is well worth saving for a warm, dry day when you can fully appreciate the utterly serene setting and glorious 360 views. The Cross Fell run (116) begins in the village of Skirwith, joining the Pennine Journey trail at Kirkland and keeping it company all the way to the top of Cross Fell. Here it joins the main Pennine Way for a short stretch before descending enjoyably down a long bridleway past dramatic Wildboar Scar, to return to Skirwith.

All too often the beautiful countryside surrounding Hadrian's Wall is passed by unnoticed by those attempting to walk the official trail, however venture just a little way from the wall and there's so much to be discovered. The wall itself is an awe-inspiring sight and circular routes limit erosion to the main trail while exploring some of the beautiful, often overlooked, places nearby. Our Hadrian's Wall route (117) visits one of the best-preserved stretches of the wall before heading out to peaceful Greenlee and Broomlee Loughs then returning on a stretch of the Pennine Way.

Routes 115-117

115 GELTSDALE

Distance 4.5 miles/7km
Ascent 297 metres
Start Jockey Shield Cottages, CA8 9NF
Info wildrunning.net/2115

Follow the track downhill and across the bridge over the River Gelt, turning R on the path to High Hynam House. Turning left here along the riverside takes you to a lovely waterfall, swimming spot and the Gelt Boulder. Our route stays L of the house, following the bridleway onto the open moor. Stay R at the next couple of path junctions to run around the base of Simmerson Hill, then bear L steeply up to its summit cairn (1.9 miles/3.1km). Continue down the other side, cross a larger path and climb to the trig point on Talkin Fell. Descend the same way but trend R and then turn R onto the bridleway. Follow this around to the R and join a larger track heading west below Talkin Fell to a path junction in Holme Gill. Turn L and take the path down to the bridge over the Gelt, crossed on the outward route. Turn R, cross the bridge and return up the hill to the start.

116 CROSS FELL

Distance 13 miles/21km
Ascent 795 metres
Start Skirwith, CA10 1RL
Info wildrunning.net/2116

Take Kirkland Road east to Kirkland, turning L at the road junction and following a bridleway past Kirkland Hall to join the Pennine Journey trail out onto the moorland up Kirkdale Beck. Trend R on the trail under High Cap, continuing uphill to the path junction with the Pennine Way at NY 684351 (5.4 miles/8.7km). Turn R onto the Pennine Way ascending to the trig point and shelter on the summit of Cross Fell. Follow the path down the other side to a path junction near Crowdundle Head. Turn R, leaving the Pennine Way and following the bridleway south-west downhill through Sturba Nook and down Wildboar Scar into Littledale. Follow the beck downstream but stay on the path following the funnel of open moor to the road in Blencarn (11 miles/17.7km). Turn R onto the road and go through the village, turning R at the junction and then L onto a footpath heading north-west across fields. Follow this back to Skirwith and the start.

117 HADRIAN'S WALL

Distance 10 miles/16km
Ascent 458 metres
Start Peel car park, North of NE47 7AN
Info wildrunning.net/2117

Turn L onto the Hadrian's Wall Path heading west past the trig point at 345 metres to Milecastle 41. Turn R onto the footpath here, crossing Melkridge Common to the road at Well House. Turn R on the road then L onto a path bearing R past Cowburn Rigg and then north to a path junction by a wall at NY 734690 (2.8 miles/4.5km). Turn R here then take the L fork off Gibbs Hill and continue along the southern edge of Greenlee Plantation to Greenlee. Turn R here and then L at the next junction, following the path to the north of Greenlee Lough across some fields to a path junction at NY 779707 (6.2 miles/10km). Turn R onto the Pennine Way and head south to Hadrian's Wall at turret 37A. Turn R onto the Hadrian's Wall Path and follow this back to the start.

Bamburgh

The North East

North-east England encompasses Northumberland, County Durham, Tyne and Wear and Cleveland. Bounded by its lengthy North Sea coast, the region has a rich history of industrial and technological innovation, from coal, steel and glass to ships and steam engines. England's most northerly county, Northumberland boasts vast skies that arch over a wonderfully varied landscape: the peaceful, sandy beaches at Bamburgh; the rugged, seabird-filled Farne Islands; the remote northern moorlands; the Cheviots and the rolling, forested hills of the picturesque Northumberland National Park. Relatively untouched by tourism, the landscape feels ancient and preserved, awaiting exploration.

Around 70 per cent of Northumberland National Park is moorland, some of which is heather-covered, but most is open grassland. Within the park, the Cheviot Hills stretch northwards from the North Pennines, separated from the Pennine Hills by the Tyne Gap. Extending over the Scottish border and merging with the Southern Uplands, the Cheviots are covered by a 'right to roam' under both the English Countryside and Rights of Way Act and the Scottish Land Reform Act. The coast path which edges the county provides spectacular scenery and enjoyable, interesting running; part of the North Sea Trail, it runs for 64 miles between Cresswell and Bamburgh. Between 1.5 and 4 miles off the coast lie the 15-20 (depending on the tide) Farne Islands, rocky and uninhabited by humans, but home to a vast number of seabirds, including over 30,000 puffins, and also a colony of grey seals.

Kielder Forest Park lays claim to both the largest artificial lake in Northern Europe and the largest working forest in England, covering an area of over 250 square miles. Vast and incredibly empty, this is a place to escape from it all, with a feeling of remoteness that sometimes borders on lonely. The Lakeside Way, a 26-mile trail around the entirety of the Kielder Water, is a great anytime running challenge, or there's an annual marathon here in October.

119

120

121

Bordering County Durham to the south and Northumberland to the north, Tyne and Wear includes the north-east's biggest city, Newcastle-upon-Tyne. Within easy access of the city are vast areas of green space – the 1000-acre Town Moor, just north of the city centre, covers a larger area than London's Hampstead Heath and Hyde Park combined.

At nearly 5000 acres, Hamsterley Forest in County Durham is managed by the Forestry Commission and is a mixture of commercial forestry and a network of great walking, running and cycling trails. Our Hamsterley Forest run (118) follows the excellent Three Becks Trail, best visited in autumn when the trails are ablaze with colour.

The National Trust-owned Souter Lighthouse stands proudly on a wide sweep of grassy headland, dazzling red and white stripes against a background of land and sea. The stretch of coast path that runs past the lighthouse comprises a section of the new 45-mile segment of the England Coast Path opened in 2018, part of a plan to complete the full 2,700-mile trail around the whole of the English coastline. The Souter Lighthouse run (119) makes full use of this new right of way, taking in the lighthouse and coastal park, the sandy stretch of Marsden Bay with its fascinating limestone sea stacks, and Frenchman's Lea.

The summit of Deadwater Fell (run 120) in Kielder Forest stands 571 metres high, overlooking Kielder Water and straddling the border between England and Scotland. A wild place popular with walkers, wildlife watchers, dark sky seekers and mountain bikers, it really is somewhere for those with a deep love of being outdoors.

The crag-topped, heather-clad Simonside Hills lie south-east of the Cheviots, a gently undulating range that reaches a high point of 440 metres. The area is rich in wildlife, and you might spot red squirrels and wild goats on your run. It is also rich in local folklore, which tells of malicious dwarves, or duergar, who hide among the rocks and lead unsuspecting visitors astray. The Simonside Hills route (121) heads straight up onto the main ridge of the hills before crossing through forest to join St Oswald's Way.

120

Routes 118-121

118 HAMSTERLEY FOREST

Distance	5 miles/8km
Ascent	239 metres
Start	Forest visitor centre, DL13 3NL
Info	wildrunning.net/2118

Take the trail north from the start, turning L on a forest track through Low Redford Wood. Follow this to the buildings at Low Redgford and turn R along Ayhope Beck and L over a footbridge at NZ 071313 (1.4 miles/2.3km). Continue, trending R to a crossroads. Turn L to Euden Beck Cottage then turn R. Don't cross the next bridge but turn L and cross the bridge after that and then cross the road, ascending to a track junction. Turn L here and continue to a crossroads. Bear L and follow the same track north-east into Windy Bank Wood. Turn L and then R, heading downhill to the Bedburn Beck, then turn R to return to the start.

119 SOUTER LIGHTHOUSE

Distance	6.5 miles/10km
Ascent	206 metres
Start	NT Souter Lighthouse, SR6 7NH
Info	wildrunning.net/2119

From the lighthouse, head to the coast path and turn R, following the coast south on a gentle loop around Whitburn Coastal Park. On re-reaching the lighthouse, run straight through car park again to the coast, this time turning L and following the path north-west on an out-and-back run all the way to the southern end of South Shields beach. You can choose to follow the intricate coastline, describing every headland and cove, or follow the straighter and slightly more inland path to cut the corners – or perhaps try going out one way and return the other.

120 DEADWATER FELL

Distance	8 miles/13km
Ascent	500 metres
Start	Kielder Castle car park, NE48 1ER
Info	wildrunning.net/2120

Follow Deadwater Fell waymarkers to the south of the Forest Road, bearing L to cross the road and climbing up through Castle Wood. Fork R then turn L and follow the trail past Ravenhill, turning R up Lightpipe Sike then L into Skellys Riggin Wood. Take the sharp R here and continue uphill and out of the forest onto Ravenshill Moor. Follow this track uphill and around the R side of the summit before curving around and reaching it from the north. Return the same way or pick up one of the forest trail maps and explore the network of forest trails.

121 SIMONSIDE HILLS

Distance	12 miles/19km
Ascent	605 metres
Start	Lordenshaw car park, NE61 4PU
Info	wildrunning.net/2121

From the car park follow the main path south-west, taking the R-hand fork up to the ridge and over The Beacon. Continue along the ridge over Dove Crag and then to Simonside at 430 metres. Run down the other side along the path heading west through woodland and out onto the Simonside Hills beyond. Turn L onto high ground over Tosson Hill to reach a path junction below Whitfield Hill. Turn L, following the bridleway south-east through Harwood Forest to a junction at Fallowlees on the south-eastern edge of the wood. Turn L again onto St Oswald's Way, following this north through woodland then bearing R over moorland back to the start.

122

123

124

Starting in the wonderfully named Happy Valley, our Cheviot run (122) stays alongside Harthope Burn for a while, a welcome warm-up for the long climb ahead. This ascent takes you first to the summit of Scald Hill at 549 metres and then steeply onwards to the top of the Cheviot at 815 metres – the highest point in the Cheviot Hills. From here there's a long, lovely descent taking in Cairn Hill, Comb Fell and Hedgehope Hill which then steepens past a number of crags before returning you, joyfully, to Happy Valley.

Bamburgh was the first part of Northumberland we explored and it's somewhere that stays with you – the great sweep of dune-backed, wave-washed sand, completely empty as we ran along it, and the massive bulk of the castle, perched high on its dolerite pedestal, dominating the skyline. It's a fantastic place to run, capturing all the qualities we want to have in our routes. Our Bamburgh run (123) starts out from Seahouses along the fabulous beach, heading inland at Bamburgh Castle, a fortification for the past 1500 years and now a privately owned, Grade I listed building. The final miles follow the combined St Oswald's Way and Northumberland Coast Path back to Seahouses.

The island of Lindisfarne lies off the Northumbrian coast at the end of a mile-long tidal causeway, only passable a couple of hours either side of low tide. Being only about 1,000 acres in size at high tide and with a population of 180, this is a fascinating and completely different place to run. Both the ruined 7th-century priory and the less ruined 16th-century castle are well worth a visit. The Lindisfarne run (124) circumnavigates the island, a great run on its own or as a fitting finale to the excellent St Cuthbert's Way, a 62-mile-long distance trail between Melrose in the Scottish Borders and Lindisfarne.

Routes 122-124

122 THE CHEVIOT

Distance 17.5 miles/28km
Ascent 1159 metres
Start Middleton Hall picnic site, near NE71 6RD. GR NT 994256
Info wildrunning.net/2122

Turn L onto the road and follow it around sharply to the R, then turn L up and over a steep hill south of Earle Hill. Stay on this road to its end at Langleeford (3.7 miles/5.9km), which is a good start point for an out-and-back ascent of the Cheviot. Fork R onto the footpath up Scald Hill and continue on to the Cheviot at 815m (6.7 miles/10.7km). Carry on over the summit and down to Cairn Hill at 777m, then turn L and head downhill to the col and up to Comb Fell. Run the ridge over Hedgehope Hill and down to Langlee Crags, joining the main path here and turning L to follow it down and around Brands Hill. Take the L fork down to the road at North Middleton (16 miles/25.7km), turning L here and following the road to the junction at Cresswell Bog. Turn L here to return to the start.

123 BAMBURGH

Distance 7.5 miles/12km
Ascent 81 metres
Start Seahouses, NE68 7SJ
Info wildrunning.net/2123

Follow the roadside path north-west out of Seahouses and along the coast until you can turn R and drop down to the beach. Run north-west along the beach, passing Bamburgh Castle then looping inland to the road just north of Bamburgh village (3.4 miles/5.5km). Turn L onto the footpath behind the castle, following this to reach the B1340 near the car park. Turn L onto this road and follow it out of Bamburgh. Turn R onto St Oswald's Way, heading south-east across fields and over the Ingram Burn to the end of the road at Fowberry. Join this road and follow it to its junction at North Cottage. Cross and join the footpath opposite, running across a couple more fields to the road to the west of Seahouses. Turn R here and then L onto the cycleway, following this back to the start.

124 LINDISFARNE

Distance 4.5 miles/7km
Ascent 42 metres
Start Lindisfarne Priory, TD15 2SH
Info wildrunning.net/2124

From the priory, follow the road back to the west coast and turn L onto the coast path, which is also St Cuthbert's Way, passing some houses to reach the south coast. Turn L and follow the coast east, turning R onto the road to the castle. Take the path to the L of the castle and run out to Castle Point in the south-east corner of the island. Turn L here, still on the coast but now heading north past the lough to the north-east corner known as Emmanuel Head. Turn L here, heading west and then L again to follow the west coast back to the road. Turn L onto the road to return to the start.

Pembrokeshire Coast

Wales

Wales is truly an incredible place to run, with its awe-inspiring scenery and wild feel. From the brooding, jagged peaks, home to giants and dragons, and peaceful hidden valleys of Snowdonia through the remote reaches of the Brecon Beacons to the breathtaking Pembrokeshire coast and the rolling grasslands of the Gower, Wales has it all.

Highlights
Wales

125-127 Run across wave-washed sands and explore coastal forest and downland on Gower.

128-130 Discover dramatic, wildlife-rich headlands in Pembrokeshire, the UK's only coastal National Park.

131-137 Find an exhilarating mountain trail to run in every corner of the Brecon Beacons.

141 Follow miles of wonderful waymarked trails through the trees at Run Coed-y-Brenin, the UK's first dedicated trail running centre.

144-152 Experience the incredible variety of running to be found in North Wales, from coastal trails around the Isle of Anglesey to Snowdonia's great mountain challenges.

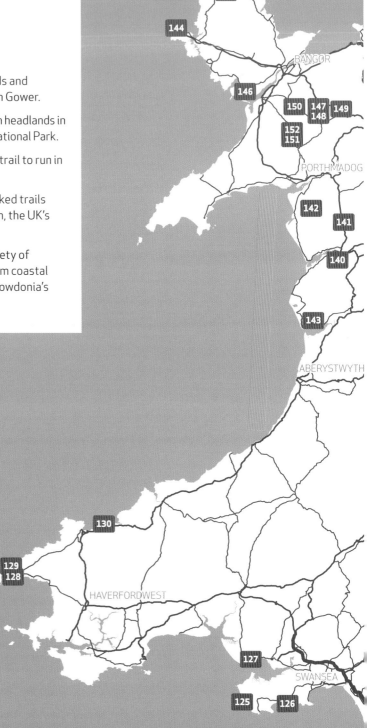

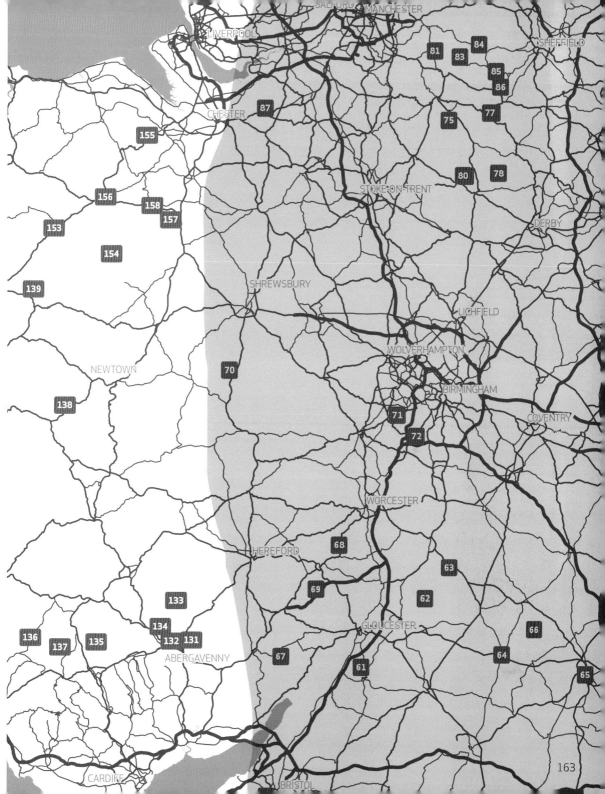

LIVERPOOL

SALFORD MANCHESTER

SHEFFIELD

81 84
83
85
86

CHESTER

87

155

75 77

156

158
157

80 78

153

154

DERBY

139

STOKE-ON-TRENT

SHREWSBURY

LICHFIELD

70

NEWTOWN

WOLVERHAMPTON
BIRMINGHAM

138

71

COVENTRY

72

WORCESTER

133

HEREFORD

68

134
132 131

63

136 137 135

ABERGAVENNY

69

62

67

GLOUCESTER

66

61

64

65

CARDIFF

BRISTOL

Rhossili

Gower & Pembrokeshire

The Gower Peninsula covers some 70 picturesque square miles of South Wales, designated in 1956 as the UK's first Area of Outstanding Natural Beauty (AONB). The peninsula's wildlife-rich countryside and lengthy coastline is dotted with nature reserves, ancient ruins and caves where the remnants of millennia of human and animal habitation can be found, including fossilised mammoths and bears and the oldest cave art in Britain, thought to be more than 16,000 years old.

Gower is a great place for adventure sport, whether you're climbing on perfect slabs of limestone – known locally as Sutton Stone – wild swimming, surfing, or enjoying some of the best coastal running to be found anywhere in Britain. Challenging and spectacular, yet also brilliantly runnable, the rockier, steeper sections are interspersed with long, flat, grassy stretches that make you feel more like you're flying. This is immensely enjoyable running, with non-stop glorious views to boot. The beaches in Gower also deserve a special mention: golden sandy crescents, many of which can be linked together at low tide. Rhossili Bay is one of our favourite beaches for running: a perfect 3-mile-long sandy sweep backed by rolling downland. Visit at low tide and you might spot the remains of the wreck of the Helvetia where it ran aground in a storm in 1887.

Bordered by the sea on three sides, Pembrokeshire is home to the UK's only coastal National Park. Some of the best running here can be found along the 186-mile stretch of the Wales Coast Path, which scales dramatic cliffs, drops into peaceful coves and traverses wide, sandy beaches between Amroth in the south and St Dogmaels in the north. Inland, the landscape is equally beautiful, with wooded estuarine valleys, rolling farmland, heath and woodland. Stackpole (explored in run 106) covers several miles of spectacular coast, with vast sandy beaches, dunes, rugged cliffs, peaceful wooded valleys and a fantastic network of trails to discover. The area is a National

125

126

127

Nature Reserve, with the Bosherston Lakes being an important habitat for wildlife and a strange and intriguing place to run.

Our Rhossili Beach run (125) begins at Rhossili village, where you'll also find an excellent café for post-run refuelling and a National Trust shop and visitor centre. This is a run of two halves that starts with a steady climb up to The Beacon, the highest point on Gower, for great views out over the Bristol Channel to Lundy. Descending enjoyably from the downs brings you to the beach and a long, lovely stretch across firm, flat sand, best run barefoot right at the water's edge. Returning to Rhossili village, the second half of the route explores the peninsula out to Worm's Head, a jutting rocky promontory that's only accessible at low tide.

Named after its three great limestone fins, which are popular with rock climbers, Three Cliffs Bay (run 126) is one of Gower's many beautiful sandy beaches, divided in two by a stream that flows down its centre. Our route takes in a stunning section of coast path and scenic countryside to the east of the bay, passing the sandy beaches at Pwlldu and Caswell and exploring the steep-sided, wooded valley at Bishopston. The long stretch down Pennard Pill and onto the wide, sandy beach at Three Cliffs is followed by wonderful dune-top running to provide a perfect finish.

Lying in Carmarthen Bay between Gower and Pembrokeshire, Pembrey Country Park covers 500 acres of woodland and 8 miles of golden sandy beaches. There's camping onsite giving you easy access to the peaceful trails, or Cynefin Eco Camping just north of Pembrey offers a wilder option. The Pembrey Forest run (127) follows the Wales Coast Path from Burry Port along the sands, with waves breaking on one side and woodland rustling on the other. At the end of the beach it heads inland, weaving through the forest on clear, runnable trails, to emerge into the main area of the country park before returning to the port.

Routes 125-127

125 RHOSSILI BEACH

Distance 6.5 miles/10km
Ascent 281 metres
Start Rhossili, SA3 1PL
Info wildrunning.net/2125

From the village centre run through the churchyard, turn L onto the Gower Way and follow this up to the trig point on the Beacon. Follow the ridge north descending to the end of the road at Hillend. Turn L onto the Wales Coast Path and follow this to the beach. Turn L and run along the sand back to Rhossili village. At very high tide you may need to stay on the coast path below Rhossili Down rather than run on the beach. Take the steep path and steps back up to the start for a 4.3 miles/6.9km loop. The second loop heads out along the coast path to the lookout station above Worms Head. At low tide you can run out and explore Worms Head itself. From the lookout station turn L, following the coast around the headland. Turn L at the first inlet and follow the path inland between fields, then take a L to return to the start.

126 THREE CLIFFS BAY

Distance 10 miles/15.5km
Ascent 517 metres
Start Southgate NT car park, SA3 2DH
Info wildrunning.net/2126

Looking out to sea, turn L to follow the Wales Coast Path over High Tor and south-east to Pwlldu Head. Continue on the coast path north from here down to Pwlldu Bay and then east to the road in Caswell Bay. Turn L on the road and at the sharp R bend continue running straight on to join a footpath trending R to the end of a road in Pyle. Turn L here on a path heading west and join a bridleway south of Backingstone Farm. Continue west through Bishopston Valley and up the other side to Hael. Take the next R and cross fields to the road by the school in Southgate. Cross and join the byway heading north down into Redden Hill Nature Reserve. Turn L and follow the valley along Pennard Pill then up onto Pennard Burrows near the remains of Pennard Castle. Continue down the stream to visit the beach or turn L onto the Wales Coast Path to return to the start.

127 PEMBREY FOREST

Distance 11.5 miles/18km
Ascent 112 metres
Start Burry Port Harbour, SA16 0ER
Info wildrunning.net/2127

Starting at the harbour, a short distance south of the railway station, take the Wales Coast Path west to the beach at Pembrey Country Park. Run on the beach or through the dunes in a north-west direction until you reach a path heading inland at SN 376024 (5.3 miles/8.5km). Still on the Wales Coast Path, turn R into Pembrey Forest to the second main R at SN 383029 (5.8 miles/9.4km). Turn R here, leaving the coast path and trending L on tracks through Pembrey Forest Nature Reserve to the south-easterly edge of the woodland. Skirt the edge of the wood into Pembrey Country Park then turn L onto St Illtyd's Walk. At the edge of the country park turn R at the track junction, returning to the coast path and the outbound route. Turn L here to return to the start.

129

129

130

The Treginnis Peninsula reaches out westwards from St David's – the UK's smallest city both in size and population – into the Celtic Sea. Forming the northern boundary of St Brides Bay, with its string of sandy beaches and rocky outcrops, this part of the Pembrokeshire coast is studded with wildlife-rich islands, many of which can be visited by regular boat services from the mainland. Our run at Treginnis (128) takes in a full loop of this picturesque peninsula, starting at Porth Clais harbour and heading inland across fields to reach St Justinian's on the opposite coast. From here it follows the undulating coast path right the way around and back to Porth Clais, passing fascinating coastal features including caves, arches, Seal Bay and the rocky cove of Porthlysgi, scene of many a shipwreck.

St David's Head (run 129) is a magical place, unreachable by car and with a remote and rugged feel. There are many ancient sites to explore, including an Iron Age cliff fort, prehistoric settlements and walls, the remains of Neolithic field systems and Coetan Arthur dolmen – Arthur's Quoit – a burial chamber dating back more than 5000 years. Our route circumnavigates the peninsula, starting from the nearest road at Whitesands Bay and heading up and down the coast path around the St David's Head promontory. The run then heads inland over the mini-mountains of Carnedd Lleithr and Carnedd Perfedd and past the rocky ridge at Carn Llidi – an enjoyable scramble – before returning to Whitesands.

Dinas Island lies within the Pembrokeshire Coast AONB. Although not quite an island, the peninsula has that feeling of remote separation found on many true islands around this part of Britain. The Dinas Island run (130) makes a perfect partner to either of the routes that precede it – or, even better, both. Looping the peninsula from the start at Pwllgwaelod beach, it climbs up and over the trig point-topped summit of the island, Pen y Fan, from where there are superb coastal views out across the rocky promontory of Dinas Head. From here the running is mostly downhill, passing Needle Rock and continuing enjoyably back to Pwllgwaelod.

Routes 128-130

128 THE TREGINNIS PENINSULA

Distance 6.5 miles/10km
Ascent 277 metres
Start Porthclais car park, SA62 6RR
Info wildrunning.net/2128

From the car park head inland along Porth Clais Road then turn L onto Treginnis Road. Bear R onto a footpath across Trefeiddan Moor, navigating vague paths to the L (west) of Pwll Trefeiddan to reach the road. Turn L, following the road past Rhosson Farm to the coast at St Justinian's. Turn L here, joining the Wales Coast Path and heading south to the tip of the Treginnis Peninsula for wonderful views across to Ramsey Island. Continue on the coast path heading east above Porthlysgi Bay and back to Porth Clais. Turn L at the harbour to return to the start.

129 ST DAVID'S HEAD

Distance 5 miles/8km
Ascent 490 metres
Start Whitesands Bay, SA62 6PS
Info wildrunning.net/2129

Turn R out of the car park following the Wales Coast Path north out to St David's Head. Continue on the coast path past Coetan Arthur, trending north-east to Penllechwen (2.5 miles/4km). Turn inland, following a zigzagging path to the saddle between Carnedd-lleithr and Carn Perfedd, detouring to the top of either for fantastic coastal views. Then continue south, turning R at the bottom of the hill and L at the next junction. Turn R at Treleddyd-fawr Farm and follow the path to reach Llaethdy. Turn R here, then L below the burial chambers on Carn Llidi Bychan (another worthwhile detour). Turn L past Upper Porthmawr and back to the B4583, turning R to return to the start.

130 DINAS ISLAND

Distance 3.5 miles/5km
Ascent 404 metres
Start Pwllgwaelod car park, SA42 0SE
Info wildrunning.net/2130

From the start join the Wales Coast Path and follow it north along the west coast of Dinas Island to Dinas Head and the summit of Pen y Fan (1.1 miles/1.8km). Continue along the coast passing Needle Rock and heading south to the beach at Cwm-yr-Eglwys. Turn inland here and follow the path across the island back to the start. The coast path is easy to follow and good running in both directions from here, or leave the car at home and begin your run at Fishguard Station, following the coast path east and around Dinas Island before continuing to Newport. The T5 bus will take you back to Fishguard in about 20 mins.

Sugar Loaf

Brecon Beacons

The Brecon Beacons National Park features some of the most spectacular and distinctive upland formations in Southern Britain, covering over 500 square miles from south to mid Wales. The running here varies greatly across the range, due to its interesting geological make-up, however many areas are remote and challenging, qualities utilised by the Special Forces in selecting and training recruits. The Central Beacons dominate the skyline to the south of Brecon, rising to 886 metres at Pen y Fan, the highest point in South Wales. Further west lies the sandstone massif of Fforest Fawr, with its steep river valleys and spectacular waterfalls, and Y Mynydd Du, The Black Mountain. Here the summit of Fan Brycheiniog is the site of the two enchanting glacial lakes of Llyn y Fan Fach and Llyn y Fan Fawr.

Much of the National Park is formed from Old Red Sandstone, resulting in the smooth, rolling outlines of the hills with brick-coloured paths that wind invitingly through bright green bracken, giving tough but straightforward running. The geology, and therefore the terrain, changes along the southern edge of the range, where outcrops of limestone and millstone grit predominate. Here there is more technical mountain running with many ridges and screes – exciting, absorbing and well-suited to those with sure feet and strong ankles. In some areas the land is pock-marked with shakeholes where the ground has sunk into the cave network below. These magnificent caves and passages that lie hidden below the surface are adorned with stalagmites and stalactites. Wales' first International Dark Sky Reserve, this region is perfect for a night run or some wild camping and stargazing as part of a multi-day jaunt. To the east of the main summits of the Brecon Beacons, the Black Mountains are a gentler range of hills close to the English border.

The distinctive outline of Skirrid (Ysgyryd Fawr in Welsh) rises on the edge of the Black Mountains, near the Herefordshire border. Our Skirrid run (131) takes the long, zig-zag trail up through the woodland that cloaks the mountain's lower slopes

131

132

132

before following the wonderful ridgeline all the way to the top. From the trig point on the summit, standing at 486 metres, there are beautiful views across the surrounding countryside and neighbouring mountains of Sugar Loaf and Blorenge.

Rising to 596 metres – just a little short of having 'official' mountain status – Sugar Loaf is the most southerly of the Black Mountains with an open, grassy summit and network of clear, inviting trails. The long summit ridge is a great viewpoint including, on a clear day, the shapely summit of Pen y Fan, the highest point in the Brecon Beacons at 886 metres. Our Sugar Loaf run (132) starts from Llanwenarth car park, which has one of the best views we've ever found from a car park, before taking in a simple but enjoyable loop following the well-defined paths up to the summit and back down again. Footpaths and bridleways crisscross the mountain, making it an ideal place to spend the day exploring. During the summer the lower slopes are carpeted with bilberries – known locally as whinberries – for some great post-run foraging.

Look at the part-ruined former Augustinian priory at Llanthony on a map or aerial photo, and the perfect horseshoe of hills that curves around the Vale of Ewas in which it sits is immediately obvious and, if you're anything like us, calling out to be explored. Our Llanthony Priory run (133) does just that, heading straight up onto the western ridge to Bal Mawr at 607 metres. It then follows the inviting line of summits to the end of the ridge, the 713-metre top of Rhos Dirion. From here the running is mostly downhill, first curving around the head of the valley to take in Twmpa and Hay Bluff, and then heading home along the eastern ridge following Offa's Dyke Path, where a well-deserved drink awaits you at the Abbey Hotel.

A perfect partner to the Llanthony Priory horseshoe, our Waun Fach run (134) traces another outstanding semicircle of summits around a parallel valley to the west. Starting and finishing along the 100-mile Beacons Way it summits Pen Cerrig-calch and Waun Fach, a high point of 810 metres, a challenging climb but one that's handsomely rewarded with glorious mountain views.

Routes 131-134

131 SKIRRID

Distance 3.5 miles/5km
Ascent 398 metres
Start Car park on B4521, near NP7 8AP
Info wildrunning.net/2131

Follow the Beacons Way north along the edge of fields and up through Caer Wood, keeping R to reach a path junction. Stay R on the Beacons Way up the ridge to reach the trig point and summit of Skirrid at 486 metres (1.2 miles/2km). Continue over the summit and down the steep hill to the valley. Turn L here, following a trail up through the notch and through woodland. Continue on boardwalk until a R turn joins the outward route.

132 SUGAR LOAF

Distance 3.5 miles/5.5km
Ascent 301 metres
Start Llanwenarth car park, NP7 7LA
Info wildrunning.net/2132

From the car park take the main path north-west bearing L to gain the path up with the south-western face of Sugar Loaf. Climb to the trig point and summit (1.7 miles/2.7km), following the ridge to its end for the best views. Return to the trig point and turn R, down the main face, trending R to avoid Cwm Trosnant. Run around the head of this cwm and curve L along the ridge of Mynedd Llanwenarth before turning R and returning to the start.

133 LLANTHONY PRIORY

Distance 18 miles/29km
Ascent 858 metres
Start Llanthony Priory, NP7 7NN
Info wildrunning.net/2133

Follow the Beacons Way south-west up Cwm Bwchel, bearing R to the trig point and summit of Bal Mawr at 607 metres. Follow the ridge path north over Chwarel y Fan and past the cairn at the Blacksmith's Anvil stone. Head north-west to Twyn Talcefn at 702 metres then cross to the trig point at 713 metres (7.1 miles/11.5km). Turn R and follow the high ground to Twmpa at 690 metres. Descend to Gospel Pass before climbing to the summit of Hay Bluff (10.4 miles/16.7km). Turn R, following Offa's Dyke Path to a path junction at SO 298285 (16.8 miles/27km). Turn R to descend to the start.

134 WAUN FACH

Distance 17.5 miles/28km
Ascent 1093 metres
Start Red Lion pub, Llanbedr, NP8 1SR
Info wildrunning.net/2134

From the pub head east past the church on a road and then footpath north to join the Beacons Way. Bear L here and then turn L at the next junction and continue to reach a road. Turn L onto this then R, still on the Beacons Way, heading south-west towards Table Mountain. Turn R before this, leaving the Beacons Way and ascending to the trig point at the summit of Pen Cerrig-calch. Continue straight on, following the ridge as it curves R to the next trig point on Pen Allt-mawr. Continue following the ridge north running past Pen Twyn Glas and over Mynydd Llysiau before curving R to Waun Fach at 810 metres (9.3 miles/15km). Follow the ridge to the south-east over Pen y Gadair Fawr then along the edge of the forest past Pen Twyn Mawr to the south-western corner of the forest near Crug Mawr. Stay on the Beacons Way curving R and dropping down the ridge to the road and outbound route, turning L onto the road to return to the start.

135

137

137

The fact that it is the highest point in the Brecon Beacons, along with its distinctive shape, well-defined paths to the top and good accessibility, means Pen y Fan is a popular mountain. Each year more than 250,000 people make their way to its 886-metre summit, often in conjunction with its two neighbours: Corn Du at 873 metres and Cribyn at 795 metres. Our Pen y Fan run (135) takes in the great, scalloped circuit of summits, climbing steeply from the forested valley at Taf Fechan up to the long ridge that leads to these three main summits. From Cribyn there's a glorious gentle descent following perfect running trails along the edge of the mountain plateau before a steep descent on the Taff Trail takes you back into the valley.

Rising at the eastern end of the Black Mountain in the Fforest Fawr area of the Brecon Beacons National Park (a different place entirely from the Black Mountains near the English border), Fan Hir, meaning 'long peak', has a magnificent 2.5-mile ridge leading up to its 760-metre summit. The dramatic landscape here, crag-topped, sprinkled with llyns and scored through by river valleys, is challenging and inspiring in equal measure. The Fan Hir Ridge run (136) begins deep in the Swansea valley and follows the Beacons Way steeply up to and along the ridge as far as Llyn y Fan Fach, where it drops off to return on a parallel, lower route.

Our next run, Blaen Llia (137) was recommended to us by friend and fellow GetOutside Champion Tracy Purnell, a passionate supporter of the Brecon Beacons National Park who spends much of her time exploring the area with her two beautiful dogs. When we ran it the route instantly became one of our all-time favourites, bringing everything we love about running in wild and beautiful places together in one incredible experience. The route begins along a stretch of the Sarn Helen, a former Roman road, through the peaceful valley of the Afon Llia before a leg-sappingly steep climb up the side of Fan Nedd brings you to its summit at 663 metres. From here there's a wonderful loop of the high plateau, culminating in superb views from the top of Fan Gyhirych at 725 metres. An exciting, involving downhill run drops you into the valley and onto the Beacons Way, which returns you to the start. Don't miss the nearby Ystradfellte waterfalls.

135 PEN Y FAN

Distance	12 miles/19km
Ascent	971 metres
Start	Pont Cwmfedwen, CF48 2UT
Info	wildrunning.net/2135

Take the track north towards the Neuadd reservoirs, but turn L on the path in front of the first dam and climb the steep hill to the ridge. Turn R and follow the ridge north, curving around to the R over Corn Du at 873 metres and up to Pen y Fan at 886 metres (4 miles/6.4km). Continue along the ridge south-east to Cribyn at 795 metres then follow the Craig Cwm Cynwyn to Fan y Big at 719 metres. Continue down the ridge to the path junction at the col below Waun Rydd, turning R and following the Graig Fan Las ridge down to a junction with the Beacons Way. Turn L and follow the Beacons Way over Craig Fan Ddu then down to join the Taff Trail on the road. Turn R and follow the Taff Trail over a cattle grid then R off the road, curving R through Taf Fechan Forest to the road and the outbound path. Turn L to return to the start.

136 FAN HIR RIDGE

Distance	13 miles/21km
Ascent	1466 metres
Start	Tafarn-y-Garreg pub and camping, SA9 1GS
Info	wildrunning.net/2136

Run north-west from the A4067 joining the Beacons Way and bearing L uphill to reach the Fan Hir Ridge. Follow this north over Fan Brycheiniog at 802 metres and on to Fan Foel at 781 metres. Turn L after this summit and continue on the ridge in a generally westerly direction over Picws Du at 749 metres and on along Bannau Sir Gaer, curving R and starting to descend as the ridge becomes less pronounced. Turn R onto a smaller path at SN 796219 (6.1 miles/9.8km). Stay on this down to the dam of Llyn y Fan Fach and continue past in the same direction to join the Beacons Way below Picws Du. Follow the trail along the bottom of the ridge below all the peaks you recently ran over, trending R below Fan Foel and reaching the northern tip of Llyn Fan Fawr (9.1 miles/14.7km). Take the path along the eastern shore and continue south to join the outbound path, following it to the start.

137 BLAEN LLIA

Distance	14 miles/22km
Ascent	935 metres
Start	Blaen Llia car park, CF44 9JD
Info	wildrunning.net/2137

From the car park return to the road and turn R. At the next junction turn L then L again, leaving the road and making your way to the trig point on Fan Nedd (2.4 miles/3.8km). Turn R down the ridge to a cairn then L on a small path north-west to reach a larger track at SN 902197 (3.7 miles/6km). Turn L onto the track and follow it across Fforest Fawr to a track junction at SN 873169 (6.5 miles/10.5km). Bear L and follow the dismantled tramway in roughly the same direction to join the Beacons Way at SN 860156 (7.8 miles/12.5km). Turn L onto the Beacons Way, following it as it curves R and heads south-east to a path junction at the corner of some woodland (SN 907143, 11.3 miles/18.2km). Turn L, still on the Beacons Way, and run north-east along the course of an old Roman road, through some woodland and back to the road. Turn R here to return to the start.

Cadair Idris

Mid Wales & South Snowdonia

The central part of Wales is dominated by the rolling Cambrian Mountains, a relatively peaceful range that lies between the Brecon Beacons in the south and Snowdonia in the north. The summit of Plynlimon (Pumlumon in Welsh) is the highest point in mid Wales and the source of the rivers Wye and Severn. Its name means 'five peaks', of which Pen Pumlumon Fawr is the highest at 752 metres. The Cambrians have been called 'the green desert of Wales' for their remote and desolate nature, however these are the very features that lend them so well to some really wild running adventures.

Many giants of folklore have dwelt upon Wales' mountains and within its ancient castles. One such giant was Idris, who appears in many guises: as giant, prince, philosopher and astronomer. It is said that the great mountain summit of Cadair Idris is his rock-hewn chair, where he would spend clear nights sitting and gazing at the stars in the vast skies that dome over Snowdonia. The chair, forming the mountain's summit plateau, is said to inflict madness, poetic inspiration or death on those who sleep upon it.

Cadair Idris lies on the southern edge of Snowdonia National Park, well away from the main tourist areas. It is a tranquil place, when the weather is clement, and a picture-perfect mountain. The three main paths, of which the Pony track is the most straightforward, lend themselves perfectly to challenging and enjoyable mountain running. The mountain's natural bowl-shaped depression and, along with the rôches moutonnées (sheep-back rocks), the teardrop shaped hills above the edge of Llyn Cau were carved by glacial action during the last ice age. Lying in lush green surrounds to the east of Cadair Idris, the little-known Aran range awaits discovery. Aran Fawddwy at its heart is a beautiful mountain with superb scenery and wonderful running terrain.

East of Harlech rises the Rhinogydd range, whose rocky, technical terrain is best suited to the fleet of foot, predominantly fell runners and walkers seeking a quieter corner of Snowdonia, along with the local population of wild goats.

138

139

140

The landscape is rugged and the running exhilarating, with challenging rocky summits and remote mountain tarns higher up and ancient woodlands of gnarled oaks on the lower slopes.

The Sarn Sabrina (run 138) is a 25-mile circular waymarked route that can be run anytime or undertaken as an annual organised challenge walk. Named after the Celtic myth of Sabrina, a water nymph said to inhabit the waters of the River Severn, the route begins in the village of Llanidloes and follows Glyndwr's Way up past the Van Pool and alongside Llyn Clywedog Reservoir to reach the source of the Severn at 620 metres. On its return trip it follows the Severn Way through Hafren Forest, meandering with the river all the way back to Llanidloes. There's also a 12-mile option, the Semi-Sabrina. Refuel with local produce from Great Oak Foods in Llanidloes. Full details for the Sarn Sabrina Challenge are available from sabrinawalk@llanidloes.com.

Aran Fawddwy (run 139), at 905 metres, is a beautiful mountain with superb scenery and wonderful running terrain, far from the crowds of Snowdon. The route starts in the beautiful valley of Cwm Cywarch, climbing up through a spectacular rocky, craggy landscape to reach a col below Glasgwm. Great running across open moorland takes you to the rocky summit of Aran Fawddwy with views to the gleaming waters of Creiglyn Dyfi 300 metres below. The descent heads over the summit of Drysgol before fast, easy running on clear paths takes you all the way back to the start.

Starting from the Dolgellau side of the mountain, the Pony path up Cadair Idris is the most straightforward and popular way to the summit, which also offers some of the best running along with outstanding views. From the start at Ty Nant the route climbs through woodland and alongside streams, eventually emerging onto open mountainside for the steep climb to the summit, where there's a shelter that's a good place to rest and refuel on a cold day. We've even seen people enjoying their Sunday roast up here. The return trip is by the same route. The Minffordd Path, from the opposite side of the mountain, is another excellent ascent, passing the beautiful Llyn Cau and with two long, steep sections that make the views from the summit even more welcome.

138 SARN SABRINA

Distance	25 miles/40km
Ascent	1526 metres
Start	Llanidloes, SY18 6AB
Info	wildrunning.net/2138

The Sarn Sabrina route is waymarked so reasonably easy to navigate. From the centre of Llanidloes take Long Bridge Street north then turn R on Church Street, following the river and crossing the B4518 bridge. Continue along Westgate Street until you can turn R onto a footpath (also Glyndwr's Way), heading north through woodland. Follow this path, trending north to Van then west, joining the B4518 at Bidffald. Turn L off the road after a short distance and head west to the Clywedog Dam. The path then hugs the western shore of Llyn Clywedog to its north-western tip before turning L, leaving Glyndwr's Way and following the Sarn Sabrina into Hafren Forest. The route crosses the forest and climbs up to the source of the River Severn where it joins the Severn Way and heads south-east back through the forest, following the course of the river to Llanidloes and the start.

139 ARAN FAWDDWY

Distance	9 miles/14km
Ascent	921 metres
Start	Cwm Cywarch, nearest postcode SY20 9JG
Info	wildrunning.net/2139

Take the track north from the end of the road, taking the L fork onto a footpath which follows a stream up the slope below Glasgwm. Turn R at the path junction and fence at the top and run north-east over several sections of boardwalk, following the path and boundary line up to the summit trig point of Aran Fawddwy (4.3 miles/6.9km). Retrace your steps down the ridge then bear L to the cairn at Drws Bach. Follow the ridge across to Drysgol and then curve R, joining a fantastic path which starts below Waun Goch and runs the length of the valley to join the outbound track. Turn L on this to return to the start.

140 CADAIR IDRIS

Distance	6 miles/9km
Ascent	858 metres
Start	Ty-nant car park, LL40 1TL
Info	wildrunning.net/2140

Leave the car park and turn R onto the road then L onto the Pony Path, heading through some woodland and onto the moor on the north of Cadair Idris. Continue on the path heading south-west around Cyfrwy. Bear L above the cliffs, gaining the ridge above Llyn y Gadair and following this to the summit of Cadair Idris with its trig point and shelter. Our route turns around and tackles the exhilarating descent back down the Pony Path; however, you could try a loop of the southern side of the mountain, heading east from the summit to Mynydd Moel then turning R to follow the wall down to the slate clapper bridge over the Nant Cadair at SH 727120. Turn R here and follow the Minffordd Path back to the top before returning on the Pony Path to the start. This makes about 10 miles/15km of running with roughly 1700 metres of ascent.

142

142

142

Coed-y-Brenin was the first of the UK's dedicated mountain biking trail centres and is still the largest. A fantastic network of trails, with levels of difficulty to suit everyone, traverses the forest, where you'll also find rivers, waterfalls and some tough climbs with airy mountain views from the top. Run Coed-y-Brenin is a more recent – and absolutely brilliant – addition to the centre, with a range of adventurous waymarked trails, from the 2.7-mile Sarn Helen short route to the challenging Half Marathon trail. There's a café and visitor centre, including a well-stocked running shop, and you can stay onsite at the excellent Mostyn Cottage self-catering or B&B, right in the heart of the trails. Our Coed-y-Brenin route (run 141) follows the Goldrush trail, a fascinating and exciting run with plenty of hills, rooty singletrack and points of interest along the way.

The Rhinogs are remote and rugged, with many excellent hard routes that make for a long day in the hills. The Rhinog Fawr swimrun (142) takes in an easier circuit, although still with plenty of ascent, that starts in woodland as it ascends the Roman Steps and then visits the summit of Rhinog Fawr at 720 metres plus three high-level mountain lakes: Llyn Morwynion, Llyn Du and Gloyw Llyn. This is a fantastic run in its own right, however on a warm, clear day there's little better than turning it into a swimrun adventure, running on perfect mountain trails and swimming each of the lakes as you reach them.

Happy Valley, the Victorian name for Cwm Maethlon, is one of the most scenic valleys in mid Wales, edged by a long, green ridge on the southern fringes of Snowdonia National Park. Our Happy Valley run (143) follows an undulating circuit taking in the adventurous high ground that encircles the valley, including a section of the Wales Coast Path, the old Roman road and the aptly named Panorama Walk with its sweeping vistas of the Dovey Estuary and coastline.

Routes 141-143

141 COED-Y-BRENIN

Distance 9 miles/14km
Ascent 760 metres
Start Coed-y-Brenin visitor centre, LL40 2HZ
Info wildrunning.net/2141

This route follows the clearly waymarked Goldrush trail clockwise from the main Coed-y-Brenin visitor centre. Maps of the different trails are available, allowing endless variations on the route. From the start head south-east on trail then bear L climbing steeply, before turning south and heading back down to reach the road by the Afon Mawddach. Cross on a footbridge and go up the hill on the other side. Recross the river and road further south-west then run up the western edge of the woods back and back to the visitor centre to finish.

142 RHINOG FAWR SWIMRUN

Distance 5 miles/8km
Ascent 703 metres
Start Cwm Bychan, LL45 2PH
Info wildrunning.net/2142

From the start, take the path signed 'Roman Steps' heading south through woodland and L up the Roman Steps. For the first swim turn L at SH 653302 after 1 mile/1.7km and drop down to the western end of Llyn Morwynion. After swimming the length, turn R and head south-east uphill back to the path. If you decide not to swim you can continue on the Roman Steps path to reach this point. Turn R onto a smaller path to Llyn Du. Swim across or run around to the L and then join the path to the summit of Rhinog Fawr at 720 metres (2.6 miles/4.1km). Return down the same path to Llyn Du. Either swim to the western end or run along the southern shore and then navigate vague paths north-west to Gloyw Lyn. Swim north or run the eastern shore to the northern end. Join the path heading north-east and down into the woodland towards Cwm Bychan and pick up the outbound path to return to the start.

143 HAPPY VALLEY

Distance 8 miles/12.5km
Ascent 698 metres
Start Happy Valley car park, LL36 9HY
Info wildrunning.net/2143

Leave the car park on a rising path heading south, then bear around to the left behind Tyddynbriddell Hill and continue north-east. Bear R onto a byway and skirt the northern edge of the forest to a path junction at SN 667986 (2.2 miles/3.6km). Turn L and run north to meet a road at a sharp bend. Turn R onto the road and stay on it briefly to the next R bend then turn L onto a byway at Pant-yr-On. Follow the byway up and west, then bear L over Bryn Dinas. Continue on the path heading south-west, descending to the road in Happy Valley. Turn L onto the road until you reach a path heading R at Dyffryn-gwyn. Follow this south and then trend L across fields to the outbound trail. Turn L on this and return to the start.

Nant Gwynant

North Snowdonia & Anglesey

The great mountain range of the Glyderau, known in English as the Glyders, stretches from Mynydd Llandygai to Capel Curig and includes five of Wales' 15 summits over 3000 feet. Together with its neighbouring range, the Carneddau, these mountains cover an incredible 21,000 acres, with over 60 miles of footpaths, the Cwm Idwal Nature Reserve and more than 1,000 archaeological sites awaiting exploration. Ogwen Cottage, a National Trust ranger base and café, is a great place for inspiration, advice and a coffee.

West of Snowdonia, the Anglesey section of the Wales Coast Path runs for 121 miles through a designated AONB, which covers 95 per cent of the coast in this area. It passes through an ancient and historic landscape with a diverse mixture of rolling green farmland, coastal heath, dunes, salt marsh, foreshore, cliffs and pockets of woodland. It's worth making the most of any opportunities to stop and admire the fine views along the coast, both out to sea and across to Snowdonia's jagged skyline. The highest point in Anglesey at 220 metres, Holyhead Mountain's rugged terrain and inviting trails make it a great place to run, exhilarating in places with narrow, twisting paths and sheer cliffs that plummet into the Irish Sea. In fact, the running all around Anglesey is enjoyable and fantastically varied, from precipitous clifftop paths to gentle, runnable trails, and from rocky scrambles to muddy, boggy tracks. The views from the summit of Holyhead Mountain are spectacular on a clear day, with a 360-degree vista of the surrounding landscape from the mountains of Snowdonia out across the glittering sea to Ireland and the Wicklow Mountains.

Llanddwyn Island, off the west coast of Anglesey, is a magical and remote place of sand dunes, rocky outcrops and rolling seas, calm and soothing in fine weather yet exciting and elemental in a storm. Not quite an island, as it can be reached on foot via a fine, sandy beach at all but the highest of tides, Llanddwyn is rich in legend and history, in particular for its associations with Dwynwen, the Welsh patron saint of lovers. There are 10 miles of trails to explore, offering great running with stunning views.

144

145

146

Our Holyhead Mountain run (144) takes in a scenic tour around Anglesey's highest point, reaching the summit at 220 metres. Starting in Breakwater Country Park it explores the dramatic rocky promontories of North Stack and South Stack, high on the coast path above sheer cliffs which rise straight out of the sea, following the Wales Coast Path between them. The out-and-back to the summit between the two headlands is steep but fun, with wonderful views from the top. Near to South Stack stands Elin's Tower, a stocky, castellated tower built between 1820 and 1850 as a summer house by a wealthy local family. It is now located in an RSPB nature reserve and used as a viewing point, information centre, shop and café.

Our Llanlleiana Head run (145) begins in Cemaes Bay, a sheltered sandy cove backed by the pretty harbourside village of Cemaes. From here it explores the Anglesey Coastal Path heading north-east on excellent trails that twist their way around the many headlands, bays and inlets of this spectacular and intricate section of coastline. Stop and take in the glorious views from Llanlleiana Head, the second most northerly point in Wales, out to the island of Middle Mouse, which is the most northerly point in Wales. There's also the Dinas Gynfor Iron Age hill fort and a lookout tower on our route to explore. The deep cleft of Hell's Mouth follows, before a climb over the headland at Craig Wen and down into Porth Wen. From here the route cuts across inland, running along quiet lanes and grassland to return to Cemaes.

Running along the well-defined trails on Llanddwyn Island feels utterly wild and magical, whether the sun is shining on a calm sea or there's a storm coming in. The island – which is in fact only a true island at the highest of tides – is located at the far end of Newborough Warren, way beyond the forests and dunes that edge this part of Wales. Twr Mawr Lighthouse, built in 1873 in the style of the local Anglesey windmills, stands proudly at the far end of the island guarding the Menai Strait. The Newborough Forest & Llanddwyn Island run (146) explores the network of trails around wildlife-rich Newborough Forest, planted in 1947 to prevent Newborough from being engulfed in sand, with a loop of beautiful Llanddwyn at halfway.

Routes 144-146

144 HOLYHEAD MOUNTAIN

Distance 5 miles/8km
Ascent 403 metres
Start Breakwater Country Park, LL65 1YG
Info wildrunning.net/2144

Join the Wales Coast Path and follow it north around Holyhead Mountain. Detour down to the promontory at North Stack then continue on the coast path, now heading south to SH 217831 where you can take a smaller path inland (1.2 miles/2km). Follow this to the trig point on Holyhead Mountain at 220 metres. Pick up a path slightly L of the ascending path to return to the coast path only a little further south than where you left it. Turn L onto the coast path and follow it to the road and viewpoint above South Stack Lighthouse. Stay on the coast path then turn L up to the car park at the seabird centre (2.9 miles/4.7km). Head east crossing moorland to the R of Holyhead Mountain, then bear L, joining the end of a road and turning L back into the country park and the start.

145 LLANLLEIANA HEAD

Distance 6 miles/9.5km
Ascent 444 metres
Start Traeth Mawr beach, LL67 0ND
Info wildrunning.net/2145

Looking out to sea, turn R and follow the Wales Coast Path to Trwyn y Parc. Continue north-east, detouring to Llanbadrig Point and the tower on Llanlleiana Head (2.4 miles/3.9km). Stay on the coast path past Hell's Mouth at 2.8 miles/4.5km and the masts on Torllwyn to a path junction at SH 403942 inland of Porth Wen (3.7 miles/6km). Turn R, leaving the coast path on a footpath ascending to the road near Ty-du. Turn R onto the road and follow it west to a footpath on the L at SH 384944 (5 miles/8.1km), then cross fields to the road near Llanbadrig. Turn R onto the road and turn L at the junction, following the road back to the start.

146 NEWBOROUGH FOREST & LLANDDWYN ISLAND

Distance 9.5 miles/15km
Ascent 116 metres
Start Llyn Rhos Ddu car park, LL61 6RS
Info wildrunning.net/2146

From the start follow the Wales Coast Path south-west to the beach at Llanddwyn Bay. Turn R and follow the beach around the lighthouse at the end of Llanddwyn Island (3.6 miles/5.8km). At very high tide this becomes an actual island so take care and check tide times before running out to the lighthouse. Continue on the coast path back along the island and then L across the sand to the western edge of Newborough Forest. Follow the path around the forest to the R and up the Afon Cefni Estuary to a track junction at SH 408660 (7.3 miles/11.7km). Turn R off the coast path heading south-east through the forest to the coast path on the far side. Turn L onto this and follow the outbound path north-east back to the start.

147

148

149

Despite being a relatively short route, our Glyder Ridge run (147) packs a lot into its 6 or so miles, with over 800 metres of ascent, the mighty twin peaks of Glyder Fawr (1001 metres) and Glyder Fach (994 metres) and breathtaking views to the Snowdon Range, Anglesey and the Carneddau on a clear day. Starting along the shores of Llyn Idwal, deep within the Cwm Idwal NNR where the extremely rare Snowdon lily (brwynddail y mynydd, meaning 'rush-leaves of the mountain') can be found, the route follows the path to the left of the Devil's Kitchen, climbing the steep mountainside to reach Llyn y Cwn. From here it heads left straight up a scree slope to the summit of Glyder Fawr. A clear path guides you across to Glyder Fach, and its famous Cantilever Stone. Continuing east off the summit brings you to the miners' track at the col of Bwlch Tryfan, from where there's an enjoyable descent past Llyn Bochlwyd and back to Idwal Cottage.

Our run around Tryfan (148) circles one of the most distinctively shaped mountains in Snowdonia – its north ridge is a classic scramble. Starting from Idwal Cottage, the route heads up past Llyn Bochlwyd and through the col at Bwlch Tryfan. Dropping down for a short way on the miners' track it then cuts straight along the eastern face of Tryfan, passing to the left of the slabby wedge of Tryfan Bach before crossing the road to reach Llyn Ogwen. The final jog back along the northern shore of the lake is a fitting finish.

On the opposite side of the Ogwen Valley from the Glyderau, the Carneddau range provides some big mountain challenges and includes the largest areas of high ground (over 900 metres) in England and Wales. The High Carneddau run (149) is a challenging route, aimed at those with good mountain and navigation skills and only to be undertaken in favourable weather conditions. If you're up for the challenge, though, it's one of the best. Starting on the outskirts of Bethesda it heads straight up onto the mighty ridge of Mynydd Du – the Black Mountain – to take in the summit of Carnedd Dafydd at 1044 metres and then the summit of Carnedd Llewelyn at 1064 metres, the highest point on the run. From here the long, curving ridge continues, taking in Foel Grach and Carnedd Gwenllian before the final steep descent back into Bethesda.

Routes 147-149

147 THE GLYDER RIDGE

Distance 6 miles/9km
Ascent 802 metres
Start Ogwen Cottage, LL57 3LZ
Info wildrunning.net/2147

Take the main path behind the visitor centre through a gate and turn R at the first main junction up to Llyn Idwal. Follow the path around to the R of the lake and up the steep, stepped path past the Devil's Kitchen and onto the col at Llyn Cwn (1.7 miles/2.7km). Turn L and follow the rocky path up to Glyder Fawr at 1001 metres. Continue along the ridge to Glyder Fach at 994 metres then around to the R and down to a path junction with the Miner's track at SH 665582 (3.7 miles/6km). Turn L and keep L, crossing the stile in Bwlch Tryfan and descending to Llyn Bochlwyd. Take the rocky path that follows Nant Bochlwyd north down the hill towards Llyn Ogwen and the road. Bear L on the main path, joining the outbound route and returning to the start.

148 AROUND TRYFAN

Distance 6 miles/9.5km
Ascent 765 metres
Start Ogwen Cottage, LL57 3LZ
Info wildrunning.net/2148

Take the main path from behind the visitor centre, heading through the gate and turning R at the first main junction up to Llyn Idwal. Turn L, following the east shore briefly then taking a smaller path L and up to Llyn Bochlwyd. Pass the lake and climb the rocky path up to the stile over the wall at Bwlch Tryfan (1.9 miles/3km). Follow the path as it curves R to reach the junction with the miners' track. Turn L here and descend Cwm Tryfan and past Tryfan Bach to a wider track along the edge of Gwern Gof Uchaf campsite. Turn L and follow this path to the A5 (4 miles/6.5km). Cross the road carefully and follow the path north, passing Tal y Llyn Ogwen and turning L across the Afon Lloer on a bridge then taking the northern shoreline path along Llyn Ogwen. Stay on this to the A5 and turn L to return to the start.

149 HIGH CARNEDDAU

Distance 9 miles/14km
Ascent 988 metres
Start Gwern Gof Isaf, LL24 0EU
Info wildrunning.net/2149

From the start follow the long uphill track north of the start point passing Ffynnon Llugwy reservoir on your L before ascending to the ridge above Cwm Eigiau (2.2 miles/3.5km). Turn L onto the ridge path above Craig yr Ysfa to reach the summit of Carnedd Llewelyn at 1064 metres (3.2 miles/5.1km). Turn L at the summit and follow the path south then around to the R to Carnedd Dafydd at 1044 metres (5 miles/8km). Continue on the ridge path, now heading south-west over Carnedd Fach to Pen yr Ole Wen at 978 metres, the prominent mountain on the right as you drive down the A5 (5.9 miles/9.5km). Turn L, taking the slightly less steep descent down to the Afon Lloer. Turn R on reaching this and follow it downhill to the A5 at Gwern Gof Uchaf. Cross the road and turn L on the path parallel to the road, back to the start.

150

151

152

Moel Eilio rises to 726 metres a couple of miles south-west of Llanberis. Bypassed by most en route to the summit of Snowdon, this is a beautiful and tranquil mountain that makes for a great day out, well away from the crowds. Our Moel Eilio run (150) begins in Llanberis and heads up along a broad, grassy ridge to its summit. From here it continues along the obvious ridge, taking in the lesser summits of Foel Gron and Foel Goch before curving around to return to Llanberis on the eastern side of Llyn Dwythwch.

Another remote and less visited corner of Snowdonia, perfect for a peaceful run when the crowds are flocking to Snowdon, the Nantlle Ridge (run 151) is considered by some to be the finest ridge walk in the National Park, and it certainly makes an outstanding run. The long line of inviting summits connected by airy edges stretches for about 6 miles from the village of Rhyd Ddu south-west to Nebo in the Nantlle Valley. The route includes a full out-and-back along the ridge, over 7 main summits each way, starting with Y Garn at 633 metres and turning around at Mynydd Graig Goch at 610 metres.

While it can be heaving on a busy day, Snowdon itself is a beautiful mountain and, if you time it right (early morning is best), an ascent even up the main Llanberis path can be a fantastically rewarding run. This is, in fact, the route of the annual International Snowdon Race, one of the most famous fell races on the calendar. But if you're looking for a different route, or perhaps staying in Rhyd Ddu and looking for a fitting run to add to the Nantlle Ridge for an epic weekend of running, this Snowdon run (152) is brilliant. It follows the adventurous Rhyd Ddu path to the summit, taking in a great stretch of ridgeline with heart-stopping views, and then descends the Ranger Path, cutting left before the road to return to Rhyd Ddu. Both paths are well-signed and well-maintained and, on a clear day, this is a truly spectacular run.

150 MOEL EILIO

Distance 8 miles/13km
Ascent 758 metres
Start Pete's Eats café, Llanberis LL55 4EU
Info wildrunning.net/2150

Head south-east along High Street and turn R onto Ceunant Street, taking the next R then L and following this road uphill to its end. Continue onto a track past Maen-llwyd-uchaf and continue up to a path junction at SH 562597 (1.4 miles/2.3km). Turn L, following the path south-west as it curves around to the L and then south to the summit of Moel Eilio at 726 metres (3 miles/4.8km). Take the ridge path over Foel Gron at 593 metres and Foel Goch at 605 metres then descend to the R to the path junction and wall at Bwlch Maesgwm (4.7 miles/7.5km). Turn L and follow this path, trending L to reach the end of a road above Hafod Lydan. Join the road, descending past the campsite into Llanberis, joining the outbound path and turning L on the main street to return to the start.

151 NANTLLE RIDGE

Distance 14 miles/22.5km
Ascent 2342 metres
Start Rhyd-Ddu car park, LL54 6TN
Info wildrunning.net/2151

Cross the A4085 and follow the straight path to the north of Llyn y Gader. Turn R after the footbridge then L at the junction with the B4418, turning straight onto a bridleway heading south-west up onto the mountainside. Turn R onto open mountainside and ascend Y Garn to the cairn at 633 metres. Turn L on the ridge and follow it south over Mynydd Drws-y-Coed and around to the R, across the col and up to Mynydd Tal-y-Mignedd at 653 metres (3.2 miles/5.1km). Turn L on the ridge south and around to the R over Bwlch Dros-bern and above Craig Pennant to the cairn at 734 metres. Follow the trail south-west from here above Craig Cwm Silyn to Garnedd-goch at 700 metres (5.3 miles/8.6km). Finally continue in the same direction downhill, turning L and climbing to Bwlch Cwmdulyn. Head R along the ridge (west) to the final summit of Mynydd Graig Goch at 610 metres (6.8 miles/11km). Turn around and retrace the route to the start.

152 SNOWDON

Distance 9 miles/14.5km
Ascent 1197 metres
Start Rhyd Ddu car park, LL54 6TN
Info wildrunning.net/2152

Pick up the Rhyd Ddu path out of the village heading roughly east up onto the open mountainside on the east face of Snowdon. Follow the path as it trends slightly L to join the ridge above Llechog. Turn R and follow the path along the ridge and L up Bwlch Main, joining the Watkin Path just before the summit of Snowdon at 1085 metres (3.6 miles/5.8km). Pass the summit and join the main Llanberis path down to the finger stone at the junction with the PYG and miners' tracks to the R, the Llanberis Path in front and the Ranger Path to your L. Turn L and follow the Ranger Path along the ridge above Clogwyn Du'r Arddu and down to the flatter ground north of Llyn Ffynnon-y-gwas. Stay L on the Ranger Path to a junction at SH 575553 (6.5 miles/10.5km). Turn L here, leaving the Ranger Path and running along a fantastic trail across moorland and through an old quarry back to the start.

Dinas Bran

Bala & North East Wales

The Clwydian Range, designated an AONB in 1985, stretches for around 20 miles across north-east Wales, from Prestatyn on the north coast to the remote Berwyn mountains in the south. These heather-clad mountains, with ancient hill forts overlooking the beautiful Dee Valley, provide some excellent running. In contrast to their open moorland summits, the surrounding valleys are lush and green, with woodland and riverside trails to explore. To the east, the foothills of the Dee Estuary and the Clwydian Range are the gateway to the wonderful and little-explored areas of the Llandegla Moors, the Ruabon Mountains, the high pastures of Esclusham Mountain, the World Heritage Site of Pontcysyllte Aqueduct and canal, and the National Trust's Chirk Castle – all encompassed by the extensive expansion of the AONB in 2011 to include much of the Dee Valley in its 389 square kilometres.

The geology in this area is fascinating and determines the shapes of the landscape and the nature of the trails here. There are excellent country parks at Moel Famau (meaning 'Mother Mountain' in Welsh), the highest point of the Clwydians at 554 metres, and Loggerheads, both with a network of waymarked trails and many other interesting features to explore. Loggerheads Country Park is nestled beneath dramatic limestone cliffs and there are limestone pavements at Bryn Alyn and Aber Sychnant, while some of the most impressive scree slopes in Britain can be found at Eglwyseg Rocks.

The Berwyn Range, tucked away in another of Wales' less visited and sparsely populated regions, also lends itself brilliantly to wild running adventures. Lower and often more runnable than many of Snowdonia's mountains, the Berwyn mountains are for the most part heather-clad with inviting, winding tracks. Cadair Berwyn, the highest in the range at 830 metres, has some outstanding ridge running, with views to match. The Clwydian Fell Race is an annual event organised by North East Wales

153

154

155

Search and Rescue in November. It involves a tough, 10-mile course with over 945 metres of ascent, including a trip to the summit of Moel Famau.

At 3.7 miles long and ½ a mile wide, Lake Bala – or Llyn Tegid – is Wales' largest natural lake. It is also the Welsh stage of the Three Lakes Challenge, requiring the swimming or kayaking of Windermere in England, Bala in Wales and Loch Awe in Scotland. Our Around Lake Bala run (153) is a full circumnavigation of the lake, which takes in a surprising wealth of landscapes and terrain including farmland, moorland and forest, with breathtaking views of the surrounding Aran, Arenig and Berwyn mountains.

The thundering falls and quirky tearooms at Pistyll Rhaeadr are a fitting start and finish to the Cadair Berwyn run (154), which takes you up into the beautiful, peaceful Berwyn mountains. At 827 metres, Cadair Berwyn is the highest in the range and the views from the long, lovely summit ridge are outstanding, as is the running on the way back down the wide, grassy slope back to the deep, wooded valley. If you enjoy foraging while running as we do, this is one of the few places in Wales where you'll find cloudberries, members of the blackberry family which are orange and look more like raspberries.

Our Clwydian Hills run (155) heads into the heart of the Clwydians, taking you to the highest point in the range, Moel Famau at 555 metres. Starting from Loggerheads Country Park it follows first the Clwydian Way and then Offa's Dyke Path, which crosses both of the main peaks on the route, Foel Fenlli and Moel Famau. From here there's an enjoyable descent taking in green lanes and tracks before following the River Alyn through its wooded valley back to Loggerheads.

Routes 153-155

153 AROUND LAKE BALA

Distance 16 miles/25.5km
Ascent 1025 metres
Start Pensarn Road, Bala, LL23 7YE
Info wildrunning.net/2153

To run the loops clockwise follow the path along the northern end of the lake, joining the B4391 and passing the train station. Turn R onto a footpath up to Cefn-ddwy-graig. Then turn R onto a path parallel to the lake heading through woodland and out onto moorland where you trend L uphill to more trees. Take the path through these to a forest road. Turn R here and follow it down to a larger road in Glyn Gower. Cross and follow a path below Cefn Gwyn to the B4403. Turn L onto the road and then R on a path into the back of Llanuwchllyn. Cross the Afon Twrch and head north, crossing the A494 and continuing up the western side of the lake. Cross a minor road at Pentre-felin and take the next path to the road. Turn L then R onto a path up to Moel y Garnedd. From here turn R and then R again following paths down to the A494 at Llanycil. Turn L and follow the road back to the start.

154 CADAIR BERWYN

Distance 6 miles/9km
Ascent 621 metres
Start Pistyll Rhaeadr, SY10 0BZ
Info wildrunning.net/2154

After visiting the waterfall, take the path north keeping R up the eastern side of Nant y Llyn. Follow the path L to the south of Llyn Lluncaws and up the spur onto the ridge above the llyn. Follow the ridge north-east to Cadair Berwyn at 827 metres (2.9 miles/4.6km). Turn around and trace the ridge back then fork R to the summit of Moel Sych at 827 metres. Follow the path south of this summit over Trum Felen and back down into the valley to the start. Why not run back up to the waterfall again, especially if it's been raining?

155 CLWYDIAN HILLS

Distance 10.5 miles/16.5km
Ascent 889 metres
Start Loggerheads Country Park, CH7 5LH
Info wildrunning.net/2155

Cross the A494 and join a track heading south past the outdoor education centre.

Take the R fork past Coed y Fedw Wood and trend south to reach Maeshafn Road. Turn L onto the road and follow it for a short distance until you can turn R on a path heading south-west through the forest to a track. Follow this west past Pentre-cerrig-bach to the A494 in Llanferres. Cross the road and join the path opposite before turning L onto a bridleway heading south-west across fields to a path junction at SJ 173594 (3.8 miles/6.1km). Turn R and follow the path west, bearing R up to Foel Fenlli at 511 metres. Continue on the path north-west, crossing the road at Bwlch Penbarras and joining Offa's Dyke Path, ascending to the trig point on Moel Famau at 555 metres (6.7 miles/10.7km). Continue north-east, leaving Offa's Dyke Path and skirting the edge of the forest to a path junction at its corner. Turn R onto the bridleway heading east along the northern edge of the forest to a path junction at Ffrith. Turn R and follow this to the road. Turn L here, then at a junction cross over onto a footpath down to a bridge over the river. Turn R and follow the riverside path back to the start.

156

157

158

The Dee Valley Way (run 156) wends its way along the high ground north of the River Dee for 15 miles between Corwen in the east and Llangollen in the west. This enjoyable waymarked trail takes in a stretch of landscape that's varied and rich in both history and wildlife, with some stretches of road but plenty of wild trails exploring the hidden beauty of this often overlooked part of the Welsh Borders. Over the summer months you can catch a steam train back along the heritage railway, or if you're up for a challenge, the North Berwyn Way takes in a parallel 15-mile route to the south of the Dee Valley, making a superb ultra-distance run or fastpacking weekender.

Taking in leafy woodland, lush grassy hills and a stretch of the Offa's Dyke Path, our next run (157) starts and finishes at the imposing medieval Chirk Castle. Now owned by the National Trust, this Grade I listed fortification was built in 1310 by the English as a statement of intent over these disputed borderlands; however, it still stands in Wales. The run explores the 480-acre estate that surrounds the castle – look out for wild ponies, a well-preserved section of Offa's Dyke and the rare and special landscape and wildlife that makes this part of the country both an Area of Outstanding Natural Beauty and a Site of Special Scientific Interest.

Heading east out of Llangollen, which is perfectly placed for a few days' exploring in this part of Wales, the Llangollen & Pontcysyllte run (158) explores some of the fascinating natural and human-built features in and around the Vale of Llangollen. The first climb is up and over the pint-sized hill at Castell Dinas Brân, once a prehistoric hill fort, now with the stone ruins remaining from a castle built in 1260 but destroyed in 1277. The views from the summit reach to the limestone escarpment of Eglwyseg in the north, the Llantysilio Mountain to the west, the Berwyn Range dominating the view south and, to the east, the Pontcysyllte Aqueduct, where the route now heads via a scenic stretch of the Offa's Dyke Path. The return trip is an enjoyable run alongside the Llangollen Canal.

Routes 156-158

156 THE DEE VALLEY WAY

Distance	14 miles/22.5km
Ascent	871 metres
Start	Corwen, LL21 0AU
Finish	Llangollen Station, LL20 8SN
Info	wildrunning.net/2156

Join the Dee Valley Way and cross the bridge to the northern side of the river. Turn R onto the B5437 then bear L past Rhagatt Hall. Turn R onto B5436. Turn R then turn L onto a smaller road through Carrog. Turn L onto the B5437 and next L, bearing L onto a path ascending through forest to a road at SJ 140441 (4.7 miles/7.5km). Turn R, following the road to Hendre-uchaf. Turn L onto a track to reach a road, turning L here and L at the next junction. The road climbs and then descends to a junction at SJ 152443. Turn R here and follow the track downhill, across the river. Bear L below Wern-ddu and follow the track north around the hill, over the col and down past Cymmo to the road near Dee Farm. Turn L on the road to Rhewl then L onto a bridleway past Llandynan and Llantysilio Farm to reach the river. Turn L, following the river and then the canal to the station in Llangollen.

157 CHIRK CASTLE

Distance	3.5 miles/5km
Ascent	247 metres
Start	Chirk Castle, LL14 5AF
Info	wildrunning.net/2157

Take the path out of the back of the car park across fields to a road near Tyn-y-groes. Follow the road L to a track heading L on the Llwybr Ceiriog Trail. Stay on this trail around Warren Wood, curving L above the Afon Ceiriog and up a spur. Turn R to join Offa's Dyke Path descending south of Gwyningar Wood to the B4500 at Castle Mill, where Offa's Dyke Path crosses the road. Don't join the road, instead turn L uphill to the Chirk Castle driveway. Turn R to visit the castle (NT members/paid entry) or go L along the drive and L back to the start. For a longer run head north on the Offa's Dyke Path to join our next route (158) on the Pontcysyllte Aqueduct.

158 LLANGOLLEN & PONTCYSYLLTE

Distance	10 miles/16km
Ascent	519 metres
Start	Llangollen Station, LL20 8SN
Info	wildrunning.net/2158

Head north from the station, crossing the canal and joining a track climbing up to Castell Dinas Brân via the top of the road at Geufron. Run down the other side and turn R onto the road and joining Offa's Dyke Path. Bear L along Panorama Walk then stay R, leaving the road but still following Offa's Dyke Path to a road by Trevor Hall. Turn R onto the road, then L onto the A539 and shortly after R onto a path crossing the old railway. When you reach the canal cross it and turn L, following the canal path, and then turn R to cross the Pontcysyllte Aqueduct. Now turn around and cross back over it. Turn L onto the canal path and, staying on the southern bank, follow it back to the start.

Scotland

Enter Scotland to discover breathtaking views from high mountain passes, meandering trails through ancient Caledonian pine forests, miles of wild heather-clad moorland, awe-inspiring glacial valleys, a scattered and wonderfully diverse mix of windswept islands, tranquil lochs and sandy beaches for waterside running and post-run swims.

Highlights
Scotland

159 Run down the Rhins of Galloway to the Mull of Galloway, Scotland's most southerly point.

165-170 Escape to the hills in and around Edinburgh and Glasgow or run between them along the Forth and Clyde and Union canals.

171-174 Explore the lochs, glens, ancient forests and mountain passes of the Cairngorm massif.

179-183 Discover the incredible contrasts of western Scotland's Argyll and Lochaber regions, with enjoyable, accessible mountains, beaches of silver sand and serene Loch Ossian, inaccessible by road.

188-191 Journey to the far north of Scotland for trails to remote mountains, wild beaches and curious sea stacks.

192-200 Experience the incredible diversity of the Scottish islands, from a loop around the tiny, eco-friendly Isle of Eigg to the Hebridean Way, taking in 10 islands and over 150 miles of running.

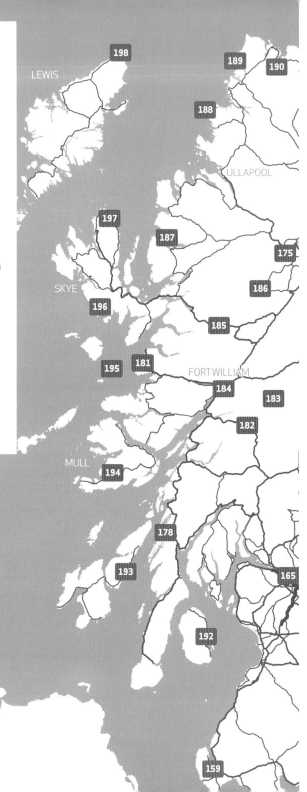

LEWIS

ULLAPOOL

SKYE

FORT WILLIAM

MULL

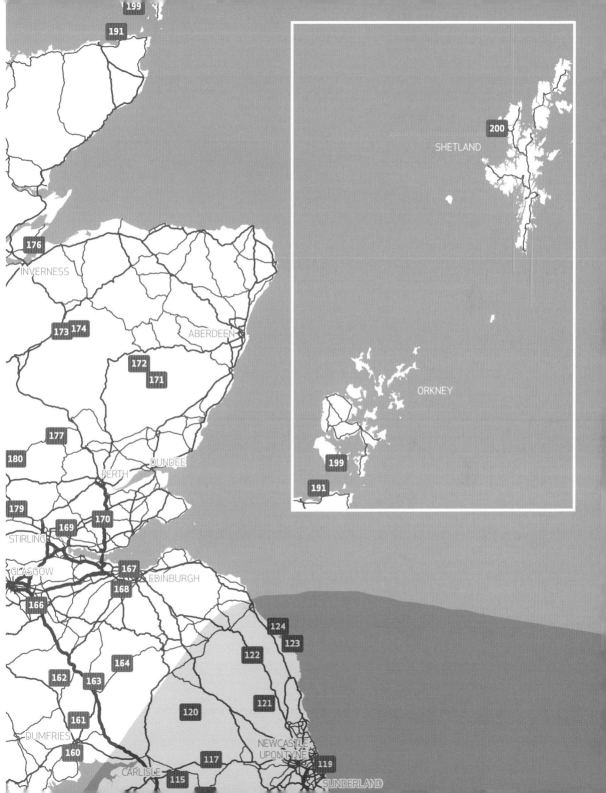

Galloway Forest

The Borders & South Scotland

Dumfries and Galloway, lying in the west of the Southern Uplands, is a lush mix of vast forest, scenic coastline, rolling hills and rugged countryside. Galloway Forest Park is the UK's first Dark Sky Park and is a haven for both trail runners and the rich diversity of wildlife that lives there. The Lowther Hills, venue for the 2007 Original Mountain Marathon, are great to explore, with their steep, tussocky hillsides and wonderfully runnable tops.

The rolling, grassy hillscapes of the Moffat Hills rise from the borders to a height of 821 metres at the summit of White Coomb, and their steep scree-covered slopes make for some exciting and adventurous running. The Annandale Way is a waymarked, 55-mile adventure, following the valley of the River Annan from its source to the sea. Starting high above the Annan's source, it takes in the dramatic hollow of the Devil's Beef Tub before descending its eastern side and following the river along the valley bottom into the pretty market town of Moffat. From here it follows the Annan river valley to its glorious end in the Solway Firth.

Miles of golden sandy beaches run along the Solway coastal edge of Dumfries and Galloway, while north of Newton Stewart lies the 5,000-year-old Wood of Cree, the largest ancient oak woodland in southern Scotland. The moss-green forest is filled with the music of babbling streams and waterfalls, while in early summer the ground is covered with bluebells; it's a magical place to run at any time of year.

The Southern Upland Way runs coast-to-coast across southern Scotland, a 212-mile waymarked trail between Portpatrick in the west and Cockburnspath in the east. Regular accommodation along the route, from recommended wild camping spots to luxury hotels, means it's a great fastpacking route, enjoyable over a couple of weeks, painful over less.

159

159

161

The Rhins of Galloway peninsula reaches down towards the Isle of Man from the far south-west coast of Scotland. At its furthest end, the Mull of Galloway is Scotland's southernmost point. Rugged cliffs, sandy beaches and a wonderful feeling of calm accompany you on our Mull of Galloway run (159), which heads from Stranraer all the way down the peninsula to its lighthouse-topped finish. On your way keep an eye out for dolphins, porpoises and seabirds. The return trip is via the same route, or catch the bus back to Stranraer. This is a special place, owned by the Mull of Galloway Trust, and well worth the detour from the main route through Scotland. Refuel at the Gallie Craig Coffee House at the lighthouse.

Popular with mountain bikers Mabie Forest is one of Southern Scotland's internationally renowned 7stanes mountain biking centres, bringing a little sculpture – seven stones carved by artist Gordon Young – to the art of shredding. This is also a wonderful place for running, following peaceful trails, well away from the bikes, through the trees with views of the Nith Estuary, the Galloway Hills, Criffel Hill and the Solway Firth. Our Mabie Forest run (160) follows the waymarked Lochaber trail, passing Dalshinnie Loch to reach a panoramic viewpoint overlooking the Solway Estuary. The trail then winds through Mabie Nature Reserve with views down to Lochaber Loch where you might spot ospreys in summer. The Nith View Trail can be added as a northern loop of the forest, extending the run to 10 miles.

From the early 14th to late-17th century, 'reivers' came from both England and Scotland to plunder the borderlands. They were livestock raiders from all walks of society, an accepted way of life for some borne out of frustration with the constant conflict of the area, as well as necessity – a way to earn a living. Starting in the Forest of Ae in Dumfries and Galloway, the Romans and Reivers route, one of Scotland's official Great Trails and our run 161, follows old Roman roads, forest tracks and drovers' roads for 52 miles through forestry and farmland of former Reivers country, making a wonderful fastpacking route through the Southern Uplands that's also suitable for bikes.

Routes 159-161

159 MULL OF GALLOWAY

Distance 25.5 miles/40.5km
Ascent 608 metres
Start Stranraer, DG9 8EJ
Finish Mull of Galloway, DG9 9HP
Info wildrunning.net/2159

Follow the Mull of Galloway trail south out of Stranraer on the A77 then L onto the A75. Turn R onto Westwood Avenue and then R off the road and onto the trail. Cross the Black Stank and the railway and head south through woodland to a road at Boreland Cottage. Turn L onto the road then R onto a track past Drumdoch to another road at Barnultoch. Turn L onto this and follow it across the B7077 to the beach at Clayshant. Turn R and follow the coast south-west to Sandhead and then south, parallel to the A716 and past Ardwell, to reach Drummore. Continue south on the coast path to the Mull of Galloway. The easiest way back to the start is to run back to Drummore where you can catch a bus to Stranraer.

160 MABIE FOREST

Distance 5 miles/8km
Ascent 316 metres
Start Mabie Forest car park, DG2 8HB
Info wildrunning.net/2160

This run follows the brown waymarkers for the Lochaber trail north out of the car park and then tracing a wide figure-of-eight. Cross Mabie Burn and run up to a footbridge near Larch Hill. Turn L here and head south, re-crossing Mabie Burn and heading south. Head R around Cragbill Hill to a main track junction at NX 927704 (2.7 miles/4.3km). Turn R and then trend L to the summit and trig point of Marthrown Hill at 249 metres. Turn around and follow the same path back initially then bearing L around to Dalshinnie Loch. Take the track east from here, crossing the outbound path and returning to the start.

161 ROMANS & REIVERS

Distance 40 miles/64km
Ascent 1748 metres
Start Ae village, DG1 1RG
Finish Craik Forest car park, TD9 7PS
Info wildrunning.net/2161

This route follows the Romans and Reivers waymarkers featuring a thistle in a hexagon. Head north-east out of the village and across the Water of Ae to join the trail. Turn R and follow it generally north-east through the Forest of Ae, meeting a road and following it R over Beattock Hill and down to the A74(M) at Beattock (15 miles/24.2km). Continue on the trail east on roads past Dumcrieff and onto forestry tracks across Eskdalemuir Forest (29 miles/47km). Turn L onto the B709 at the Samye-Ling Tibetan Centre and follow it for half a mile to a R back onto forest trails past Dumfedling. Continue generally east through the forest and up Craik Muir at 384 metres (34.5 miles/55.6km). Join the old Roman road along this ridge, crossing over Lamblair Knowe at 406 metres and Craik Cross Hill at 449 metres before dropping down to the finish.

162

163

164

The Lowther Hills stretch across the Southern Uplands, mostly lying within Dumfries and Galloway. The hills are the source of the mighty River Clyde and the area is bordered by river valleys and cut through by several mountain passes. It is southern Scotland's only skiing area. Our Green Lowther run (162) is an enjoyable loop of the hills, with their steep sides and gentle summits. Starting in Wanlockhead, it heads up the grassy flanks of Whiteside to the summit of Lowther Hill at 725 metres, with its golf ball-shaped radar station. From here it follows the wide ridge across to the mast-topped Green Lowther, the highest point in the hills at 732 metres. The route now takes you over three further summits: Dungrain Law (669 metres), Dun Law (677 metres) and Glen Ea's Hill (649 metres), before descending to the road and following this back to the start.

The deep hollow of the Devil's Beef Tub lies hidden in the hills north of Moffat. Over 150 metres deep, the dramatic scoop is formed by four hills, Great Hill, Peat Knowe, Annanhead Hill, and Ericstane Hill. Its name comes from its former use by the Reivers – also known as the Devils – for hiding stolen cattle. Run 163 follows a loop of the Annandale Way, a 55-mile waymarked route between Moffat and Annan, around the Beef Tub and all of the main surrounding hills. It starts and finishes with the two highest: Annanhead Hill at 478 metres and Great Hill at 466 metres.

Run 164 is a longer, wilder route; one for those with good navigation skills, particularly in poor weather. It follows a long stretch of the 212-mile Southern Upland Way, starting out along the shores of St Mary's Loch, the largest natural lake in the Scottish Borders, on a tranquil trail bordered by high hillsides. From here it weaves its way up into the higher hills, leaving the main trail and gaining a long, beautiful ridge at Stake Law, climbing to Dun Rig at 744 metres. An awesome row of summits follows, taking you over White Cleuch, Blackhouse Heights, Black Law, Conscleuch Head and Deer Law, all over 600 metres. The final descent over Broomy Law drops down to the Lochside and follows this back to the start – and the Tibbie Shiels Inn.

Routes 162-164

162 GREEN LOWTHER

Distance 11.5 miles/18km
Ascent 782 metres
Start Wanlockhead Village, ML12 6UZ
Info wildrunning.net/2162

Follow the Southern Upland Way south-east out of the village, over Stake Hill and Whiteside to the top of Lowther Hill at 725 metres (2 miles/3.3km). Turn L and, leaving the Southern Upland Way, take the track north-east towards the masts and trig point at 732 metres on Green Lowther. Continue over Dungrain Law at 669 metres to Dun Law at 677 metres (4.7 miles/7.5km). Turn L and follow the ridge through a col and up to Glen Ea's Hill at 549 metres. Bearing R, descend to the track, turning R onto this and following it around to the L and down to the B7040 (6.9 miles/11.1km). Cross the road and turn L onto a track that tracks the road south-west, crossing again at NS 895149 and continuing around the golf course and past the steam train station near Leadhills. Stay on the track heading south-west, parallel to the railway and the B797 past Glengonnar Station, and then turn R across the road and back to the start.

163 DEVIL'S BEEF TUB

Distance 11 miles/17.5km
Ascent 743 metres
Start Layby nr Corehead Farm, DG10 9LT
Info wildrunning.net/2163

Follow the Devil's Beef Tub signs to the R of the farm then around to the L behind it, south of the Coreknowe Plantation. Bear R, following finger posts to the Beef Tub, and keep R up the side to the lip at NT 065134 known as Strait Step (1.1 miles/1.7km). Turn L, joining the Annandale Way and running along the lip of the Beef Tub over Annanhead Hill and past the trig point at 478 metres to the A701. Turn L onto this briefly then head R over Ericstane Hill and back to cross the A701. Still on the Annandale Way, head south down the valley to cross the River Annan and join the valley road at Howslack. Turn L and follow the road north, bearing R on the Annandale Way just before the start. Follow the path up to Spout Craig and turn L along Chalk Rig Edge. Continue to Strait Step where you turn L and follow the outbound path back to the start.

164 ST MARYS LOCH

Distance 21.5 miles/34km
Ascent 1097 metres
Start South St Mary's Loch, TD7 5LH
Info wildrunning.net/2164

Follow the Southern Upland Way north along the eastern shore of St Mary's Loch to the A708 (3.7 miles/5.9km). Cross and continue to Blackhouse Tower (6 miles/9.6km). Turn L, leaving the Southern Upland Way and ascending to Douglas Burn, bearing R into the forest to the northern edge. Turn L onto a path over Peat Hill to a track junction into the forest. Turn R over Banks Burn and Kirk Burn and above Stake Law then L at a path junction, heading to the summit of Stake Law at 681 metres. Continue up the ridge to the trig point on Dun Rig at 744 metres then south-west over White Cleuch Hill to Blackhouse Heights at 675 metres. Turn L following the ridge over Black Law, Conscleuch Head, Deer Law and Broomy Law before descending L to the road. Turn L to Cappercleuch, turn R and follow path parallel to the A708 south to return to the start.

Loch Lomond southern shore

Around Edinburgh & Glasgow

Edinburgh could be a city designed with runners in mind, it has so many excellent routes within easy reach. Right from the city centre rises the inviting challenge of Arthur's Seat, the main peak of the hills of Holyrood Park, perfect for an early morning excursion, often in the company of other runners. There are some fantastic trails around Holyrood, taking in Salisbury Crags and the summit of the Seat itself, all with amazing views out over Edinburgh and beyond.

Looking out from the city, the hills of Corstorphine, Blackford and the Braids that form the skyline stand waiting to be explored. To the east lies East Lothian, with its beautiful coastline, sandy beaches, dunes and nature reserves. Aberlady Bay, Britain's first Local Nature Reserve, has a stunning beach that can be relatively busy in summer, but out of season or at daybreak it's a wonderfully serene place to run. The conservationist and 'Father of the National Parks', John Muir, was born in Dunbar on this coast in 1838; the fully waymarked John Muir Way runs for 45 miles from Musselburgh, east of Edinburgh, to the East Lothian border near Cocksburnpath. The country park in Dunbar, which also bears his name, is a great place for exploring both trails and the local wildlife, either running or walking with the family. The Pentland Hills dominate to the south of Edinburgh, stretching in a south-westerly direction for around 20 miles from the city's outskirts towards Biggar and the Upper Clydesdale. The northern hills are a designated Regional Park with over 62 miles of waymarked trails that are ideal for running and exploring.

Glasgow, too, is perfectly placed for easy access to great running, from rolling hills to interesting woodland trails, also the West Highland Way, which starts in Milngavie in the north of the city and heads for the Highlands. The Clyde Walkway is a 40-mile route taking you from the city centre out through Strathclyde to the spectacular gorge and waterfalls at Clyde. This route can be linked with the West Highland Way, using the Kelvin Walkway.

165

166

167

There's something about a point-to-point run that makes it even more of an adventure than one that starts and finishes in the same place. They are often, however, a logistical problem. Not so for this Glasgow to Edinburgh run (165), which travels along the fascinating Forth and Clyde and Union canals, following the towpaths through Bonnybridge, Falkirk, Linlithgow, Broxburn and Ratho. There are excellent public transport links at the start, finish and along the route. At an inviting 100km (62 miles) you could do it all in one go, however the route lends itself brilliantly to a multi-day fastpacking, sightseeing adventure.

Chatelherault Country Park is only 20 minutes by train from central Glasgow and the location of our Chatelherault run (166). The large house around which the park is set was only built in the 18th century, as a hunting lodge for the Duke of Hamilton. His much larger palace, which once stood at the opposite end of the drive, was demolished in 1927. Starting from the visitor centre, where there's a café and great views to the ruins of Cadzow Castle, the route takes in a wide loop of the estate, following both wooded banks of the meandering River Avon. Chatelherault Station is a few minutes away.

The 640 acres of Holyrood Park lie just a short distance from Edinburgh's Royal Mile in the heart of the city. The highest point in the park is Arthur's Seat, an ancient volcano and ancient fort that rises to 251 metres above sea level. The Arthur's Seat run (167) includes all the best bits of the park, starting at sparkling Dunsapie Loch then climbing steeply to the summit of Arthur's Seat where you'll have to pause to catch your breath and appreciate the glorious views. From here there's a fun descent followed by a run along the ridgeline of Salisbury Crags. The final stretch passes St Margaret's Loch and St Anthony's Chapel before returning to Dunsapie Loch.

Routes 165-167

165 GLASGOW TO EDINBURGH

Distance 60.5 miles/97km
Ascent 852 metres
Start Clydebank Station, G81 1RZ
Finish Edinburgh Waverley Station, EH1 1BB
Info wildrunning.net/2165

Turn R out of the station then L onto Argyll Road, heading north until you can turn R onto the canal to path. Follow the canal path east on the southern side to the lochs near Maryhill (5.1 miles/8.3km). Cross at a loch and turn R to pick up the canal path east on the northern side of the canal. Continue on the path passing Possil Loch and heading out of Glasgow on the Forth and Clyde Canal. Run through Kirkintilloch at 12.5 miles/20km and under the M80 at 22.1 miles/35.6km. Turn R at 26.5 miles/42.7km past the Falkirk Wheel and up to the Union Canal. Turn L and follow this east on the northern bank. Run through Falkirk and past Linlithgow Station at 37.9 miles/61km. Pass the Ratho climbing centre at 50 miles/80.6km and run into Edinburgh. Follow the canal past Kingsknowe Station to its end in Lochrin. To reach the station turn L then R onto Fountainbridge Road and follow

this onto West Port, which then becomes Grassmarket. Turn L onto Cowgate and then L onto Bank Street, L on North Bank Street and R onto Market Street, to Edinburgh Waverley Station.

166 CHATELHERAULT

Distance 5 miles/8km
Ascent 310 metres
Start Chatelherault Country Park, ML3 7UE
Info wildrunning.net/2166

This run takes in a clockwise loop of the country park, running down the eastern side of the valley and back up the west. Start by turning L at the top of the car park and following the trail south between the country park and the golf club. Continue on this path around the edge of the woodland to Fairholm Bridge which crosses Avon Water at the south-eastern tip of the park (1.9 miles/3.1km). Cross it and join the path trending R and uphill to join the Avon Walkway trail along the western edge of the woodland. Continue on the path to the old earthworks and the Cadzow Oaks at NS 734534 (4.3 miles/7km). Follow the path north, trending R, and then fork R downhill

and cross the bridge, and turn R at the top of this path to return to the start.

167 ARTHUR'S SEAT

Distance 3 miles/5km
Ascent 340 metres
Start Dunsapie Loch layby, EH8 8JD
Info wildrunning.net/2167

Head west uphill on one of the obvious paths, and trend L to reach the trig point on Arthur's Seat at 251 metres. Descend to the L or south over the smaller hill at 237 metres and onto the path to the south. Turn R and follow this around and down to the terrace path below Salisbury Crags. Take this path around Holyrood Park in a clockwise direction, to a path junction just south of St Margaret's Loch. Turn R and follow the dry dam uphill and around to the L on the hill north of Arthur's Seat. Turn L to return to the start. An enjoyable extra loop can be run by turning L and following the road past Dunsapie Loch, then R away from the road and around the small fort hill back to the road, then turning R back to the start.

168

169

170

Our Pentland Hills run (168) is a scenic loop that begins up the long ridge of the hills from Flotterstone, just outside Penicuik, climbing first to Carnethy Hill and then to its neighbouring Scald Law, the highest point in the range at 579 metres. From here there's a fantastic descent on grassy trails all the way down to Loganlea Reservoir. The gentle final miles follow the Logan Burn down the dramatic, steep-sided valley, rounding the right-angled Glencorse Reservoir to finish.

With their steep sides and rounded tops, the Ochil Hills (run 169) rise to the north of the Forth valley, near to Stirling. The route starts from Tillicoultry, climbing out from the steep-sided Mill Glen to ascend the long ridge to Ben Ever at 622 metres. Continuing along the obvious wide ridge it reaches the summit of Ben Cleuch, the highest point in the Ochils at 721 metres, before making its way down the well-trodden trail over The Law and down past a series of waterfalls to finish. There are many other ways to ascend Ben Cleuch, all of which are rewarded by fine views on a clear day.

Loch Leven, near Kinross, is a fascinating place to explore, dotted with islands, on one of which stand the ruins of Loch Leven Castle where Mary, Queen of Scots, was imprisoned in 1567. The loch lies within the 4700-acre Loch Leven National Nature Reserve, managed by Scottish Natural Heritage and the RSPB. Our run here (170) follows the Loch Leven Heritage Trail around the lake – the trail is flat and multi-user-friendly so it's perfect for running buggies and bikes as well – in the company of thousands of waterbirds. Look out for ospreys in the summer and the 20,000 pink-footed geese that fly here from Iceland in the autumn.

Routes 168-170

168 PENTLAND HILLS

Distance	8 miles/12.5km
Ascent	835 metres
Start	Flotterstone Ranger Centre, EH26 0PR
Info	wildrunning.net/2168

Take the path west following Glencorse Burn then bear L to climb Turnhouse Hill. Join the ridge path and follow it south-west past a cairn at 506 metres and down to the col at White Craig Heads. Continue on the ridge up Carnethy Hill at 573 metres, down to another col and up to the trig point at 579 metres on Scald Law (3.3 miles/5.3km). Turn around and descend back to the col then turn L, heading downhill to reachLogan Burn at the top of Loganlea Reservoir. Turn R and follow the path along the northern shore of the reservoir, past the dam and down the Logan Burn to Glencorse Reservoir. Run along the northern shore of the reservoir to Glen Cottage. Stay on the path heading south-east back to the burn and down the outbound path to the start.

169 OCHIL HILLS

Distance	6 miles/9km
Ascent	797 metres
Start	The Woolpack Inn, Tillicoultry, FK13 6AR
Info	wildrunning.net/2169

From the start follow the road and then path north, following the burn up Mill Glen and bearing L uphill before the burn forks into two. Take the path west, heading up onto the rounded ridge and then bearing R to the top of Wood Burn and up the hill above at 558 metres (1.4 miles/2.2km). Follow this ridge north-west above Calf Craig to Ben Ever at 622 metres. Run around the ridge, curving R down to the col at 584 metres and then up to Ben Cleuch with its trig point at 721 metres (3.2 miles/5.1km). Trace the ridge south-east to the boundary point and junction at NN 910003 (3.7 miles/5.9km). Turn R and head south over The Law at 638 metres then downhill to the confluence of the Gannel Burn and Daiglen Burn. Cross this then bear L onto a higher path than the outbound one, which also returns you to the start.

170 LOCH LEVEN

Distance	12.5 miles/20km
Ascent	79 metres
Start	Kirkgate Park, KY13 8ET
Info	wildrunning.net/2170

This is a clockwise circumnavigation of the loch along the easy-to-follow lakeside path, only deviating from the shore slightly in the south-west corner. Our route starts at the Kirkgate Park car park in Kinross but you could start the run at any point around its circumference. From the Kirkgate car park head north along the lochside path to the Tarhill car park at 1.7 miles/2.8km. Continue along the northern shore and down the east shore to the Findatie car park in the south-east (6.9 miles/11.1km). Follow the southern shore close to the B9097 to a R turn near East Brackley (8.6 miles/13.9km). Head north, reaching the loch shore again and following it to Kinross, turn R out to Kirkgate Park and back to the start.

Lairig Ghru

Central & Eastern Highlands

The Cairngorm massif is Britain's highest and largest mountain range. It is home to five of the six highest mountains in Scotland, with the highest in the range, Ben Macdui, standing at 1,309 metres. Rugged and remote, the Cairngorms are a serious undertaking, particularly in the colder months when they become a snowy, icy arena, popular as a venue for winter climbing, mountaineering and snow sports. Cairn Gorm itself lies within a vast plateau that is the snowiest place in Britain. A wild summit, exposed to the most extreme elements, this was the site of the greatest wind speed ever officially recorded in Britain, at 173 miles per hour, in March 1986. The lower slopes of these mountains are forested and tranquil, and within the valleys are sparkling lochs and wide, meandering rivers. The mountains themselves form only part of the Cairngorms National Park, the biggest National Park in Britain, covering some 1,748 square miles.

There are some fantastic waymarked long-distance trails in this part of the country: the East Highland Way runs for 83 miles from Fort William, and the Speyside Way is 66½ miles from Buckie on the Moray coastline, both ending in Aviemore on the western edge of the Cairngorms. Many sections of these routes make great out-and-back or linear runs, generally on excellent paths. The Moray coastline has superb sandy beaches interspersed with cliffs, rocky arches and sea stacks. Moray Firth dolphins can be spotted playing in the sea, and there is abundant birdlife here. The Moray Way, the Dava Way, the Moray Coast Trail and the Speyside Way together form a circular route of around 95 miles.

North of Inverness and lying between the Firth of Cromarty and the Beauly Firth, the Black Isle peninsula reaches out into the North Sea. It is neither black nor an island, getting its name from the fact that its warmer climate means snow doesn't settle here so it looks black in comparison to its surrounding landscapes during winter. There's much to discover here, from mountain

171

172

173

biking at Learnie Red Rocks and wildlife watching at Chanonry Point, the best place in Britain to see dolphins, to the delights of the Black Isle Brewery, set within its own organic farm.

Glen Esk is the longest and most easterly glen in Angus, and Mount Keen, at its furthest point, is Scotland's most easterly Munro. Our Glen Esk run (171) heads down the glen alongside Loch Lee before a climb past tumbling waterfalls brings you out high on the open mountainside at Cairn Lick at 682 metres. From here there's an exhilarating zig-zag descent down to the valley floor and back along Loch Lee, a perfectly peaceful stretch of water for a post-run dip.

Deep in the heart of the Cairngorms, overlooked by the mighty Lochnagar which rises to 1,155 metres, Loch Muick lies within the Balmoral estate. Our Loch Muick run (172) takes in a full circumnavigation of the loch, starting from Spittal of Glenmuick and following a rough track to its north-eastern tip. From here it tracks the northern shore, taking in the utter serenity of the place with its dramatic mountain surrounds. At the far end of the loch you can turn right, signposted to Lochnagar, to climb the mountain, adding 4 miles each way and nearly 800 metres of ascent. Otherwise, continuing around the edge of the loch brings you pleasantly along the southern shore, following the track back to the start.

Loch an Eilein lies hidden deep within the ancient Caledonian pine forests of Rothiemurchus, considered by many to be one of the finest remaining examples of this vast swathe of temperate rainforest which once covered much of this part of Scotland. Our Loch an Eilein run (173) takes you through the forest around the edges of the loch, with its ruined 15th-century castle and inviting shingle beach. At the far end of the loch a short detour leads you around Loch Gamhna, but this is worth missing out after particularly heavy rainfall as it can get boggy. The return route takes you along the northern shore of Loch an Eilein, with great views out to the castle. Cool off with a swim and an ice cream from the café and gallery.

Routes 171-173

171 GLEN ESK

Distance 10 miles/16km
Ascent 731 metres
Start Invermark car park, DD9 7YZ
Info wildrunning.net/2171

Follow the road over the bridge and then take the estate track past Invermark Castle, heading west along the northern shore of Loch Lee. Stay R at the junction at the west of the loch and take the track curving R, following the Water of Lee north-west to a L onto a footbridge (3.6 miles/5.7km). Cross the bridge and take a much smaller path west to reach the impressive Falls of Unich. Take the scrambly path to the R of the falls and follow this on the north and then west bank of the river up to the Falls of Damff. Continue up the burn then cross at a footbridge. Take the path south-east towards the col between Craig Maskeldie and Cairn Lick then turn R, navigating vague paths south to the estate track south of Cairn Lick. Turn L onto this and descend to Inchgrundle. Follow the track north from here back to the outbound track at the western end of Loch Lee. Turn R onto this back to the start.

172 LOCH MUICK

Distance 7.5 miles/12km
Ascent 592 metres
Start Spittal of Glenmuick, AB35 5SU
Info wildrunning.net/2172

Run up the path heading south-west to the eastern corner of Loch Muick. Turn R and follow the lochside path around the loch past the boathouse at the northern tip then down the northern shore to Glas-allt-Shiel at NO 276823. To extend this route and increase its challenge level, turn R here and follow the path north-west up Glas Allt. Bear R to the cairn at Cac Carn Mor where you turn R following the edge of the cliff north to the trig point at 1155 metres on the summit of Lochnagar. Return to Loch Muick by the same route. This detour is an extra 7 miles/11.2km and adds 769 metres of ascent. Continuing around Loch Muick from Glas-allt-Shiel, follow the path to the southern end and turn L along the loch shore to the south-western point. Turn L here and trace the shore north-east back to the start.

173 LOCH AN EILEIN

Distance 5 miles/7.5km
Ascent 208 metres
Start Loch an Eilein Gate car park, PH22 1QT
Info wildrunning.net/2173

From the car park pick up the path south to the L of Loch an Eilein and along the north-east shore to a path junction and footbridge. Cross and turn R, continuing south-west through the forest to another path junction and footbridge, over the burn that runs between Loch Gamhna and Loch an Eilein. Turn L and follow the path south-west initially and then bear R around the southern end of Loch Gamhna. Head back north-east up the other side of the loch and then L along the southern shore of Loch an Eilein. Turn R along the shore through a gate and past the castle in the loch. Finally, follow the path back north along the loch shore and back to the start.

174

175

176

The Lairig Ghru trail bisects the Cairngorms between Aviemore and Linn of Dee; although the original route continued to Braemar this now follows a tarmac road. Rising to 835 metres at its highest point and taking in long stretches of remote and exposed mountain terrain, it is both a fantastically enjoyable high-level traverse of this majestic plateau and a serious and challenging undertaking that requires careful planning. The Lairig Ghru run (174) takes in the full traverse, a good day's running or a two-day fastpack with a wild camp along the way – alternatively overnight at the Corrour bothy, which sits at the foot of Cairn Toul and the Devil's Point at halfway. For an absolutely epic adventure the return can be made along the parallel pass, the Lairig an Laoigh.

The River Orrin rises in the East Monar Forest and winds its way eastwards through the Strathconon and Corriehallie forests to join the River Conon near Dingwall. Just to the west of Muir of Ord are the Falls of Orrin, a delightful series of tumbling waterfalls set in a hidden wooded valley. Our Falls of Orrin run (175) starts at the tiny hamlet of Aultgowrie, heading up the northern bank of the river past the falls – which are well worth taking some time to explore with their wide, white chutes and intriguing weir – and below the ruined Fairburn Tower.

Our next route visits the Black Isle with a circumnavigation of Chanonry Ness, stopping to see the views, and perhaps even a pod of dolphins, at Chanonry Point (run 176). Refuel at the Fortrose Café or The Anderson, both in Fortrose and, for the best possible chances of dolphin sightings, camp nearby at Fortrose Bay Campsite.

Immortalised in Robert Burns' 1787 poem, the Birks of Aberfeldy rise steeply from the Moness Burn with its fast-flowing waters and series of stepped waterfalls. Our Birks of Aberfeldy run (177) takes in the popular loop of the gorge, climbing steeply for awe-inspiring views from the bridge at the top before weaving its way back down forest trails and rocky steps. It's a magical place, best summed up by the Bard himself: "The braes ascend like lofty wa's, The foaming stream deep-roaring fa's, O'erhung wi' fragrant spreading shaws – The birks of Aberfeldy."

174 LAIRIG GHRU

Distance	18.5 miles/29.5km
Ascent	855 metres
Start	Glenmore Lodge, PH22 1QZ
Finish	Linn of Dee car park, AB35 5YG
Info	wildrunning.net/2174

From the Lodge head south and cross a footbridge in the forest, turning R at the track junction and following this to the road. Turn L on the road heading south then bear R onto a path following the Allt Mor. Once above the forest, turn R and cross a footbridge and head south-west up and over the Chalamain Gap. Drop down into the valley and turn L following the Lairig Ghru up to the Pools of Dee (7.1 miles/11.5km). Continue down the valley trending L below Carn a Mhaim and following the Allt Preas nam Meirleach down to Lui Water. Turn R, descending to reach the Linn of Dee.

175 FALLS OF ORRIN

Distance	4 miles/6km
Ascent	116 metres
Start	Parking area at Aultgowrie, IV6 7XA
Info	wildrunning.net/2175

From Aultgowrie follow the road north across the bridge and turn L onto the track heading west through woodland to the north of the River Orrin. Follow the riverside path to some buildings and a footbridge at NH 453524 (1.8 miles/2.9km). Cross the bridge and turn L, following the minor road along the southern bank of the river. Bear L at the top of a small hill off the road onto a path that leads down to the weirs and Falls of Orrin. Continue on the path east back to the road and L to the start.

176 CHANONRY POINT, BLACK ISLE

Distance	5 miles/7.5km
Ascent	171 metres
Start	Car park central Fortrose, IV10 8TD
Info	wildrunning.net/2176

Follow High Street north-east then turn L onto East Watergate Street and bear R out of Fortrose. Ascend to reach a R turn onto a footpath down Swallow Den (0.6 mile/1km). Turn R and follow this path down through woodland into Fairy Glen. Turn R again, following the stream and crossing the A832 before turning R onto Well Road. Turn L on Mill Road and R along the coastal Marine Terrace. Bear L onto a footpath along the coast out to Chanonry Point. Trace the headland around the point, looking out for dolphins, and then head back along the southern coast to the start.

177 BIRKS OF ABERFELDY

Distance	3 miles/4.5km
Ascent	320 metres
Start	Aberfeldy Square, PH15 2DA
Info	wildrunning.net/2177

From the square in central Aberfeldy follow the main road west then turn L, signed to the Birks, and run through a small park and up to the A826. Cross this and run through the car park on the R and come to the Moness Burn. A little further upstream cross the bridge to the L and follow the eastern bank of the Moness Burn uphill through the woodland. Pass the viewpoint of the waterfall and then turn R across a small footbridge at the top of the gorge. Follow the west side back down heading north across the waterfall bridge and back down to the start.

Descending from Ben More

Lochaber, Argyll & Trossachs

The Lochaber region, diverse and spectacular in landscape and scenery, reaches from Rannoch Moor and Glencoe in the south to the Great Glen in the north, and from Fort William along the west coast to Mallaig, including the small isles of Eigg, Rum and Muck. Westwards it extends out into the Atlantic to Ardnamurchan Point, the most westerly part of the UK mainland. Lochaber also includes the Glen Spean area, and Loch Laggan and part of Argyll in the south-west.

Fort William is something of a hub for outdoor enthusiasts. Runners, climbers, walkers and mountain bikers flock here to explore the wonders of the surrounding landscapes. The Great Glen Way and the West Highland Way both start or end here. The Nevis Range is startlingly beautiful, from the brooding form of Ben Nevis, its summit often obscured by swirling cloud, to the tranquil, golden valley of Glen Nevis with its cascading waterfalls, woodland trails and bracken-covered hillsides.

Lying across the Highland Boundary Fault, and often considered to be the boundary between the lowlands and highlands of Scotland, the great, glassy expanse of Loch Lomond seems to accompany you for an eternity as you travel the busy, twisting A82 north. Loch Lomond is the largest area of inland water in Britain, its 27 square miles dotted with wooded islands, yachts and kayaks. The West Highland Way gives you a different view of the loch, tracing its eastern shores, wending through forest and often dipping right down to the water's edge. It is a glorious place to be in early spring, but can be a war with the midges during the summer months.

The Trossachs lie to the east of Ben Lomond, the landscape gentler than that of the Highlands, and scattered with quiet lochs and forested glens. West of Loch Lomond and the Trossachs National Park lies Argyll, with its intricate coastline and remote peninsulas, reaching out towards the islands of Mull, Bute, Islay and Jura.

180

180

181

The Crinan Canal crosses the Mull of Kintyre, linking the Atlantic with Loch Fyne at Ardrishaig. Opened in 1808 it meant boats no longer had to make the perilous journey around the Mull of Kintyre. Our Crinan Canal run (178) begins at the pretty harbour village of Crinan, following the surfaced towpath as it draws a line between the canal and the sea before passing the locks at Cairnbaan. A long, quiet stretch alongside woodland brings you to Lochgilphead, after which you emerge onto the shores of Loch Fyne at Ardrishaig. A bus service links the start and finish.

Rising to 760 metres above Loch Lubnaig and the town of Callander, Ben Ledi is the highest peak in the central part of the Trossachs. A beautiful mountain, set in picturesque surroundings, the path to the top is paved and relatively straightforward and the views all the way up are outstanding. Our Ben Ledi route (179) starts in Callander along a gentle section of the Rob Roy Way, which runs for 92 miles between Drymen and Pitlochry. Shortly after the Falls of Leny the route heads up on a delightful trail through woodland, emerging onto open mountainside and continuing all the way to the top. The return trip is by the same route, back down the mountain into Callander.

Our Ben Lawers route (180) is another fantastic run to a summit and back, this time scaling the mighty Ben Lawers, Scotland's 10th-highest Munro at 1214 metres, with another Munro – Beinn Ghlas – ticked off on the way. This is a high and exposed mountain so best kept for favourable weather, however the high-level car park and clear path to the summit mean that, on a good day, it's a great way to experience some of the highest ground in Britain.

The Silver Sands of Morar (run 181) stretch like a string of pearls around the coastline between Arisaig and Morar, each beach affording spectacular views of the rugged skylines of the Small Isles – Rum, Eigg, Muck and Canna. Our route links the beaches by running between them – at low tide this is straightforward but at high tide you may need to scramble over some of the rocky sections that divide the beaches, or swim around. Any of the three options makes for a highly enjoyable wild run. The return can be done by the same route, alternatively take the quiet road that runs parallel to the coast, with great views along its length.

Routes 178-181

178 CRINAN CANAL

Distance	9 miles/14km
Ascent	248 metres
Start	Crinan village centre, PA31 8SR
Finish	Ardrishaig, PA30 8EA
Info	wildrunning.net/2178

Follow the canal path east along the shore of Loch Crinan, crossing the first bridge and continuing along the southern side before re-crossing with the B8025. Turn R and stay on the northern bank, heading south-east past the parking at Dundary Locks and through Cairnbaan to the B841. Cross and stay on the northern bank, heading south-east along the towpath past Lochgilphead following the A83 south to the finish.

179 BEN LEDI

Distance	11 miles/17.5km
Ascent	1142 metres
Start	Callander, FK17 8BB
Info	wildrunning.net/2179

Head west out of Callander on the Rob Roy Way, continuing over the River Garbh Uisge and along the course of an old railway, before crossing the A821 and follow the river to the parking at Creagna h-Airde (3.1 miles/5km). Turn L off the trail onto a footpath rising through young woodland. Cross the forest road and continue uphill along a stepped path which becomes rocky higher up. Trend L then R onto the ridge towards the summit then up the final climb to the trig point at 879 metres on Ben Ledi. Return by the same route.

180 BEN LAWERS

Distance	7 miles/11km
Ascent	1038 metres
Start	Ben Lawers car park, FK21 8TY
Info	wildrunning.net/2180

From the car park cross the road and follow the signed path north-east through the gated Ben Lawers nature reserve and out onto the mountainside above. Stay R on the main path zigzagging uphill to the first summit of Beinn Ghlas at 1103 metres. Run down the wonderful, exposed ridgeline and then up the steeper rocky path to the trig point at 1214 metres on the summit of Ben Lawers (3.2 miles/5.2km). Turn around and return along the ridge to Beinn Ghlas, then turn R and descend to the col below Meall Corranaich. Turn L and run on a superb path down the Burn of Edramucky to the outbound trail. Turn R and return through the nature reserve to the start.

181 SILVER SANDS OF MORAR

Distance	5½ miles/8.5km
Ascent	86 metres
Start	Morar beach car park, PH39 4NT
Info	wildrunning.net/2181

This run traces the coast at the high water mark; at the lowest tide there is only one section of scrambling to be done, but at high tide most of the rocky headlands will need to be scrambled over. You can avoid some scrambles by getting wet feet or even swimming, but this is an adventurous 5½ miles. Head north-east out of the car park and down to Morar beach. Turn L and follow the sands out through Morar Bay to the Sound of Sleat. Turn L along the coast south-west below Beinn an Achaidh Mhoir, along Camusdarach Beach and south past several headlands and smaller beaches to Camas Rubha a' Mhurain where you can turn L inland to the road near Traigh House. Turn L onto the road and follow it back to the start.

182

183

184

Deep in dramatic Glencoe, the Lairig Gartain and Lairig Eilde trails encircle the long ridgeline of Buachaille Etive Beag, the little brother to its better known neighbour, Buachaille Etive Mor. These two trails together make one of the best low-level runs in the area, with outstanding vistas down Glen Etive. Our run around Buachaille Etive Beag (182) is a clockwise loop, heading straight into the glorious steep-sided Lairig Gartain and finishing down the Pass of Glencoe.

Remote and serene, Loch Ossian (run 183) is inaccessible by road but has its own train station and SYHA hostel. It is an incredibly peaceful place, surrounded by the imposing Munros of Ben Alder, Carn Dearg, Sgor Gaibhre and Sgor Choinnich. Running the loop around the loch gives you wonderful views of the mountains and a feeling of complete release from everyday life – wild running at its finest.

Starting at the end of the West Highland Way, the Great Glen Way (run 184) stretches 73 miles coast to coast across the Highlands, linking Fort William in the west with Inverness in the east. The route follows the natural fault line of the Great Glen, running alongside Loch Lochy, Loch Oich and Loch Ness as well as the Caledonian Canal. With clearly waymarked trails, most of the route is low-level, however there is a higher level option between Fort Augustus and Drumnadrochit where steeper climbs are rewarded with dramatic views. Our route takes in the full length of the Great Glen Way, for a perfect multi-day fastpacking adventure with plenty of places to rest and refuel along the way.

Routes 182-184

182 BUACHAILLE ETIVE BEAG

Distance	9 miles/14.5km
Ascent	716 metres
Start	Cnoc nam Bocan car park, west of PH49 4HY
Info	wildrunning.net/2182

Follow the path south-west out of the back of the layby, roughly following the River Coupall up the Lairig Gartain between Buachaille Etive Beag to the north and Buachaille Etive Mor to the south. Reach the col at 489 metres and descend the Allt Gartain trail to a path junction just north of the road at NN 172516 (3.8 miles/6.1km). Turn R and follow the valley north along the Lairig Eilde trail, bearing to the R down the Allt Lairig trail. Trend R back to the A82 by a cairn and layby parking at NN 187562 (7.1 miles/11.4km). Turn R onto the road to the next parking area where you can fork L on a track that runs parallel to, but a bit further away from, the road. Follow this to just past the start and take a sharp R to cut back to the road and the start.

183 LOCH OSSIAN

Distance	9 miles/14.5km
Ascent	331 metres
Start	Corrour Station, NN 356664
Info	wildrunning.net/2183

Take the main track north-east to the south-western tip of Loch Ossian. Turn L at the track junction, following the path clockwise around the loch along the wooded northern shore to Corrour Shooting Lodge at the northern end (4.4 miles/7.1km). Continue on the lochside path around the northern end and back along the southern shore to the Loch Ossian Youth Hostel at NN 371670 (7.9 miles/12.8km). Follow the track to meet the outbound route and return to the start. For a great weekend run in from either Loch Rannoch, Kinlochleven or Dalwhinnie, climbing Ben Alder and wild camping or staying at the SYHA.

184 GREAT GLEN WAY

Distance	75 miles/121km
Ascent	2863 metres
Start	Fort William Station, PH33 6TQ
Finish	Inverness Station, IV1 1LF
Info	wildrunning.net/2184

Join the waymarked Great Glen Way north of the station and follow it along the coast to the mouth of the Caledonian Canal. Turn R inland on the southern bank, past the series of lochs known as Neptune's Staircase, to join the B8005 and cross the canal at Gairlochy (10.4 miles/16.7km). Turn R and follow the trail north-east along the west shore of Loch Lochy to the Laggan Locks at the northern end (22 miles/35.3km). Cross at the loch and turn L along the eastern bank of the Caledonian Canal, heading north-east to the southern end of Loch Oich. Cross the A82 and follow the loch's eastern shore to the A82 at the Bridge of Oich (27.8 miles/44.8km). Cross the bridge and follow the canal north on the western bank to the A82 in Fort Augustus (33 miles/52.5km). Turn L onto the road and follow roads then forest trails slightly west but keeping to the edge of Loch Ness. The trail diverts away from the loch in Invermoriston at about 40 miles/65km and Drumnadrochit at about 56 miles/90km, but generally follows Loch Ness north-east. Head inland on the trail at Abriachan at 61 miles/97.5km. Stay on higher ground to the north of the loch into Inverness, descending to follow the River Ness to the station.

Torridon Coire Mhic Nobuil behind Liathach

Northern Highlands

Tucked into the far north-western corner of Scotland, the landscape around Assynt and neighbouring Coigach is truly extraordinary. From a vast, undulating, loch-studded moorland rises a series of steep-sided mountains, each standing separate from the rest. The coastline around Assynt is equally astounding – a stunning combination of rugged cliffs and white sandy beaches fringed by clear seas and impressive sea stacks. One such stack is the awe-inspiring Old Man of Stoer, a classic rock climb and nesting ground for fulmars – stiff-winged seabirds related to the albatross.

Beloved by climbers, walkers, cyclists and wild runners alike, Torridon is an ancient and enchanting wilderness, with jagged mountains formed from ancient Torridonian sandstone dating back 750 million years. To the west the hilly landscape is even older, formed from Lewisian gneiss over 2,600 million years old. This is a place that inspires adventures on a grand scale, from lengthy fastpacking epics to mountain summits to long days that finish with a long swim in a clear, cool loch.

The landscapes of north-west Sutherland are remote and hauntingly beautiful, filled with vast moors and shimmering lochs edged by sandy beaches and craggy mountains. The epic Cape Wrath Trail runs for 200 miles from Fort William to the dramatic sea cliffs at Cape Wrath. Sandwood Bay, reached along a lengthy track with no vehicle access, is a mile-long stretch of sand backed by dunes and Sandwood Loch. Although popular for its wonderful remoteness, this is a place that never feels busy, with visitors lost within the vastness of the landscape. This area is kept beautiful through the fine work of the John Muir Trust, and a donation in return for your visit will help fund this important work in the future.

Unlike John o' Groats, which lies some 11 miles away in an east-southeasterly direction, Dunnet Head is the most northerly point in mainland Britain. With its stunning sandstone sea cliffs, coastal grassland and great views out to Hoy, the headland is a nature reserve and home to a vast number of seabirds.

185

186

187

Glen Shiel runs for about 9 miles from the Cluanie Inn at the western end of Loch Cluanie to the village of Shiel Bridge and Loch Duich. South of the River Shiel, the Glen Shiel ridge rises above the glen in an inviting and awe-inspiring jagged line. Our Glen Shiel run (185) takes on the full traverse, including no fewer than seven Munros, with minimal descent between them. A long day out requiring good mountain fitness and navigation and some kind weather, this is one of the best multi-summit mountain ridges in the country. You will need to plan logistics to return you along the glen to your start point but it's well worth the effort.

Considered by many to be the most beautiful glen in Scotland, Glen Affric is a place of wild and spectacular landscapes. The River Affric spans its full length, surrounded by lochs, moorland, mountains and a large area of ancient Caledonian pine forest. Our Glen Affric run (186) takes in a full circumnavigation of serene Loch Affric, starting between it and neighbouring Loch Beinn a' Mheadhoin and following the northern shore around the rugged hillside to reach the River Affric. From here it returns on the Affric Kintail Way, a 44-mile cross-country route from Drumnadrochit on Loch Ness to Morvich in Kintail by Loch Duich.

Our Diabaig Torridon run (187) takes you on a brilliantly adventurous route around the coastal outcrop of Diabaig on the shores of Loch Torridon. It's a tougher run than it looks from the map, with rocky ground and plenty of ascent, but it's thoroughly enjoyable and the setting and views are unbeatable. From the start in the village of Diabaig opposite the Gille Brighde café it heads up alongside a stream to reach the road, where a section of road running, interspersed with trails, is a good warm-up for the rest of the route. At Wester Alligin (Alligin Shuas on the map), the run leaves the road and heads over moorland and rocky outcrops, with some boggy sections, then traces the coastline back to Diabaig.

Routes 185-187

185 GLEN SHIEL

Distance	20 miles/31.5km
Ascent	1869 metres
Start	Cluanie Inn, IV63 7YW
Finish	Shiel Bridge, IV40 8HW
Info	wildrunning.net/2185

Cross the road and follow the track south past Cluanie Lodge to a path junction at NH 101072 (4 miles/6.4km). Turn R off the main track and head north-west up onto the ridge to the first summit, Creag a Mhaim at 947 metres. Follow the ridge curving to the R over Druim Shionnach at 987 metres then Aonach air Chrith at 1021 metres (7.7 miles/12.4km). Continue over Maol Chinn-dearg at 981 metres to Sgurr Coire na Feinne at 902 metres (9.5 miles/15.3km). Run north-west, detouring north to Sgurr an Doire Leathain at 1010 metres, then carrying on over Sgurr an Lochain at 1004 metres to Sgurr Beag at 896 metres (12 miles/19.3km). Run down through the col and up to Creag nan Damh at 918 metres then north to Sgurr a' Chuilinn at 755 metres (13.5 miles/21.7km). Descend from here north-west along the rounded ridge to join and follow Allt Mhalagain to the car park on

the A87 at NG 971138 (15.2 miles/24.4km). Turn L and follow the road down to Shiel Bridge where you can get a bus back to the start.

186 GLEN AFFRIC

Distance	11 miles/17.5km
Ascent	521 metres
Start	Glen Affric car park, near IV4 7LN
Info	wildrunning.net/2186

Note, the postcode is for Cannich village, from there follow the signed road up Glen Affric along the northern shore of Loch Beinn a' Mheadhoin to the car park at the end of the road.

This route circumnavigates Loch Affric in an anti-clockwise direction. Start by heading north out of the car park and following the driveway to Affric Lodge. Turn R onto a smaller path around to the north of this and then onto a larger track going west above the loch. Follow this to Loch Coulavie where the path becomes less distinct. Continue to a junction with the Affric Kintail Way at NH 127208 (5.4 miles/8.7km). Turn L onto this clearer track and follow it south-east across a bridge and past Athnamulloch then L onto a larger track along the southern shore of the

loch, then head north-east above the loch and into woodland. Take the large trail L at the eastern end of the loch, crossing a bridge and turning R up a hill back to the start.

187 DIABAIG TORRIDON

Distance	8.5 miles/13.5km
Ascent	780 metres
Start	Lower Diabaig, IV22 2HE
Info	wildrunning.net/2187

Follow the path from the southern end of the road and turn L up Allt an Uain to the road north of Loch a' Mhullaich. Turn R and follow this road to a fork R onto a path north of Loch Diabaigas Airde, around the north-eastern end of the loch and south down to the road and down Bealach na Gaoithe. Straightline the road's curves and take the first R to Glachacro (3.4 miles/5.5km). Turn R here off the road and follow a path south-west to Rubha na h-Airde Glaise (5.2 miles/8.3km). Turn around and return on the same path to a L turn that follows the coast north-west to Lochan Dubh. Pass to the L or west of this and take the path around to the R, north of Loch a' Bhealaich Mhoir and then north back to the start.

188

189

190

The Old Man of Stoer is a 60-metre-tall sea stack of Torridonian sandstone, standing off the Sutherland coast. Popular with rock climbers and wildlife watchers alike, the area is home to thousands of seabirds and is also one of the best places in Assynt to spot whales and dolphins. Our Old Man of Stoer run (188) explores the wild and windswept headland on rough, rocky grassland, including a climb over the trig point-topped summit of Sithean Mor (Big Fairy Hill) which, at 161 metres, offers superb views of the coast and mountains of Assynt.

Remote and beautiful Sandwood Bay is the location of run 189, with its freshwater loch and sea stack, Am Buachaille. Starting from Blairmore it heads along a rugged moorland track past Loch Aisir, Loch na Gainimh and Loch a Mhuilinn, crossing several minor streams. As the path rises towards Sandwood Loch the coastline to Cape Wrath comes into view. Passing the loch and dunes to reach the bay you're greeted by the stunning mile-long sweep of white wave-washed sand. The return, if you can ever drag yourself away, is by the outward route.

Ben Hope is Scotland's most northerly Munro, rising in splendid isolation to 927 metres south-east of Loch Hope. The Ben Hope run (190) takes on the awesome, steep ridge from the south of the mountain to the summit and back. Signs from the roadside car park at the foot of the mountain lead you on clear paths all the way to the top, where an incredible panorama awaits. Return the same way. Although the route is short and relatively straightforward, Ben Hope is a remote and exposed mountain and route finding can still be tricky in poor visibility – and conditions at the top can be extremely challenging.

Dunnet Head (run 191), the most northerly point in mainland Britain, is a superb and challenging run with a great feeling of wildness. Starting at Dwarwick Pier, a mile from Dunnet village, it loops anticlockwise around the loch-strewn moorland, close to the precipitous edge of the high, sandstone cliffs – take care in high winds. The lighthouse on the point is well worth a visit, built by Robert Stevenson, grandfather of the writer Robert Louis Stevenson.

189

Routes 188-191

188 THE OLD MAN OF STOER

Distance 4.5 miles/7km
Ascent 319 metres
Start Stoer Head Lighthouse, west of
IV27 4JH
Info wildrunning.net/2188

From the lighthouse, follow the coast path
north-east from the lighthouse passing
the headlands at Seana Chreag and Cirean
Geardail. The impressive sea stack of the
Old Man of Stoer appears off the coast
at NC 017351 (2 miles/3.2km). Continue
north-east to the Point of Stoer and then
turn R inland up to the trig point at 161
metres on Sithean Mor (2.9 miles/4.6km).
Continue over the hill and follow paths
south-west back to the start.

189 SANDWOOD BAY

Distance 9.5 miles/15km
Ascent 292 metres
Start John Muir car park, IV27 4RU
Info wildrunning.net/2189

Head north-east out of the John Muir car
park on a path to the R (east) of Loch na
Gainimh and then north to Loch a' Mhuilinn
(2.4 miles/3.8km). Curve around to the R
from here past Loch Meadhonach and Loch
Clais nan Coinneal then bear L to the beach
past the bothy and Sandwood Loch. Turn
L on the beach and follow the coast south-
west, out to Rubh' a Bhuachaille and along
to a stream. Turn inland and run over Carn
an Righ at 133 metres before trending L to
join the outbound path by Loch a' Mhuilinn.
Turn R onto the path and follow it back to
the start.

190 BEN HOPE

Distance 5 miles/7.5km
Ascent 961 metres
Start Layby north of Alltnacaillich,
IV27 4UL
Info wildrunning.net/2190

From the layby at NC 461476 follow the
path signed to Ben Hope heading north-east
uphill. Follow the signed path as it climbs
up to the ridge then turns L and leads to the
trig point at 927 metres on the summit. The
return is by the same route, taking in fast,
technical terrain to return to the start.

191 DUNNET HEAD

Distance 11 miles/17km
Ascent 705 metres
Start Dunnet Head lighthouse, KW14 8XS
Info wildrunning.net/2191

From the lighthouse head west, following
the coast path around to the south to reach
the road and car park at West Dunnet (5.3
miles/8.6km). Turn L onto the road and run
north-east through the village. After the
village bear R off the road and continue until
you meet the B855 just west of St John's
Loch (6.4 miles/10.3km). Turn L onto the
road and follow it north past Brough and L
past Courtfall to return to Dunnet Head and
the start.

Mull

The Scottish Islands

Scotland's islands, scattered along the country's north and west coasts, are unlike anywhere else in Britain. Each one has a unique character with a landscape and culture all of its own. If you come here island-hopping, make sure you spend at least a few days on each island, to give yourself time to really experience the great diversity here, meeting the people, eating the food and, of course, exploring the trails.

Arran is the most southerly of the inhabited islands, lying just off the coast of Ayrshire within the Firth of Clyde. North of Arran the Inner Hebrides stretch northwards from Islay in the south through Mull up to Skye, the largest and perhaps best known of the islands.

The Outer Hebrides – the Western Isles or Long Island, as they are sometimes known – include Lewis and Harris, North Uist, Benbecula, South Uist, and Barra. This cluster of islands is a magical place, with its huge range of landscapes and terrain creating vast scope for on-foot exploration. The delicate pink rock is ancient Lewisian gneiss and forms the bedrock of the islands. It is amongst the oldest in Europe, created by bubbling Precambrian volcanoes some 3 billion years ago. The variety and abundance of wildlife on the islands are awe-inspiring – the calls of dunlins, lapwings and ringed plovers fill the air, puffins and razorbills huddle noisily on the rocks and surf on the waves. Inland, the rasping cries of the corncrake, a rare summer visitor, can sometimes be heard, but these are shy and elusive birds and seldom seen. Fulmars scythe their way around the sea cliffs, and hen harriers and golden eagles arc majestically over the rough-hewn landscape. There are 7,500 lochs in the Outer Hebrides alone; salmon and trout swim in the crystal-clear water, and otters can be spotted playing in the shallows. The seas are home to basking sharks, whales and dolphins.

The island archipelagos of Orkney and Shetland lie 10 miles and 90 miles respectively off the north-east coast of mainland Scotland. With around 20,000 people living on each, these

192

193

194

wildlife-rich islands are a joy to visit, with close knit communities interspersed throughout their beautiful landscapes.

At 874 metres Goatfell is the highest point on Arran, its prominent pyramidal peak rising above the surrounding forested hills, clearly visible as you approach the island by boat. Our Goatfell run (192) climbs the mountain from Brodick, passing the castle and heading up through woodland to emerge onto open mountainside just below the summit. A run along the airy summit ridge to neighbouring Cir Mhor gives breathtaking views over the summits of Arran, the Clyde Estuary and even across to Ireland on a clear day. The descent takes the direct line off fell, heading straight down Glen Rosa to return to Brodick.

The island of Jura, with its three distinctive peaks, is visible from miles around. Our next route takes on the challenge to traverse this famous skyline: the Paps of Jura (run 193). Starting deep in the valley at the Corran River it heads up the rugged hillside to reach Loch an t-Siob. Turning right there's a steep climb to the first summit, Beinn Shiantaidh at 757 metres, before you descend steeply and then climb back up to Beinn an Oir at 785 metres. Descending to the small lochs at Na Garbh-lochanan brings you to the final ascent, Beinn a' Chaolais at 734 metres. A direct descent takes you down to Loch an t-Siob, joining your outward route for the return journey.

Mull is a surprisingly large and diverse island, from the dramatic high mountains at its centre and the peaceful sandy beaches of the Ross of Mull to the vast lochs of the north and the pretty harbour town of Tobermory. The Ardmeanach peninsula juts out from the west coast of the island, to the west of Ben More, Mull's highest peak at 966 metres. Our run to the Fossil Tree on Mull (194) follows Ardmeanach's wild-feeling southern coastline out to its wild, remote westernmost point to find MacCulloch's fossil tree, thought to be 50 million years old when it was engulfed by the lava flows from the Ben More volcano. The final section of the route is tidal so check tide times before you leave.

Routes 192-194

192 GOATFELL, ARRAN

Distance 13 miles/21km
Ascent 1034 metres
Start Brodick pier, KA27 8AY
Info wildrunning.net/2192

Turn R out of the ferry terminal and follow the A841 to the southern end of the beach. Turn R onto a path running just inland of the beach and then meeting the A841. Turn R onto this and follow it north to a L turn onto a track at Cladach, going past the castle and uphill north-west through Cnocan Wood and onto the mountainside. Continue uphill to the ridge and cairn at 607 metres. Turn L here and follow the ridge to the trig point at 874 metres on Goatfell (5 miles/8.1km). Descend the ridge north of the summit to North Goatfell at NR 989423 (5.5 miles/8.9km) where the ridge splits. Take the L fork heading down to the Saddle at NR 978430. Turn L and run down the stream into Glen Rosa, following Glenrosa Water south into Brodick and back to the start.

193 PAPS OF JURA

Distance 11 miles/17km
Ascent 1562 metres
Start Layby at Corran River Bridge, near PA60 7XZ
Info wildrunning.net/2193

From the layby follow the path north-west to Loch an t-Siob'. Turn R at its eastern tip and head north on vague paths to the east of Beinn Shiantaidh. Turn L onto a better path around to its south and up to the summit at 757 metres (3.2 miles/5.1km). Descend to the west and then climb up Beinn an Oir to the north-eastern summit at 763 metres then run along the ridge to the trig point at 785 metres (4.8 miles/7.7km). Descend the south-west ridge on indistinct paths to reach the valley floor south of Na Garbh-lochanan. Cross the valley to the east of Beinn a' Chaolais and turn R, heading straight for the summit at 733 metres (6.3 miles/10.2km). Follow the same path back to the valley but continue east down Gleann an t-Siob to Loch an t-Siob. Take the path around the south of the loch back to the outbound track. Turn R onto this to return to the start.

194 FOSSIL TREE, MULL

Distance 12.5 miles/19.5km
Ascent 622 metres
Finish Tiroran car park, PA69 6ES
Info wildrunning.net/2194

An out-and-back route to visit the incredible fossil tree, with wildly differing views in each direction. Turn R out of the car park and follow the main track west, bearing R at the first junction and continuing to Tavool House (2.8 miles/4.5km). Stay L and follow the track to the monument just west of Burg Farm. Descend to the grassland and run along the coast, joining singletrack paths contouring below the cliffs to reach a metal ladder (5.5 miles/8.8km). Descend the ladder and boulder-hop along the breach past a big waterfall and around the corner to find the fossil tree in an alcove next to a large cave. Turn around and return by the same route.

195

196

197

The Isle of Eigg is a beautiful and fascinating place, owned and managed by the island's Heritage Trust since 1997 and considered to be the most eco-friendly island in Britain. At its centre rises the distinctive volcanic peak of An Sgurr, with its steep sides and narrow summit. Our Northern Eigg run (195), recommended to us by runner, Eigg resident and co-owner of Eigg Adventures, Laraine Wyn-Jones, is in an enjoyable tour of the craggy north of the island from Cleadale.

Wild and wonderful Glen Brittle campsite on Skye, right by the beach and with a great café next door, is a perfect base for exploring the island. The Coire Lagan run (196) starts from your tent and takes you right into the heart of Coire Lagan, a great, rocky amphitheatre bordered by towering gabbro crags, including the infamous Inaccessible Pinnacle, part of the classic Cuillin Ridge traverse. Looping the tiny loch at the base of Sgurr Mhic Choinnich, the descent takes you to the north of Loch an Fhir-bhallaich and back to Glen Brittle.

At the opposite end of Skye, the Trotternish peninsula reaches northwards into The Minch. The long, beautiful, awe-inspiring ridgeline that runs north-south forming the peninsula's jagged backbone is widely considered to be one of the best mountain traverses in Britain. Our Trotternish Ridge run (197) takes on the main part of the ridge, starting at Flodigarry and heading south to finish beyond the Old Man of Storr, the much-photographed pinnacle of rock that stands proud on the ridge. For the full traverse you can continue onwards to finish in Portree.

Routes 195-197

195 NORTHERN EIGG

Distance	4 miles/6km
Ascent	582 metres
Start	Cleadale, PH42 4RL
Info	wildrunning.net/2195

Follow the road north through Cleadale and onto a track heading in the same direction above the fields onto the open mountainside below Dunan Thalasgair. Turn R and climb the zigzagging path onto the ridge and turn L to the trig point at 336 metres. Follow the ridge south-east over Sgorr an Fharaidh and across the Allt Bidein an Tighearna. Continue around to the R and descend on vague paths down to the road to the south of the start point, turn R to return to the start. Assuming you are staying on Eigg, a great route for the second day is an ascent of An Sgurr from Galmisdale – the summit offers one of the best views in the country.

196 COIRE LAGAN, SKYE

Distance	5.5 miles/8.5km
Ascent	584 metres
Start	Glen Brittle campsite, IV47 8TA
Info	wildrunning.net/2196

Begin by running through the campsite to the beach side of the shop then following the path onto the mountainside. Continue to head east at the first path junction and then bear L at the next one, heading into Coire Lagan. Continue up the valley to the small lochan. Run around this clockwise then return on the outbound path. This time bear R at the fork, taking the path north of Loch an Fhir-bhallaich to the hill above the Eas Mor waterfall on the Allt Coire na Banachdich. Continue west to the road at Glenbrittle House. Turn L onto the road and back to the start. An excellent extension here is to run up onto the Cuillin Ridge and, with good weather and mountain skills, traverse north to Sligachan.

197 TROTTERNISH RIDGE, SKYE

Distance	17 miles/27km
Ascent	1840 metres
Start	Flodigarry car park, south of IV51 9HZ
Finish	Loch Leathan car park, south of IV51 9HX
Info	wildrunning.net/2197

Join the main tourist path south-west from the car park and through the Quiraing to the parking area on the road at NG 440679 (2.7 miles/4.4km). Cross and follow the much quieter path up the ridge to Bioda Buidhe at 466 metres. Continue south on the ridge keeping the steep cliffs to your L past Bealach nan Coisichean at 4.7 miles/7.6km and Bealach Uige at 5.6 miles/9km. Climb up to the trig point at 611 metres on Beinn Edra (7.2 miles/11.6km) and continue south over Beinn Mheadhonach then Groba nan Each at 575 metres. Continue south over Flasvein at 599 metres and then Creag a' Lain at 609 metres where the ridge curves L (9.9 miles/15.9km). Follow it south-east, detouring to the summit of Sgurr a Mhadaidh Ruaidh at 593 metres then around to Baca Ruadh at 639 metres (11.3 miles/18.2km). Run south along the ridge bearing L over Hartavel at 669 metres then ascend to the trig point at 719 metres on The Storr (15 miles/24.2km). Follow the ridge down to Bealach Beag at NG 492531, turning L and descending the ridge to reach the A855 at Loch Leathan.

198

199

200

The Hebridean Way (run 198) covers 156 miles of stunning, wildlife-rich Outer Hebridean scenery, visiting 10 islands, crossing 6 causeways and with 2 ferry rides taking you the whole length of the archipelago. There's a marvellous range of culture, nature and landscape here, from deserted beaches and pretty fishing villages to rugged mountain and moorland, with each island having its own, unique mix. Our route takes on a fastpacking adventure of the Hebridean Way, starting on Vatersay and ending in Stornoway. Be prepared for challenging terrain, extremes of weather and the experience of a lifetime.

Hoy is the second-largest island in the Orkney archipelago, famous for its 137-metre sea stack, the Old Man of Hoy. The tallest stack of its kind in Britain, the Old Man was climbed by Tom Patey, Rusty Baillie and Chris Bonington in 1966. The Old Man of Hoy run (199) is a circuit of the wild and windswept north of Hoy from the ferry port at Moaness, and visits St John's Head which, at 335 metres, is the highest vertical sea cliff in the UK.

In the far north-west of Shetland, the Esha Ness Peninsula experiences the full force of the North Atlantic, which has sculpted the coastline into an intricate series of stacks, caves, blowholes and geos. The peninsula is the remains of the Eshaness volcano, with layers of rock and lava formed by a volcanic eruption 350 million years ago still visible. The Esha Ness run (200) starts at the lighthouse, perched high on a rocky outcrop (and available as a holiday let), then strikes out along the dramatic coast to the head of Calder's Geo, a deep inlet carved by the sea into the rock. It then passes the great hole of Grind of the Navir with its boulder beach and remote sea loch. Heading back along the western shore, it takes you past the twin inlets of Drid Geo and Calder's Geo before returning to the lighthouse.

Routes 198-200

198 THE HEBRIDEAN WAY

Distance 156 miles/251km
Ascent 5160 metres
Start Vatersay, HS2 0XF
Finish Stornoway, HS2 0XP
Info wildrunning.net/2198

Split into 12 sections of between 3 and 17 miles each, the Hebridean Way makes an outstanding 2-week fastpacking adventure and is the first dedicated, waymarked pedestrian route across the archipelago. It runs across 10 Hebridean islands, starting at Vatersay in the south and crossing Barra, Eriskay, South Uist, Benbecula, Grimsay, North Uist, Berneray and Harris, before finishing on Lewis in the north. The islands are linked by 6 causeways and 2 ferry rides. Full details, including logistics for planning travel and accommodation for the trip, can be found at www.visitouterhebrides.co.uk. There are also several dedicated guidebooks for exploring the Hebridean Way both on foot and by bike.

199 OLD MAN OF HOY, ORKNEY

Distance 12.5 miles/20km
Ascent 750 metres
Start Moaness Pier, KW16 3PG
Info wildrunning.net/2199

Follow the B9047 south-west from the pier to the car park at the sharp bend below Round Hill. Turn L off the road then, trending R, ascend steeply R up Cuilags at 435 metres. Descend the other side to Enegars then turn L and follow the ridgeline past a trig point at 374 metres and over Sui Fea. Turn R and descend to the coast path at St John's Head. Turn L and follow the coast south-west to Tuaks of the Boy above the Old Man of Hoy sea stack (5.8 miles/9.4km). Take the larger path from here, cutting the corner of Rora Head and following the coast around to the L then inland into Rackwick. Turn L onto the road here and follow it briefly before forking L onto the track north-east up the Rackwick Burn and around to the north-east to join the outbound path by Sandy Loch. Turn R onto this and follow the road back to the start.

200 ESHA NESS, SHETLAND

Distance 4 miles/6km
Ascent 133 metres
Start Esha Ness Lighthouse, ZE2 9RS
Info wildrunning.net/2200

From the lighthouse return along the road back past Loch of Framgord and then bear L away from the road onto the coast heading north. Follow the coast to the west of the Lochs of Dridgeo and past several sea stacks and arches. Continue north up the coast to the Head of Stanshi and around Croo Loch. Turn R inland down the east shore of the loch and then south-west past another loch and south to the Holes of Scraada. Run around to the L of these and then south past the Loch of Houlland and carry on in the same direction to the road and the outbound route. Turn R onto the road to return to the start.

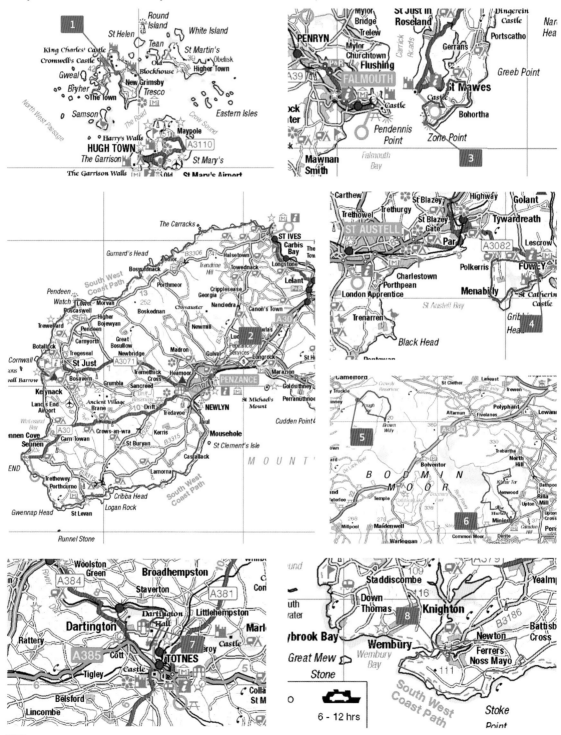

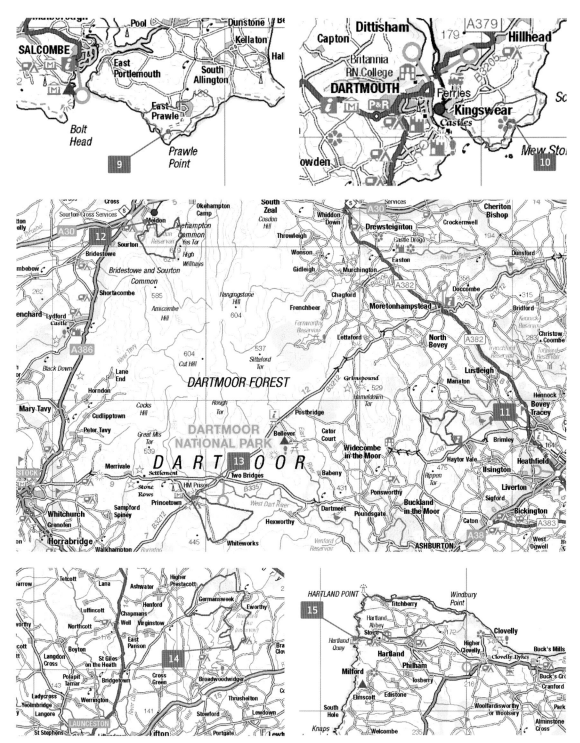

239

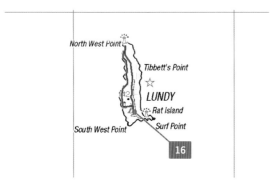

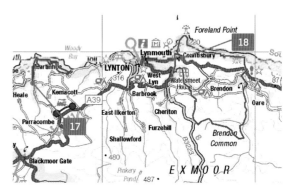

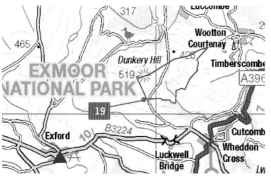

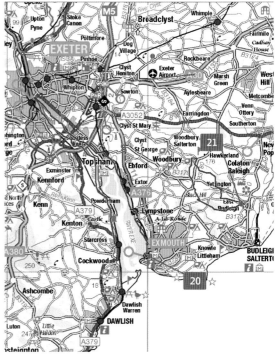

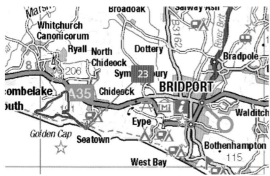

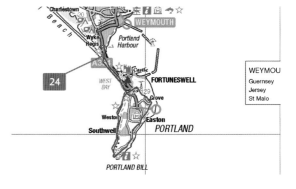

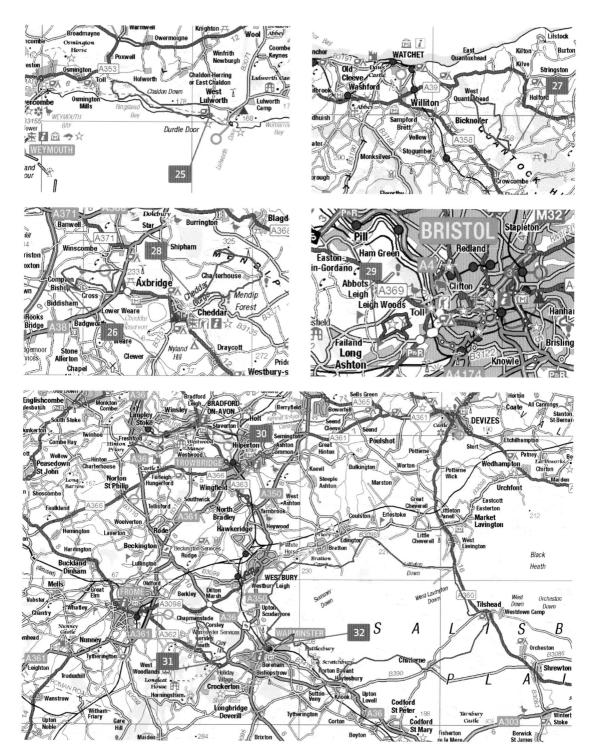

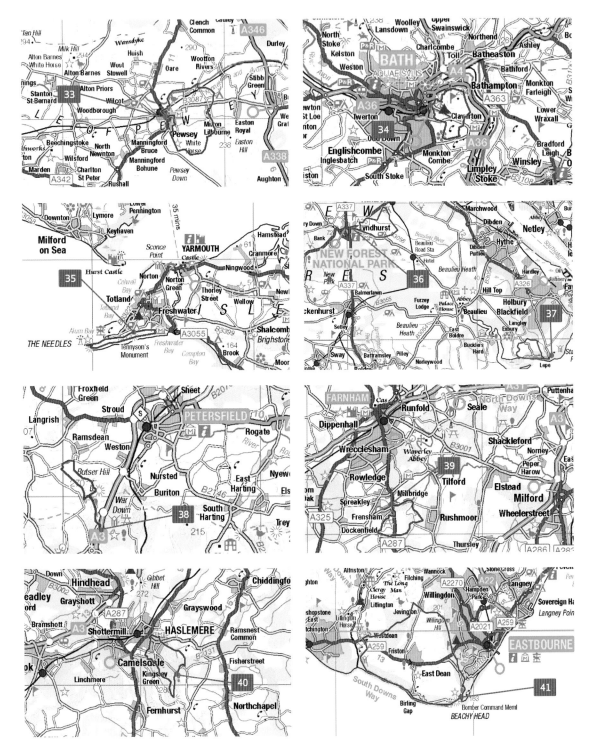

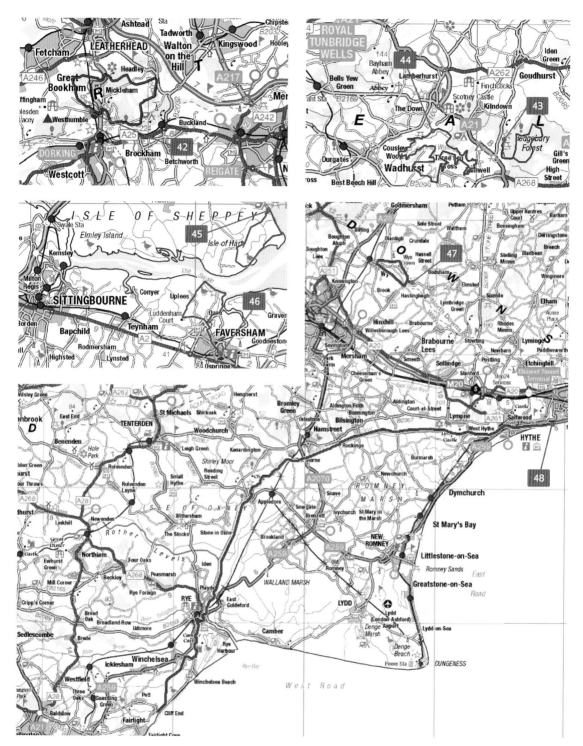

243

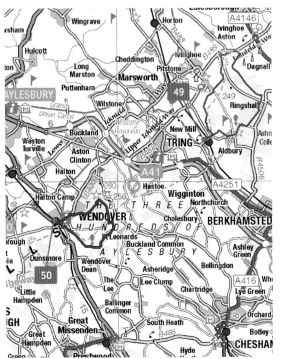

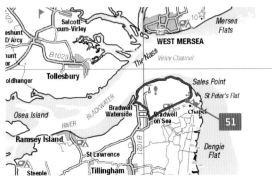

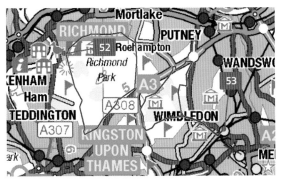

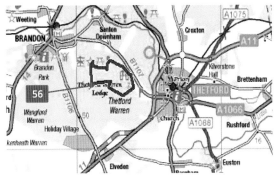

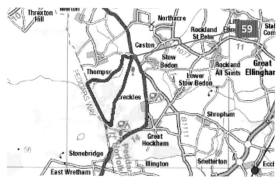

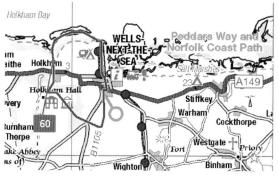

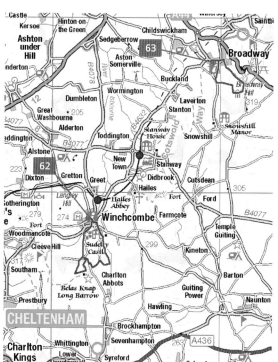

245

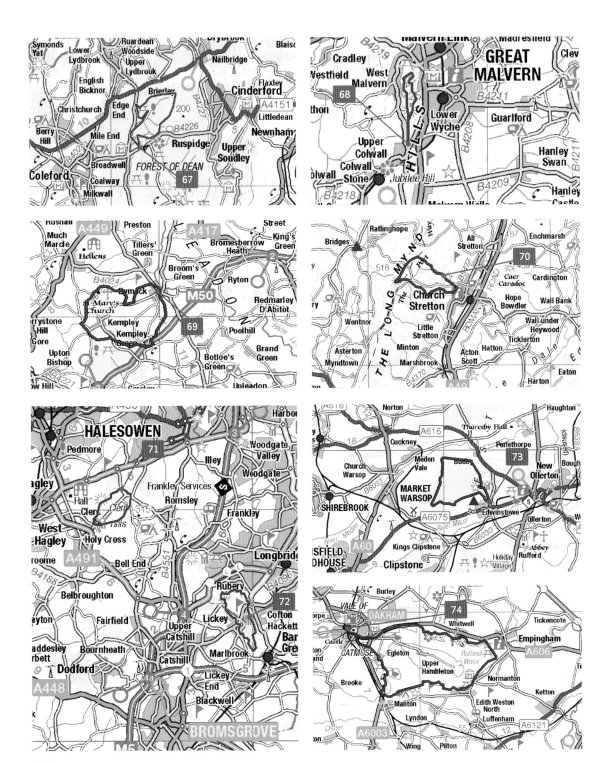

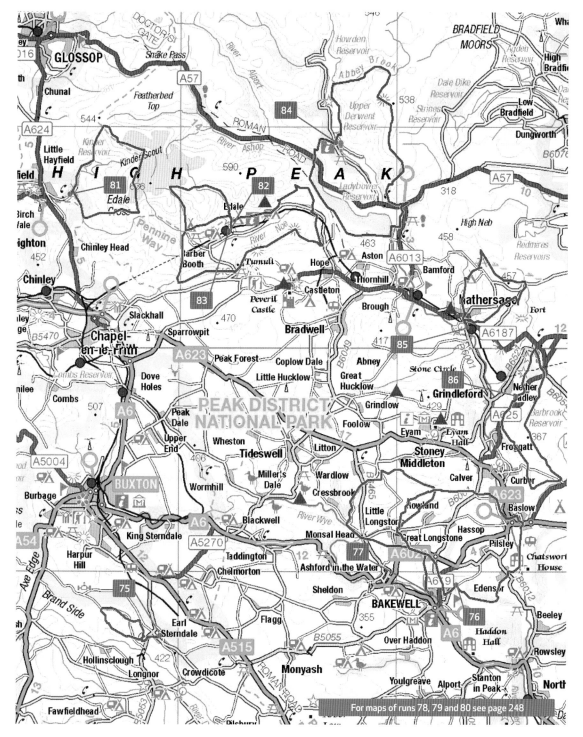

For maps of runs 78, 79 and 80 see page 248

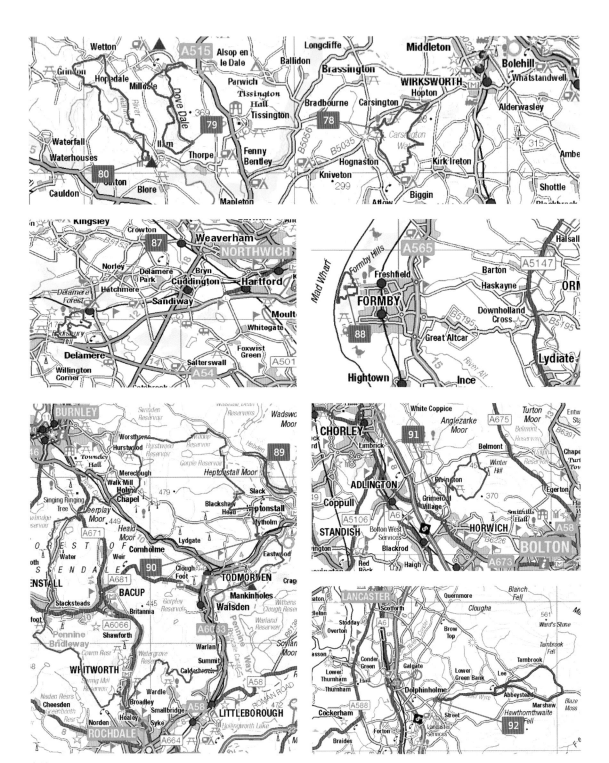

248

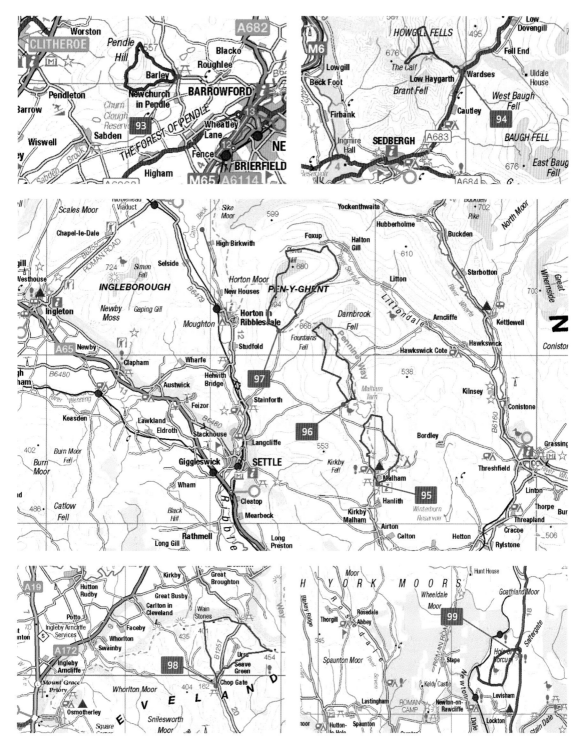

249

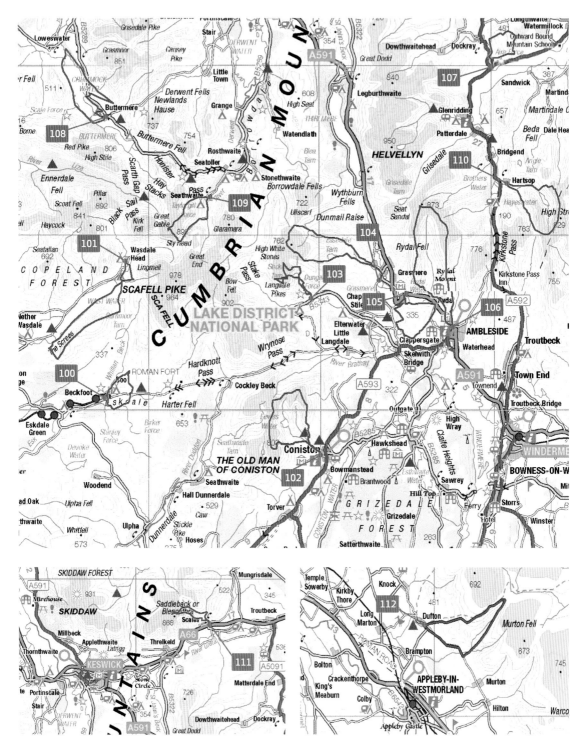

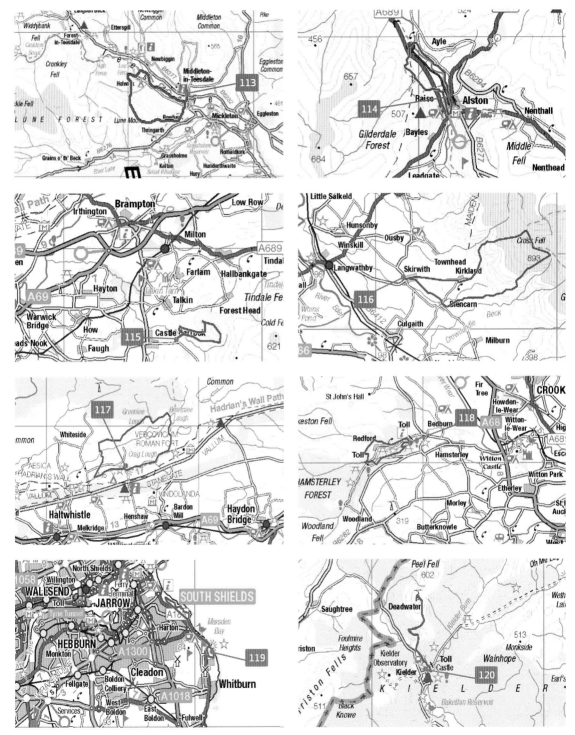

113

114

115

116

117

118

119

120

251

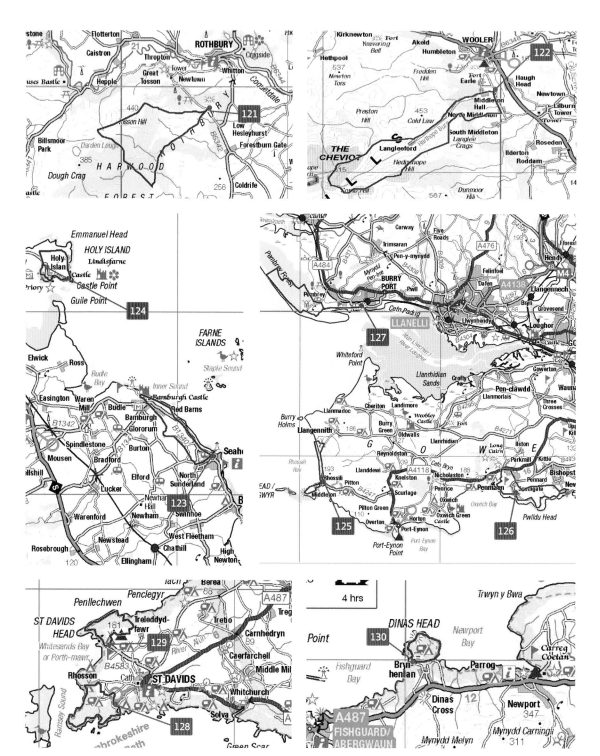

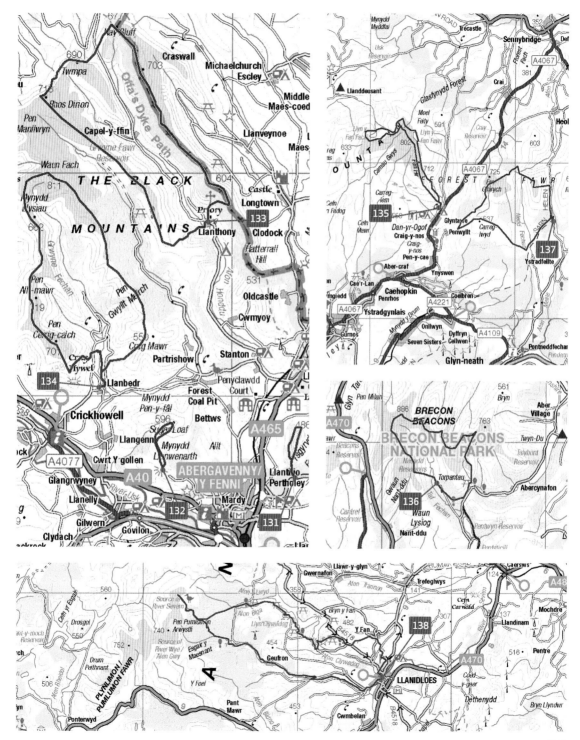

253

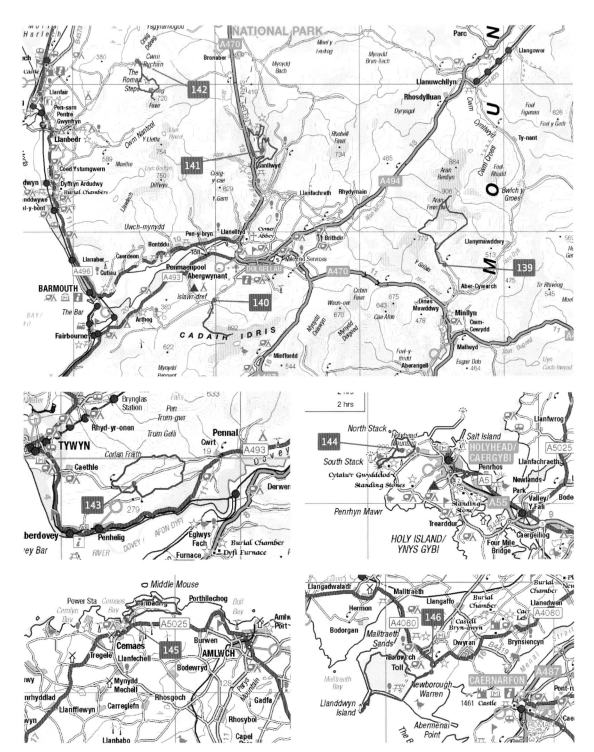

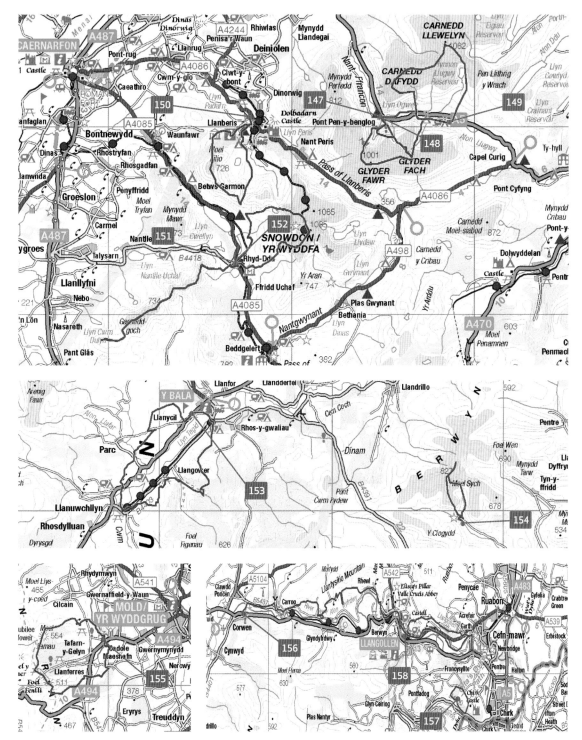

255

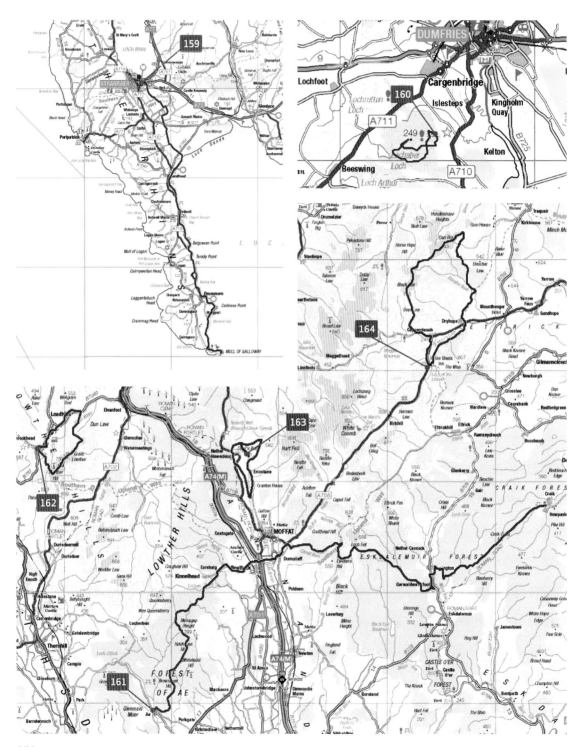

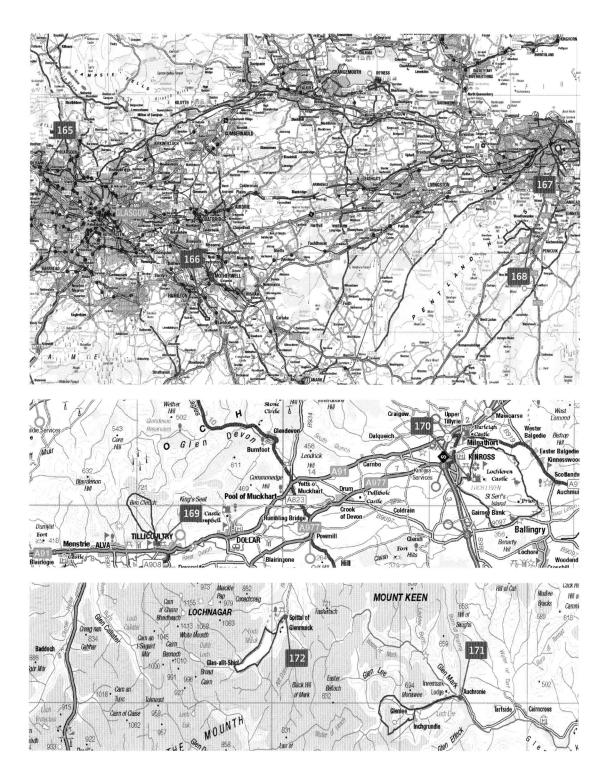

257

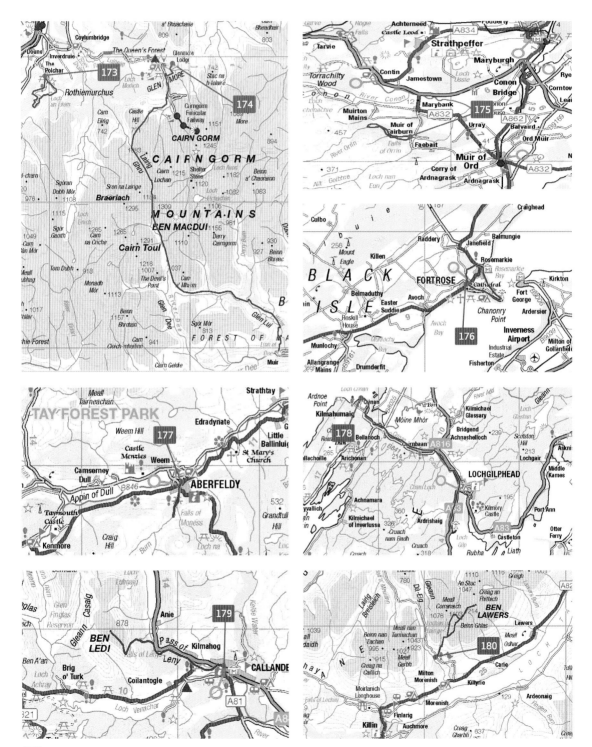

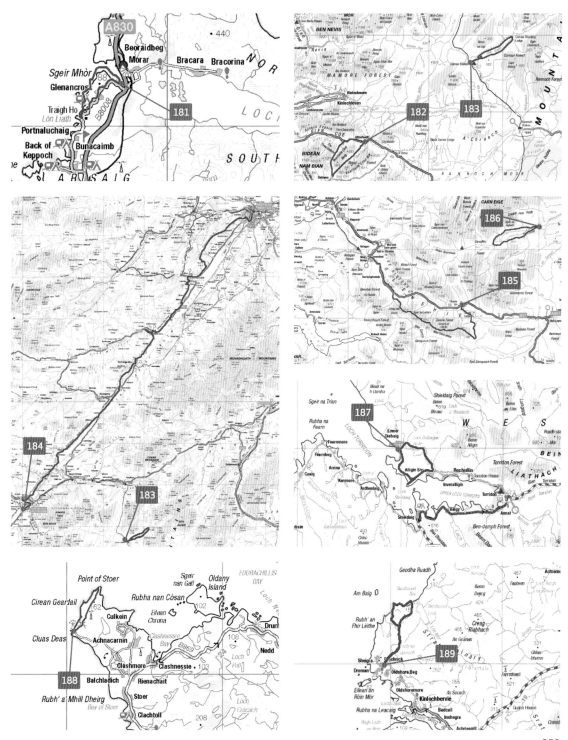

259

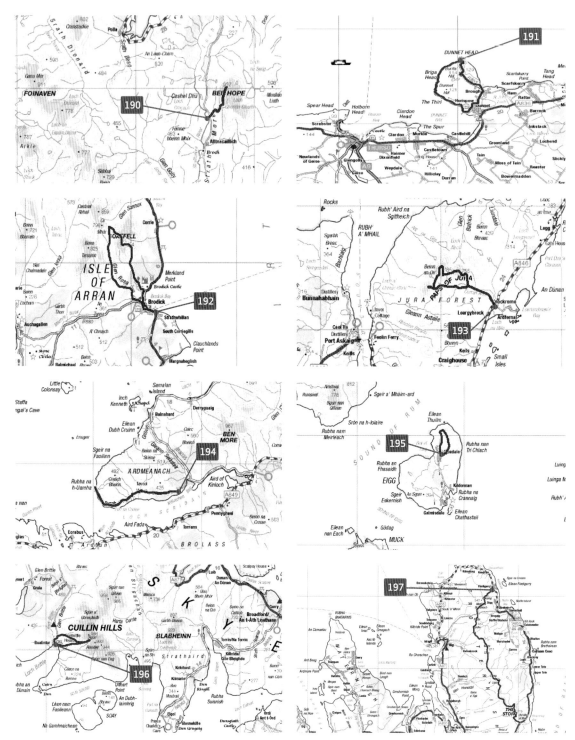

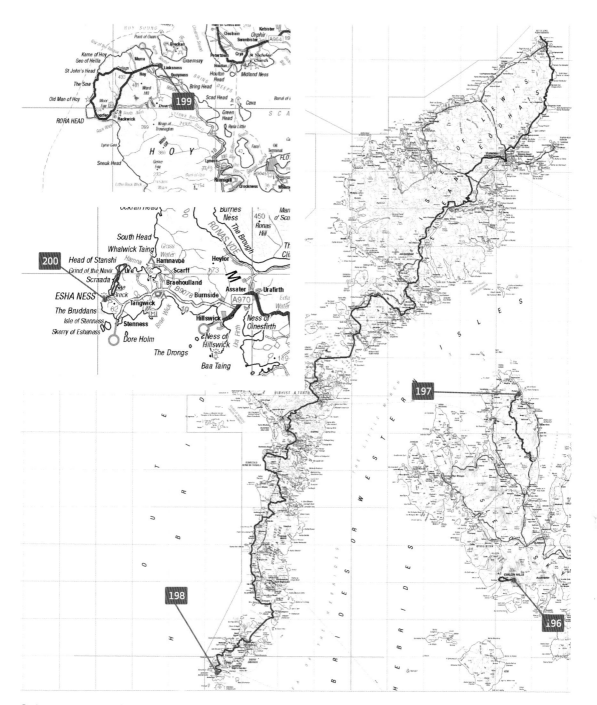

Grid squares represent 10 km. Maps are for guidance only and do not contain all footpaths or names. To help improve these maps for a future edition please contribute to OpenStreetMap. For more accurate mapping insert the LatLong into *bing.com/maps* and choose the Ordnance Survey layer. **Ordnance Survey maps © Crown copyright and database right 2016.**

Grid References of start points

Run	Lat Long	Grid Ref	Run	Lat Long	Grid Ref	Run	Lat Long	Grid Ref
1	49.9556, -6.3416	SV887152	51	51.7324, 0.9296	TM024078	101	54.4644, -3.2573	NY186084
2	50.1079, -5.5323	SW476305	52	51.4499, -0.2961	TQ185737	102	54.3673, -3.0804	SD299974
3	50.1417, -5.0145	SW847312	53	51.4207, -0.2000	TQ217706	103	54.4177, 3.0902	NY294063
4	50.3323, -4.6486	SX116514	54	51.5550, -0.1667	TQ272856	104	54.4567, -3.0273	NY335073
5	50.6061, -4.6328	SX138818	55	52.2618, 0.1965	TL500649	105	54.4497, -3.0070	NY348065
6	50.5128, -4.4569	SX259710	56	52.4339, 0.6626	TL811851	106	54.4330, -2.9650	NY375046
7	50.4527, -3.6931	SX799628	57	52.1554, 1.4808	TM382565	107	54.5716, -2.9296	NY400200
8	50.3086, -4.0419	SX547474	58	52.2070, 1.6181	TM473627	108	54.5433, -3.2814	NY172172
9	50.2059, -3.7194	SX774354	59	52.5327, 0.8588	TL940966	109	54.4984, -3.1827	NY235121
10	50.3506, -3.5348	SX909512	60	52.9663, 0.8128	TF890447	110	54.5080, -2.9127	NY410129
11	50.5805, -3.7457	SX765771	61	51.7749, -2.2463	SO831085	111	54.6348, -3.0116	NY348271
12	50.7071, -4.0393	SX561917	62	51.9541, -1.9679	SP023284	112	54.6174, -2.4769	NY693248
13	50.5433, -3.9913	SX590734	63	52.0349, -1.8629	SP095374	113	54.6237, -2.0836	NY947254
14	50.7021, -4.2119	SX439915	64	51.8079, -1.6330	SP254122	114	54.8143, -2.4434	NY716467
15	50.9941, -4.5336	SS223247	65	51.7531, -1.2713	SP504063	115	54.8923, -2.6922	NY557555
16	51.1657, -4.6660	SS137441	66	51.8721, -1.4901	SP352194	116	54.6870, -2.5972	NY616326
17	51.2162, -3.9286	SS654481	67	51.8044, -2.5612	SO614119	117	55.0023, -2.3924	NY750676
18	51.2319, -3.7889	SS752496	68	52.0930, -2.3400	SO768439	118	54.6758, -1.8604	NZ091312
19	51.1540, -3.5814	SS895406	69	51.9775, -2.4382	SO700311	119	54.9690, -1.3658	NZ407640
20	50.6210, -3.4150	SY000811	70	52.5482, -2.8273	SO440948	120	55.2352, -2.5802	NY632936
21	50.6554, -3.3226	SY066848	71	52.4243, -2.0926	SO938807	121	55.2824, -1.9197	NZ052987
22	50.6413, -2.0593	SY959824	72	52.3757, -2.0044	SO998753	122	55.5241, -2.0111	NT994256
23	50.7220, -2.8244	SY419917	73	53.1973, -1.0689	SK623671	123	55.5821, -1.6542	NU219321
24	50.5783, -2.4702	SY668755	74	52.6720, -0.7355	SK856090	124	55.6749, -1.8012	NU126424
25	50.6230, -2.2685	SY811804	75	53.2000, -1.8667	SK090670	125	51.5685, -4.2898	SS414880
26	51.2909, -2.8733	ST392550	76	53.2176, -1.6690	SK222690	126	51.5669, -4.0891	SS553874
27	51.1322, -3.2162	ST150377	77	53.2176, -1.6795	SK215690	127	51.6798, -4.2520	SN444003
28	51.2873, -2.7442	ST482545	78	53.0620, -1.6433	SK240517	128	51.8705, -5.2843	SM740242
29	51.4380, -2.6430	ST554712	79	53.0552, -1.7836	SK146509	129	51.8962, -5.2964	SM733271
30	51.3442, -2.2526	ST825606	80	53.0534, -1.8075	SK130507	130	52.0207, -4.9090	SN005398
31	51.1968, -2.2347	ST837442	81	53.3789, -1.9293	SK048869	131	51.8412, -2.9768	SO328163
32	51.2068, -2.1789	ST876453	82	53.3644, -1.8166	SK123853	132	51.8441, -3.0640	SO268167
33	51.3398, -1.7674	SU163601	83	53.3644, -1.8166	SK123853	133	51.9441, -3.0372	SO288278
34	51.3808, -2.3462	ST760647	84	53.4003, -1.7443	SK171893	134	51.8761, -3.1069	SO239203
35	50.6692, -1.5429	SZ324856	85	53.3254, -1.6531	SK232810	135	51.8441, -3.4008	SO036171
36	50.8716, -1.5693	SU304081	86	53.2956, -1.6189	SK255777	136	51.8406, -3.6735	SN848171
37	50.7852, -1.3545	SZ456986	87	53.2287, -2.6770	SJ549704	137	51.8358, -3.5602	SN926164
38	50.9615, -0.9790	SU718185	88	53.5654, -3.0976	SD274082	138	52.4484, -3.5405	SN954845
39	51.1576, -0.7959	SU843405	89	53.7583, -2.0197	SD988291	139	52.7457, -3.6947	SH857178
40	51.0673, -0.6855	SU922306	90	53.7322, -2.0485	SD969262	140	52.7187, -3.9291	SH698152
41	50.7409, 0.2521	TV590959	91	53.6194, -2.5639	SD628138	141	52.8193, -3.8786	SH735263
42	51.2534, -0.3291	TQ167518	92	53.9744, -2.7379	SD517534	142	52.8630, -4.0142	SH645314
43	51.0716, 0.4480	TQ716331	93	53.8586, -2.2706	SD823403	143	52.4873, -4.0043	SN640896
44	51.0782, 0.3898	TQ675337	94	54.3640, -2.4678	SD697966	144	53.3159, -4.6660	SH225832
45	51.3886, 0.9364	TR044696	95	54.0601, -2.1543	SD900627	145	53.4150, -4.4480	SH374937
46	51.3116, 0.8884	TR014609	96	54.1024, -2.1774	SD885674	146	53.1561, -4.3555	SH426647
47	51.1691, 0.9725	TR079453	97	54.1382, -2.2418	SD843714	147	53.1227, -4.0218	SH648603
48	51.0708, 1.1218	TR188348	98	54.3861, -1.1407	SE559993	148	52.5681, -4.0078	SN640986
49	51.8004, -0.6237	SP950122	99	54.3318, -0.6913	SE852937	149	53.1227, -3.9665	SH685602
50	51.7622, -0.7495	SP864078	100	54.3950, -3.2752	NY173007	150	53.1208, -4.1279	SH577603

Run	Lat Long	Grid Ref	Run	Lat Long	Grid Ref	Run	Lat Long	Grid Ref
151	53.0506, -4.1348	SH570525	168	55.8550, -3.2268	NT233631	185	57.1567, -5.1811	NH077118
152	53.0506, -4.1333	SH571525	169	56.1578, -3.7500	NS914975	186	57.2649, -4.9846	NH201233
153	50.1420, -5.0141	SH921355	170	56.1999, -3.4086	NO127017	187	57.5753, -5.6861	NG797599
154	52.8541, -3.3751	SJ075294	171	56.9107, -2.9114	NO446803	188	58.2376, -5.4018	NC004327
155	53.1545, -3.2008	SJ198626	172	56.9520, -3.1376	NO309851	189	58.4907, -5.1002	NC194600
156	52.9800, -3.3732	SJ079434	173	57.1541, -3.8250	NH897085	190	58.3897, -4.6344	NC461476
157	52.9362, -3.0921	SJ267382	174	57.1642, -3.6766	NH987094	191	58.6698, -3.3776	ND202766
158	52.9714, -3.1719	SJ214422	175	57.5279, -4.5468	NH476515	192	55.5765, -5.1393	NS022359
159	54.9052, -5.0197	NX065609	176	57.5814, -4.1307	NH727566	193	55.8784, -5.9282	NR544720
160	55.0215, -3.6454	NX949709	177	56.6188, -3.8659	NN856490	194	56.3723, -6.0875	NM477275
161	55.1875, -3.6004	NX982893	178	56.0901, -5.5573	NR788943	195	56.9198, -6.1473	NM477886
162	55.3971, -3.7794	NS874129	179	56.2446, -4.2204	NN625080	196	57.2027, -6.2917	NG409206
163	55.3949, -3.4667	NT072122	180	56.5116, -4.2637	NN608378	197	57.6563, -6.2546	NG463709
164	55.4706, -3.2069	NT238203	181	56.9616, -5.8244	NM676921	198	56.9270, -7.5367	NL633954
165	55.9005, -4.4055	NS497701	182	56.6606, -4.9188	NN212559	199	58.9157, -3.3144	HY244039
166	55.7610, -4.0143	NS737538	183	56.7601, -4.6909	NN356664	200	60.4888, -1.6288	HU205784
167	55.9446, -3.1544	NT280730	184	56.8205, -5.1083	NN104742			

Wild Running (2nd edition)
Britain's 200 greatest trail runs

Words and Photos:
Jen Benson & Sim Benson

Editing and Proofing:
Siobhan Kelly
ProofProfessor

Design and Layout:
Tania Pascoe

Distribution:
Central Books Ltd
Freshwater Road, Dagenham
RM8 1RX, United Kingdom
Tel +44 (0)208 525 8800
orders@centralbooks.com

Published by:
Wild Things Publishing Ltd.
Freshford, Bath,
BA2 7WG, United Kingdom

WildThingsPublishing.com
WildRunning.net

Copyright © 2019 Jen Benson & Sim Benson. This second edition published in the United Kingdom in 2019 by Wild Things Publishing Ltd, Bath, BA2 7WG, United Kingdom. ISBN: 978-1910636152. The moral rights of the authors have been asserted.

Photographs © Jen & Sim Benson except the following (all reproduced with permission or with CC-BY-SA): Mark Bullock @mark_bullock: p10, p54 (bottom), p186 (middle), p187, p263. Ben Winston for Trail Running: p12 (top), p180. Zana and Joe Benson: p12 (bottom), p78 (middle and bottom), p79, p160, p164, p168 (top), p210 (middle), p211, p216 (bottom). Paul Mitchell wildman-media.com: p22, p144 (bottom), p145. Daniel Start: p32, p36 (top), p52 (top), p166 (middle), p168 (bottom), p184 (top). Mark Brooks puretrail.uk: p46 (middle & bottom). Jorge Malkin @jorgemalkin: p50, p55. Alison Ingleby: p54 (middle). Alun Ward: p62 (top), p236 (bottom), p237. Adam & Becky Lockyear: p70 (top). Kate Jamieson: p70 (bottom). Lucy Perkins & Sam Foggan: p71. Eva Rose Benson: p76 (top). Grassroots groundswell: p76 (bottom). Stefan Czapski: p78 (top). Trevor Harris: p82 (bottom). Leges Romanorum: p84 (middle). John Weller jeweller.co.uk: p84 (bottom). Duncan Grey: p88 (top). Dudley Miles: p88 (bottom). Katy Walters: p90 (middle). Ethan Doyle White: p98 (middle). David Purchase: p100 (bottom). Tim Green: p128 (bottom). Joe Hayhurst: p138 (middle). Robert J Heath: p148. Trevor Littlewood: p150 (top), p192 (top). Ian S: p152 (middle). Andrew Curtis: p156 (bottom). Matt Pearce: p158 (top). Robert Tilt: p158 (bottom), p176, p184, p190, p194 (bottom), p195. Alistair Hare: p166 (bottom). Wildman Media for BRECA Swimrun: p167. Tracy Purnell @asher.marley: p174, p175. Russ Coleman: p178 (top). Nigel Brown: p178 (middle). Dave Taylor Fell Running Guide: p186 (top). Ian Loombe Mountain Pursuit: p186 (bottom). Kate Worthington RAW Adventures: p188 (middle). Espresso Addict: p192 (middle). David Mellor pottyadventures.com: p192 (bottom), p194 (top). Lee Beel: p193. Andrew: p194 (middle), p228 (bottom). Graham Thomson: p200. Dr Gordon Baird: p202 (top). A M Hurrell: p202 (middle). David Parker: p204 (top). Brian Sharp: p204 (bottom). Rude Health: p205. Anne Burgess: p208 (top). Richard Webb: p210 (top). James Clapham: p214 (middle). Paul Raistrick: p216 (top). Michael Taylor: p218. Graham Grinner Lewis: p222 (middle). Tim Heaton: p222 (bottom). National Trust for Scotland: p224, p232 (top). Ally Beaven: p226 (top). Defacto: p226 (bottom). Paul Hermans: p228 (top). Kevin Lelland johnmuirtrust.org: p228 (middle), p229. Jens Mayer: p232 (middle). Laraine Wyn-Jones eiggadventures.co.uk: p234 (top). Kasman: p234 (middle). Kevin Marshal: p236 (top). Colin Keldie Orkney.com: p236 (middle).

Authors' acknowledgements: Huge thanks to everyone involved in editing and production at Wild Things Publishing, in particular to Daniel and Tania for everything – you guys rock. A massive thank you to everyone who has given generously of their time, expertise, photography skills and company, in particular Mark Bullock; Paul Mitchell at Wildman Media; Kate Worthington at RAW Adventures; Joe and Zana; Lucy, Sam and Osker; Robert Tilt; David Mellor at Potty Adventures; Tracy Purnell, Asher and Marley; Renee McGregor; the Pryer family; the Ordnance Survey team and our fellow GetOutside Champions; and Steve and Mark at PureTrail.uk. Grateful hugs to our families for their unwavering support. Thanks to awesome ethical brands Howies, Vaude and Thule for kitting us out, Trail Running and Outdoor Fitness magazines for having us on board for the past few years and the National Trust, Forestry Commission and John Muir Trust. Finally, thanks to the Flickr and Geograph community of photographers.

Other books from Wild Things Publishing:

Scottish Bothy Bible
Bikepacking
France en Velo
Hidden Beaches Britain
Lost Lanes Southern England
Lost Lanes Wales
Lost Lanes west
Lost Lanes West Country
Only Planet
Wild Garden Weekends
Wild Ruins & Wild Ruins B.C.

Wild Guide - Devon, Cornwall
and South West
Wild Guide - Lake District and
Yorkshire Dales
Wild Guide - Southern and
Eastern England
Wild Guide Wales and Marches
Wild Guide Scotland
Wild Guide - Scandinavia
(Norway, Sweden, Iceland
and Denmark)

Wild Guide Portugal
Wild Swimming Britain
Wild Swimming France
Wild Swimming Italy
Wild Swimming Spain
Wild Swimming Sydney
Australia
Wild Swimming Walks
Around London
Wild Swimming Walks
Dartmoor and South Devon

hello@wildthingspublishing.com